Windows® 8

FOR

DUMMIES®

eLEARNING KIT

Windows® 8

FOR

DUMMIES®

*e*LEARNING KIT

by Faithe Wempen

WILEY

John Wiley & Sons, Inc.

Windows® 8 eLearning Kit For Dummies®

Published by
John Wiley & Sons, Inc.
111 River Street
Hoboken, NJ 07030-5774
www.wiley.com

Copyright © 2013 by John Wiley & Sons, Inc., Hoboken, New Jersey

Published by John Wiley & Sons, Inc., Hoboken, New Jersey

Published simultaneously in Canada

For general information on our other products and services, please contact our Customer Care Department within the U.S. at 877-762-2974, outside the U.S. at 317-572-3993, or fax 317-572-4002.

For technical support, please visit www.wiley.com/techsupport.

Wiley publishes in a variety of print and electronic formats and by print-on-demand. Some material included with standard print versions of this book may not be included in e-books or in print-on-demand. If this book refers to media such as a CD or DVD that is not included in the version you purchased, you may download this material at http://booksupport.wiley.com. For more information about Wiley products, visit www.wiley.com.

Library of Congress Control Number: 2012954125

ISBN 978-1-118-20287-6 (pbk); ISBN 978-1-118-22831-9 (ebk); ISBN 978-1-118-23347-4 (ebk); ISBN 978-1-118-26544-4 (ebk)

Manufactured in the United States of America

10 9 8 7 6 5 4 3 2 1

WILEY

About the Author

Faithe Wempen, MA, is a Microsoft Office Master Instructor and the author of more than 100 books on computer hardware and software, including *The PowerPoint 2013 Bible* and *Microsoft Office For Dummies eLearning Kit.* She is an adjunct instructor of Computer Information Technology at Purdue University, and her corporate training courses online have reached more than one-quarter of a million students for clients such as Hewlett-Packard, Sony, and CNET.

Dedication

To Margaret

Author's Acknowledgments

Thanks to the wonderful editorial staff at Wiley for another job well done. You guys are top-notch!

Publisher's Acknowledgments

We're proud of this book; please send us your comments at http://dummies.custhelp.com. For other comments, please contact our Customer Care Department within the U.S. at 877-762-2974, outside the U.S. at 317-572-3993, or fax 317-572-4002.

Some of the people who helped bring this book to market include the following:

Acquisitions, Editorial, and Vertical Websites

Senior Project Editor: Paul Levesque

Senior Acquisitions Editor: Katie Mohr

Copy Editor: Heidi Unger

Technical Editor: Keith Underdahl

Editorial Manager: Leah P. Michael

Vertical Websites Supervising Producer: Richard Graves

Sr. Editorial Assistant: Cherie Case

Cover Photos: © Comstock Images / Getty Images

Composition Services

Project Coordinator: Patrick Redmond

Layout and Graphics: Jennifer Henry, Jennifer Mayberry

Proofreader: Sossity R. Smith

Indexer: BIM Indexing & Proofreading Services

Publishing and Editorial for Technology Dummies

Richard Swadley, Vice President and Executive Group Publisher

Andy Cummings, Vice President and Publisher

Mary Bednarek, Executive Acquisitions Director

Mary C. Corder, Editorial Director

Publishing for Consumer Dummies

Kathleen Nebenhaus, Vice President and Executive Publisher

Composition Services

Debbie Stailey, Director of Composition Services

Contents at a Glance

Table of Contents

On the Web

Introduction

*I*f you've been thinking about taking a class online (it's all the rage these days) but you're concerned about getting lost in the electronic fray, worry no longer. *Windows 8 eLearning Kit For Dummies* is here to help you, providing you with an integrated learning experience that includes not only the book and CD you hold in your hands but also an online version of the course at www.dummieselearning.com. Consider this Introduction your primer.

About This Kit

Each piece of this eLearning kit works in conjunction with the others. Whether you pop the CD into your computer to start the lessons electronically, follow along with the book (or not), or go online to see the course, this kit teaches you how to

- ✔ Sign in and out of Windows with your user account, and create new accounts as needed so everyone who uses your computer can have his or her own.

- ✔ Install and run applications, both the traditional desktop type and the new touchscreen-friendly Windows 8 type.

- ✔ Customize the Start screen and desktop with your favorite pictures, colors, font sizes, and formatting themes.

- ✔ Store and manage files and folders using File Explorer, both locally in your own libraries and in the cloud with SkyDrive.

- ✔ Use Internet Explorer 10 to browse the web, save favorite pages for later viewing, and take control of security and privacy settings.

✔ Create and use a home network to share files and printers and stream music and videos to any PC in your home.

✔ Configure Windows security settings to prevent attacks from hackers and viruses, and use Windows Update to keep your system files up to date.

✔ Control how children use the PC by implementing web restrictions, time limits, and application blocking.

✔ Troubleshoot common errors that can occur with applications, system files, and data corruption.

✔ Explore the new apps available in Windows 8 for checking the weather, managing photos, tracking appointments, sending e-mail, and more.

How This Kit Is Organized

In addition to containing 10 lessons, this book has a CD and a companion website. I describe all these elements here:

✔ **Lesson 1: Getting Started with Windows 8:** This lesson introduces you Windows 8, starting with signing in and out of Windows. You'll tour the Windows 8 workspace, including both the Start screen and the desktop, and learn about mouse and touch actions for controlling Windows.

✔ **Lesson 2: Running and Managing Applications:** This lesson is all about working with apps. You'll find out the difference between Windows 8 apps and desktop apps, and learn how to start up, switch between, and shut down both types. You'll learn how to install, repair, and remove both types of apps too.

✔ **Lesson 3: Customizing the Start Screen and Desktop:** Here you'll find out how to customize the Start screen by pinning and unpinning items from it, and sizing and arranging tiles. You'll also learn how to create, arrange, and delete desktop shortcuts, how to customize the taskbar, and how to control display options including resolution, fonts, colors, and themes.

✔ **Lesson 4: Storing and Managing Files and Folders:** Here's where you will learn about file storage in Windows 8. You'll learn how to organize your local files and folders, work with libraries, use your SkyDrive to store content online, and set file properties. You'll also learn how to change the File Explorer layout and customize how it shows files and folders.

↙ **Lesson 5: Using Internet Explorer 10:** In this lesson, you'll learn about Internet Explorer, Windows 8's built-in web browser. You'll find out how to use it to browse and search the web, and how to recall previously viewed content and guard your privacy and security.

↙ **Lesson 6: Networking Your PCs:** In this lesson, you'll learn how to assess your existing network, and set up a home network if you don't have one already. You'll learn how to browse shared resources between PCs, and how to share files and printers with others on the network and stream audio and video clips between computers.

↙ **Lesson 7: Managing Accounts and User Settings:** Here's where you learn about the different account types in Windows, and find out how to set up new accounts of any type. You'll also learn how to customize some Windows settings, including mouse operation, date and time, and power usage.

↙ **Lesson 8: Keeping Your System Healthy and Secure:** This lesson covers the various security and maintenance features in Windows 8. You'll learn how to prevent virus attacks, tidy up your hard drive, use Windows Update, and impose parental controls (a set of tools that Microsoft now calls Family Safety) on accounts belonging to children.

↙ **Lesson 9: Troubleshooting Common Problems:** Turn to this chapter for help fixing errors with the file system, applications, or Windows 8 itself. Windows 8 includes some great new tools for repairing and reinstalling when major problems occur, and you'll learn how to use them here.

↙ **Lesson 10: Exploring the Windows 8 Apps:** Windows 8 apps are the touchscreen-friendly apps launched from tiles on the Start screen, and in this chapter you'll learn the basics of several of the most popular ones.

↙ **About the CD appendix:** The appendix briefly outlines what the CD that accompanies this book contains and what you'll find in the online course, which is available here:

www.dummieselearning.com

The appendix also contains a few technical details about using the CD and troubleshooting tips, should you need them.

↙ **About the companion website:** The companion website holds a bonus chapter titled "Using Windows Media Player." If you like listening to music using your computer, you'll appreciate this chapter, which provides all the details about using Windows Media Player to play, organize, and manage your music collection. You'll learn how to rip and burn music, create playlists, and copy your music to a portable device. You can download this chapter here:

www.dummies.com/go/windows8elearningkit

How This Book Works with the Electronic Lessons

Windows 8 eLearning Kit For Dummies merges a tutorial-based *For Dummies* book with eLearning instruction contained on the CD and in an online course. The lessons you find in this book mirror the lessons in the course, and you can use the two together or separately. Both the book and the course feature self-assessment questions, skill-building exercises, illustrations, and additional resources.

In each lesson in the book, you'll find these elements:

- **Lesson opener questions:** The questions quiz you on particular points of interest. A page number heads you in the right direction to find the answer.
- **Summing Up:** This section recaps the content you just learned.
- **Know This Tech Talk:** Each lesson contains a brief glossary.

Foolish Assumptions

I assume you know what eLearning is and want to learn how to use Windows 8 for all the normal things that people do with it: run programs, manage files, surf the web, and so on. Although you may have used other Windows versions before, I don't assume you have much, if any, experience with Windows. I also assume you want to learn the fun and easy way, using the online course and book together to support your learning.

Conventions Used in This Book

A few style conventions will help you navigate the book piece of this kit:

- Terms I truly want to emphasize are defined in Lingo sections.
- Website addresses, or URLs, are shown like this: www.dummies.com.
- Numbered steps that you need to follow, and characters you need to type (such as a user ID or a password), are set in **bold**.

Icons Used in This Kit

The familiar and helpful *For Dummies* icons guide you throughout *Windows 8 eLearning Kit For Dummies,* in the book and in the electronic lessons, too.

The Tip icon points out helpful information that's likely to make your job easier.

This icon marks an interesting and useful fact — something you probably want to remember for later use.

The Warning icon highlights lurking danger. When you see this icon, you know to pay attention and proceed with caution.

The Practice icon highlights where I've provided you with a short exercise to perform.

In addition to the icons, you also find these friendly study aids in the book that bring your attention to certain pieces of information:

- ✔ **Extra Info:** This box highlights something to pay close attention to in a figure or points out other useful information related to the discussion at hand.
- ✔ **Lingo:** When you see the Lingo box, look for a definition of a key term or concept.

Class Is In

Now that you're primed and ready, it's time to begin. If you're altogether new to using Windows 8, this course starts at the beginning (see Lesson 1) and helps you lay the groundwork for later activities. You can also jump right to a topic that interests you. Whichever path you choose, you can use the book in tandem with the CD and the online course — the content of each reinforces the other.

Lesson 1

Getting Started with Windows 8

✔ Log into and out of Windows 8.

✔ Shut down your computer safely without losing any work.

✔ Get to know the Windows 8 workspace.

✔ Master mouse and touchscreen actions.

*W*indows 8 is your computer's *operating system.* You can think of Windows as the taskmaster of your computer — you tell Windows what you want to do, and it directs your computer to do it. You don't typically talk to your computer to get it to do something (although a few grumbles now and then don't hurt); instead, you make selections from what you see onscreen using the computer's mouse, keyboard, or touchscreen.

Windows 8 brings a certain commonality to everything you do with the computer. You might compare learning Windows 8 to learning to drive a car. After you figure out how to start a car, switch gears, apply the gas and the brake, and turn the steering wheel, you have the basic idea and can apply these same concepts to any car you want to drive.

With this book, you learn how to "drive" Windows 8 and then apply that knowledge to anything you want to do on the computer, whether that's writing a letter, adding up a bunch of numbers, listening to music, or browsing the Internet. This lesson gets you started by showing you how to log in and out of Windows 8, work with the user interface, and master the mouse and/or touchscreen actions that you'll need to perform to use Windows 8.

Signing In and Out of Windows

When you turn on your computer, Windows 8 displays a pretty picture, along with today's date and time. At this point, you aren't signed in yet. In other words, you're standing on the front porch waiting to be let in. To do anything useful, you must sign in.

Signing in identifies you to the computer. Because your login is password-protected in most cases, signing in also prevents other people from using your computer without your permission. Signing out is the opposite — it shuts down any applications that you're running and returns to the pretty picture that greets visitors on the front porch.

LINGO

Signing in logs you onto the computer, and **signing out** logs you off. Earlier versions of Windows called these activities logging in (or on) and logging out (or off).

TIP

Where do user accounts come from? Well, when you installed Windows 8 (or when you turned on your computer for the first time with Windows 8 preinstalled), you were prompted to create a user account. That may be the only one you have at this point, or you may have others. You'll learn how to create more user accounts, change their passwords, and exercise other account-related skills in Lesson 10.

Signing in

Signing in to Windows gives you access to the computer. After you sign in, you can run applications, manage files, use the Internet, and more.

When you create your user account, you choose whether you want your local Windows account to be connected to your Microsoft online account. If you choose to do so, you have access to additional benefits when you sign in. For example, Windows remembers your display preferences across different PCs and enables you to easily access online storage and social media friends lists. You learn how to create user accounts, and how to connect or disconnect them from Microsoft accounts, in Lesson 10.

LINGO

A **Microsoft account** is an online-enabled login that is associated with a particular email address. Logging into Windows with a Microsoft account enables many free services and conveniences within Windows 8.

1. **If the computer isn't on, press the Power button to turn on the device.**

   After a few seconds, Windows displays the current date and time and a background graphic, as shown in Figure 1-1.

Figure 1-1

2. **Press the spacebar to display the sign-in screen.**

   Alternatively, you can point to the bottom of the screen with your mouse pointer (or with a fingertip if you're using a touchscreen) and drag upward to reveal the sign-in screen. That's called *swiping up,* and you'll learn more about it later in this lesson.

3. **If more than one user is listed, as shown in Figure 1-2, click (tap) the account you want to use to sign in.**

   Note: Throughout this book, *click* is used to mean selecting something. If you're working with a touchscreen, you *tap* instead of clicking. See the explanation of touchscreen actions at the end of this lesson for more details.

   If the account is password-protected, a password prompt appears. If the account isn't password-protected, that account is signed in immediately.

4. **If you're prompted for a password, click in the Password box, as shown in Figure 1-3, type the password, and press Enter.**

   Instead of pressing Enter, you can click (or tap) the Submit button (the right-pointing arrow) to the right of the Password box.

   The Start screen appears. See Figure 1-4. You may have different items on your Start screen than the ones shown here, and you may see it at a different resolution, with more or fewer tiles visible.

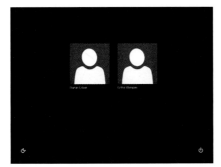

Figure 1-2

Figure 1-3

Figure 1-4

Signing out

When you're through working in Windows, you can sign out. This enables some other user to sign in, and it also provides some security and privacy protection when you leave your computer unattended. Signing out shuts down any running programs, so you should save your work before you sign out. Signing out doesn't shut down the computer. If you want to turn the computer's power off, you must use the Shut Down command, covered later in this lesson in "Shutting down the computer."

To sign out, follow these steps:

1. **If the Start screen (shown earlier in Figure 1-4) doesn't already appear, press the Windows key on the keyboard to make it appear, or on a touchscreen PC, swipe in from the left to display the Charms bar, and then click the Start icon.**

2. **Click (tap) your name in the upper-right corner of the screen.**

   A menu appears. See Figure 1-5.

Click Sign Out

Figure 1-5

3. **Click (tap) Sign out.**

You are signed out — and the graphic with the date and time reappears, so your screen now looks like it did before you signed in. Press the spacebar or swipe up if you want to sign in with a different account.

Locking and unlocking the computer

If you want to password-protect your computer when you step away from it, but you don't want to shut down your running applications, use the Lock feature instead of signing out. Locking the computer makes it unusable until you retype the sign-in password, but it leaves open applications exactly as they were.

To lock and unlock the computer, follow these steps:

1. **If the Start screen (shown in Figure 1-4) doesn't appear (for example, if the desktop appears instead), display it by pressing the Windows key or swiping in from the right and then clicking the Start icon.**

2. **Click your name in the upper-right corner of the screen.**

   A menu appears. Refer to Figure 1-5.

3. **Click Lock.**

   The Date and Time screen reappears (shown earlier in Figure 1-1).

4. **Press the spacebar or swipe up to redisplay the sign-in screen.**

   Notice that under your name, the word *Locked* appears. This indicates that you're still signed in, but your account is locked.

5. **Type your password in the Password box and press Enter.**

   The Start screen appears. Any applications that were previously open are still open, so you can resume your work.

Restarting Windows

Sometimes Windows misbehaves: It runs sluggishly, crashes applications that you try to run, fails to recognize certain hardware devices, and so on. In many cases, such misbehavior can be corrected by a restart. Restarting Windows shuts Windows down and then reloads it into the computer's memory.

To restart the computer, follow these steps:

1. **Sign out.**

   You learned to sign out earlier in this lesson. Here's a quick reminder: Press the Windows key or swipe in from the right and tap Start to open the Start screen, click or tap your name in the upper-right corner, and click or tap Sign Out.

2. **Press the spacebar, or swipe up from the bottom.**

   The sign-in screen appears.

3. **Click (tap) the Power icon in the lower-right corner of the screen.**

   The Power icon looks like a circle with a short vertical line through the top. A menu appears with three choices: Sleep, Shut Down, and Restart. See Figure 1-6.

4. **Click (tap) Restart.**

   The computer restarts.

Some older computers without much extra memory may not offer a Sleep option. Without enough memory, they can't store your work until you return.

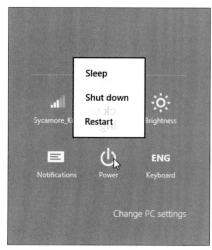

Figure 1-6

Shutting down the computer

Shutting down the computer turns its power off. You might want to do this when you are going to be away from the computer for a long time, to save electricity, or in preparation for moving the computer.

To shut down the computer, follow these steps:

1. **Sign out.**

   You learned to sign out earlier in this lesson. Here's a quick reminder: press the Windows key to open the Start screen, click your name in the upper-right corner, and click Sign Out.

2. **Press the spacebar or swipe up from the bottom.**

   The sign-in screen appears.

3. **Click (tap) the Power icon in the lower-right corner of the screen.**

   A menu appears with two choices: Shut Down and Restart.

4. **Click (tap) Shut down.**

   The computer shuts down.

Putting the computer to sleep

Theoretically, you could leave your computer on almost all the time. However, an always-on computer uses quite a bit of electricity, which is neither environmentally nor financially sound. That's why some people choose to shut their computers off when they don't intend to use them for a day or two.

The only problem with shutting off the computer is that it takes a few minutes for it to start back up again when you're ready to resume using it. If only there were a way to make the computer use less power temporarily without having to shut it down completely . . . oh wait, there is!

> **LINGO**
>
> Putting a computer into **Sleep mode**, sometimes called *sleeping a computer,* shuts off the electricity to almost all of the computer, but leaves the memory powered.

The Sleep feature keeps the memory powered, so you don't lose whatever you're working on in Windows and in applications — and so the time required to start it back up again is much shorter. All other components are turned off to save electricity.

There are two ways to "sleep" the computer. One way is to sign out, as you learned earlier in this lesson, and then to select Sleep from the Power icon's menu (rather than selecting Shut Down, as you did in the preceding section). That's great for saving power and saving a bit of startup time, but since you have to sign out in order to use that method, you have to close all your open applications and data files anyway.

The other way to make the computer go to sleep requires you to use a feature in Windows 8 that you haven't seen yet: charms. These are icons that pop up on the right side of the Windows desktop when you hover the mouse pointer in the lower-right corner of the screen. The Charms bar has a transparent background at first, but then if you move the mouse upward slightly, its background becomes solid black so that you can see it better, as shown in Figure 1-7.

Charms

Figure 1-7

There are five charms, but the one I'm talking about at the moment is the bottom one, which looks like a gear. It's called the Settings charm. When you click the Settings charm, a panel appears on the right side of the screen. That panel has a Power button on it, and that Power button opens a menu from which you can choose Sleep. When you sleep the computer this way, everything you have open remains open. When the computer wakes back up again, it's all just as you left it.

TIP

Many portable computers are set up so that if you shut the lid, they automatically go into Sleep mode. In addition, computers often put themselves to sleep after so many minutes of inactivity to save power. You can adjust these settings to suit the way you want to use your computer. See Lesson 10.

To put the computer to sleep without signing out, follow these steps:

1. **Point the mouse pointer at the lower-right corner of the screen, or swipe in from the right.**

   The Charms bar appears. (Refer to Figure 1-7.)

2. **Click (tap) the Settings charm, which is the bottommost charm.**

   A panel of settings appears.

TIP

Because the Start screen was active when you opened the panel, settings appear that apply to the Start screen; if you opened Settings from some other location, you might see different options.

3. **Click (tap) the Power icon.**

   A menu appears. See Figure 1-8.

4. **Click (tap) Sleep.**

   The computer goes into sleep mode.

5. **When you're ready to use the computer again, press its Power button.**

   The computer immediately wakes up and displays the sign-in screen. The computer wakes up locked, for your privacy, even though you're still signed in.

6. **Type your password in the Password box and press Enter or click (tap) Submit.**

   The computer resumes, just as you left it.

Understanding the Windows 8 Workspace

If you were previously a Windows 7 (or earlier) user, Windows 8 is going to take some getting used to. It's very different! Don't panic, though, because I'll take you through it step-by-step in this section.

Figure 1-8

Working with the Start screen

Earlier versions of Windows had a Start menu that you accessed from the lower-left corner of the screen. Windows 8, in contrast, has a Start screen, which is like a bulletin board on which you can pin shortcuts to your favorite applications and locations for easy access. By default, many items are already pinned there for your convenience, but the Start screen is thoroughly customizable, and the items already on it are just suggestions. You'll learn how to make the Start screen your own in Lesson 3.

The Start screen is part of Windows 8's tablet-like interface, which is designed to be easy to use with either a touchscreen or a mouse. In the section "Mastering Mouse and Touch Actions" later in this lesson, you'll learn the details of touchscreen operation.

To browse the content of the Start screen, follow these steps:

1. **Display the Start screen if it doesn't already appear. To do so, press the Windows key, or swipe in from the right and tap the Start icon.**

2. **Move the mouse pointer to the right edge of the screen, and then keep moving it toward the right.**

   If there are more tiles than will fit onscreen at once, the Start screen display scrolls to the right, showing any items that weren't visible before, as shown in Figure 1-9. You may have items on your Start screen that are different from the ones shown here.

Scroll bar

Figure 1-9

3. **Move the mouse pointer to the left edge of the screen, and then keep moving it toward the left.**

   The display scrolls to the left, returning to the original view of the Start screen.

TIP

If you're using a touchscreen, you can also scroll the display with your finger or a stylus by dragging across the screen. You'll learn about touchscreen use later in this lesson, in the section "Mastering Mouse and Touch Actions."

4. **Move the mouse pointer to the bottom of the screen.**

   A scroll bar appears. (It's also shown in Figure 1-9.) You can drag the lighter area of the scroll bar to move the display.

5. **Right-click an empty area of the Start screen background, or swipe up from the bottom on a touchscreen.**

   A command bar appears across the bottom of the Start screen. The bar has one icon in it at the moment: All Apps. (See Figure 1-10.) If something were selected other than the Start screen in general, the options on the command bar would pertain to that item, and would be different.

Command bar

Figure 1-10

6. **Click (tap) the All Apps icon.**

   A list of all the applications installed on the computer appears. See Figure 1-11.

   If you were wondering what happened to the programs that came with earlier versions of Windows, like Calculator and Notepad, they're still here, and this Apps screen is how you find and run them. You'll learn more about this list in Lesson 2.

Figure 1-11

7. **Move the mouse pointer to the right edge of the screen, or on a touch-screen, drag to the right.**

The list of applications scrolls to the right, just like the Start screen contents did earlier.

8. **Press the Windows key on the keyboard, or swipe in from the right and tap Start.**

The Start screen appears again.

Understanding the Windows desktop

The desktop, along with the Start screen, forms the main interface of the Windows operating system. By default, the desktop is rather bare. It consists of a colored or graphical background with a single icon on it: Recycle Bin. (You'll learn about the Recycle Bin in Lesson 4.) You can customize the desktop by adding shortcut icons to your own favorite applications, files, or locations too, as you'll learn in Lesson 3.

The desktop interface also includes a *task-bar,* which is the thin horizontal bar at the bottom of the screen, as shown in Figure 1-12. The taskbar serves multiple purposes, as the following list makes clear:

LINGO

The **desktop** is the main interface of Windows. It contains a **taskbar** along the bottom, which serves multiple purposes, including managing running programs.

Icon   Open program windows

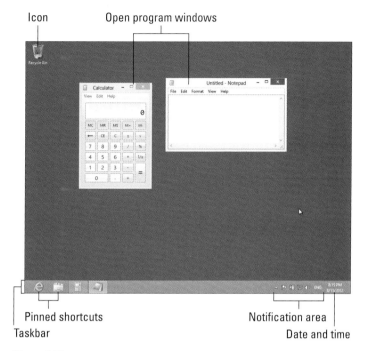

Pinned shortcuts   Notification area

Taskbar   Date and time

Figure 1-12

✓ Shortcuts to frequently used applications can be *pinned* to the taskbar. By default, two shortcuts are pinned to the taskbar: Internet Explorer and File Explorer. Pinned shortcuts appear at the far left of the taskbar. You'll learn about these two applications in Lessons 5 and 4, respectively.

✓ When applications are running, icons for them appear immediately to the right of the pinned shortcuts. For example, in Figure 1-12, two applications are running: Calculator and Notepad. Notice that the icons for these two appear with a lighter background than the background of the taskbar itself; this indicates that those icons are for running programs, not just pinned shortcuts.

✓ At the far-right end, the current date and time appear.

✓ To the left of the date and time are icons for utilities or features that are running in the background, such as the volume control, the battery monitor (on a portable PC), and the network connection indicator. This area is called the notification area, or system tray.

LINGO

The **notification area**, or **system tray**, is the area of the taskbar just to the left of the clock. It holds icons for programs that are running in the background.

Note: Does Figure 1-12 look a little plain to you compared to what you see on your own screen? You may have a picture background on the desktop, and a different window border color. I've turned off the picture background in this book's figures, and toned down the window color to a nice relaxing pale gray, for maximum readability. To learn how you can change the desktop's appearance, including adding or changing the background image, see Lesson 3.

Using the Charms bar

The Charms bar is a new feature in Windows 8. It is a pop-up vertical bar along the right side of the screen that displays five special icons, called charms. See Figure 1-13.

LINGO

Charms are icons that appear on the **Charms bar** that open commonly used sections of Windows 8, like the Search utility and the Start screen. The Charms bar appears when you move the mouse pointer to the lower-right corner of the screen or swipe in from the right.

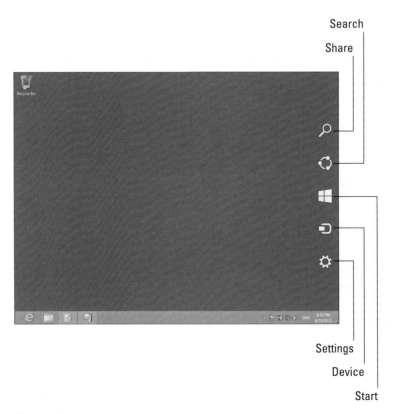

Figure 1-13

Each of the charms performs some special function that Windows 8 users frequently need. From top to bottom, they are

- ✔ **Search:** Opens a Search screen, from which you can search for any applications, settings, or files on your computer or online.

- ✔ **Share:** Enables you to share links, photos, and more with your friends and social networks without leaving the app you're in.

- ✔ **Start:** Takes you to the Start screen, or if you're already on the Start screen, back to the last app you were working with.

- ✔ **Devices:** Enables you do things like sending files and streaming movies to printers and TVs.

- ✔ **Settings:** Provides access to many common system settings, such as brightness, volume control, and notifications, as well as access to the Control Panel. You also can shut down your PC from here, as you learned earlier in the lesson.

The exact options that appear when you click a certain charm depend on the context — that is, they depend on what's on the screen at the moment. For example, when you choose the Settings charm with the desktop displayed, you get different choices than when you choose it with the Start screen displayed. You can do the following exercise from either the Start screen or the desktop.

To display the Charms bar and select a charm, follow these steps:

1. **Move the mouse pointer to the bottom-right corner of the screen.**

   The Charms bar appears. Its background is transparent at this point, as shown in Figure 1-13. If you pause here for a few seconds, the Charms bar goes away again, so move on to Step 2 quickly.

2. **Move the mouse pointer straight up, so that it touches one of the charms.**

   The background of the Charms bar changes to black. When the Charms bar is black, the Charms bar stays open until you close it, so acting quickly isn't important anymore once you get to this step.

TIP

If you're using a touchscreen, you can swipe from the right side toward the center of the screen to open the Charms bar instead of using Steps 2 and 3.

3. Click the Search charm.

The Apps list appears, with a search bar to its right. From here, you can search for an application you want to run. See Figure 1-14.

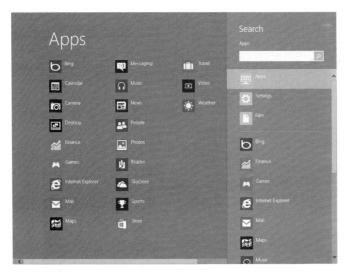

Figure 1-14

4. Press Esc once to clear the Search bar from the Apps list, and then press Esc again to return to the desktop.

If the desktop doesn't appear when you press Esc, click the Desktop tile on the Start screen.

5. Display the Charms bar again, and click the Settings charm.

A panel appears containing settings for the desktop.

6. Click the Volume Control icon (the speaker).

A vertical slider appears. See Figure 1-15.

7. Drag the slider up or down slightly to adjust the speaker volume. Then click on the background behind the slider to close the slider.

8. Click on the desktop, away from the Settings panel, to close the Settings panel.

For more practice, explore the remaining three charms on your own. Return to the desktop when you are finished.

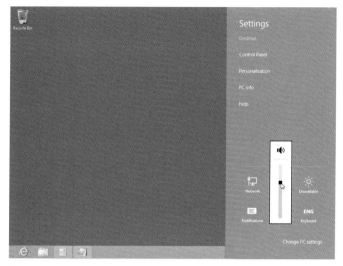

Figure 1-15

Mastering Mouse and Touch Actions

Windows 8 has been designed from the ground up to be easy to use with a variety of input devices, including keyboard, mouse, and touchscreen. That last one, touchscreen, is a significant change from earlier Windows versions. Whereas earlier Windows versions had touchscreen capabilities added on as an afterthought, Windows 8 has them in mind from the get-go. In fact, some would say that Windows 8 is actually easier to use with a touchscreen than with a mouse!

Understanding basic mouse actions

The basic mouse actions haven't changed much from earlier versions of Windows — and you're probably already familiar with them — but here's a very brief review:

✔ **Point:** To move the mouse pointer over an item without touching any of the mouse's buttons.

✔ **Click:** To press and release the left mouse button once. Clicking usually selects an item, such as a file or folder in File Explorer. On the Start screen, clicking opens apps.

✔ **Double-click:** To press and release the left mouse button twice in quick succession. Double-clicking usually activates the item being clicked, such as a shortcut icon on the desktop.

✔ **Right-click:** To press and release the right mouse button once. Right-clicking usually opens a shortcut menu from which you can select commands relevant to the item you right-clicked.

✔ **Drag:** To press and hold down the left mouse button on an item, and then move the mouse. Dragging relocates items, such as icons on the desktop, and in some of the new Windows apps, dragging the top of the window down to the bottom of the screen closes the app.

✔ **Right-drag:** To press and hold down the right mouse button on an item, and then move the mouse. Right-dragging also relocates items, but when you release the mouse button, a menu pops up asking what you want to do. For example, when you right-drag an icon to the desktop, a menu appears from which you can choose to create a shortcut for that icon.

In this exercise, you'll practice using mouse actions.

1. **Display the desktop if it isn't already displayed.**

2. **Point the mouse at the Recycle Bin icon.**

   The background around the icon lights up.

3. **Hold down the left mouse button and move the mouse to the center of the desktop; then release the button.**

   The Recycle Bin icon moves to the center of the desktop.

   Note: If the Recycle Bin icon doesn't move when you drag it, the Auto Arrange Icons feature may be enabled. To disable it so you can do this exercise, right-click the desktop, point to View, and click Auto Arrange Icons.

4. **Right-click the Recycle Bin icon.**

   A shortcut menu opens. See Figure 1-16.

5. **Click away from the menu to close it without making a selection.**

6. **Drag the Recycle Bin icon back to its original location.**

7. **Point to the recycle Bin icon and hold down the right mouse button.**

Figure 1-16

8. Drag to the center of the screen and release the mouse button.

A shortcut menu appears.

9. Click Cancel.

The shortcut menu closes.

Learning touchscreen navigation

Touchscreen navigation may be less familiar, at least to most people. Touchscreens haven't been widely used on Windows computers in the past, but Windows 8 may change that. Here are the basic touchscreen commands you need to know:

- ✔ **Tap.** To press and release your finger or stylus once on the item. This is equivalent to clicking with the mouse.

- ✔ **Double-tap.** To press and release your finger or stylus twice quickly in succession on the item. This is equivalent to double-clicking with the mouse.

- ✔ **Press and hold.** To press your finger or stylus down and hold it there for a few seconds, and then release. This is equivalent to right-clicking with the mouse.

- ✔ **Pinch.** To touch two fingers to the screen in different spots and then drag the fingers together. Pinching zooms out. It works only in certain situations, like when you're viewing a web page or graphic.

- ✔ **Stretch.** To touch two fingers to the screen together and then drag the fingers apart. Stretching zooms in. Like pinching, it works only in certain situations.

- ✔ **Slide (drag):** To touch your finger or the stylus down and then slide it, maintaining contact with the screen. There are different kinds of sliding:

  - *Slide to scroll.* Drag your finger on the screen.

  - *Slide to rearrange.* Drag an item in the opposite axis compared to how you would scroll. For example, if the window has a vertical scroll bar, drag the item horizontally.

  - *Slide to close.* To close a Start screen app, drag from the top of the screen all the way down to the bottom.

- ✔ **Swipe to select.** Slide an item a short distance in the opposite direction compared to how the page scrolls. Use a quick, short movement. This selects an item, such as an app in the Start screen or a photo, and often brings up related commands for an app.

✔ **Swipe from edge.** Starting with the edge of the screen, swipe in. This does different things depending on which edge you start at:

- *From right:* Opens the Charms bar.
- *From left:* Shows open apps (mostly the Start screen apps) or switches between open apps and the desktop.
- *Top or bottom:* In a Start screen app, shows the command bar, which contains commands such as Save, Edit, and Delete.

✔ **Snap an app.** Drag an app window to change its size. You can snap an app to take up one-third or two-thirds of the available screen space. This works only with Start screen apps.

In this exercise, you practice using touchscreen actions. Skip this exercise if you don't have a touchscreen.

1. **Display the Start screen if it's not already displayed. To do so, swipe in from the right edge and click Start.**

2. **Swipe in from the right edge.**

   The Charms bar appears. See Figure 1-17.

Figure 1-17

3. **Tap a blank area of the Start screen background.**

   The Charms bar disappears.

4. Swipe up from the bottom edge.

The command bar appears, containing the All Apps button. See Figure 1-18.

Figure 1-18

5. Tap a blank area of the bar at the bottom.

The bar disappears.

6. Tap the Calendar app on the Start screen.

The Calendar app opens. See Figure 1-19.

Note: The first time you open the Calendar app, you may be asked a question about whether the e-mail address you signed into Windows with is an Exchange ActiveSync (EAS) account. Click No — unless, of course, you're sure that it is. If you're working on a PC at your workplace, ask your network administrator.

7. Slide (drag) from the top of the screen all the way down to the bottom of the screen.

The Calendar app closes and the Start screen reappears.

8. Tap and hold the Calendar app.

The app's rectangle shifts slightly, becoming slightly smaller to indicate it is selected.

9. Drag the Calendar app to a different spot on the Start screen.

If the whole Start screen scrolls instead of the Calendar app's tile moving, try dragging it in a different direction at first.

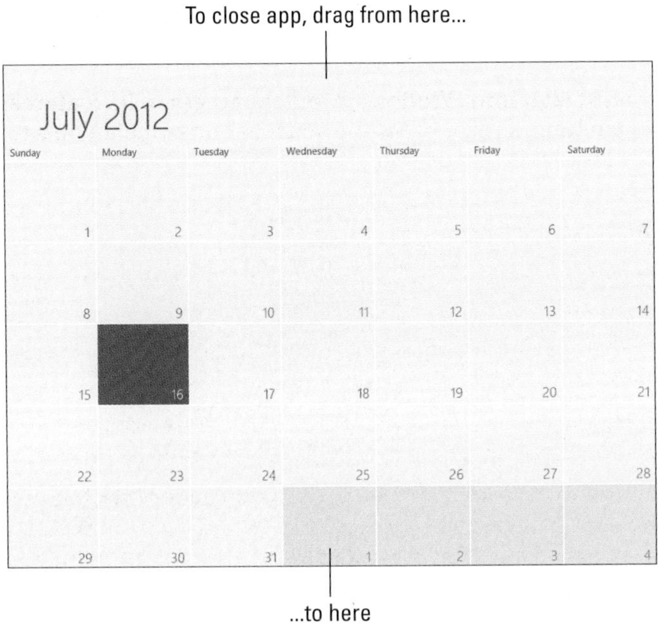

To close app, drag from here...

July 2012

Sunday	Monday	Tuesday	Wednesday	Thursday	Friday	Saturday
	1	2	3	4	5	6	7
8	9	10	11	12	13	14
15	16	17	18	19	20	21
22	23	24	25	26	27	28
29	30	31	1	2	3	4

...to here

Figure 1-19

Most of this book uses mouse-based terminology when giving instructions as to what to do, but keep in mind that you can use a touchscreen instead of a mouse whenever you like. Just make the following mental translations:

✔ Click = tap.

✔ Double-click = double-tap.

✔ Drag = slide.

✔ Right-click = tap and hold for a few seconds, then release.

Summing Up

In this lesson, you learned the basic information you need to get started using Windows, such as how to start your computer safely and how to shut it down, how to get around the Windows 8 workspace, and how to use the mouse or a touchscreen. Here are the key takeaways for this lesson:

- ✓ **You must sign into Windows 8 to gain access to its features.** From the date and time screen, press the spacebar or swipe up on a touchscreen to access the Sign-in prompt.

- ✓ **To sign out, from the Start screen, click your name in the upper-right corner and click Sign Out.**

- ✓ **To lock the computer, from the Start screen, click your name and click Lock.**

- ✓ **To restart or shut down, sign out and then press the spacebar.** Click the Power icon and click either Restart or Shut Down.

- ✓ **The Start screen replaces the Start menu from previous Windows versions.** To access it, press the Windows key on the keyboard.

- ✓ **The desktop is similar to the desktop in earlier Windows versions.** To access the desktop, select the Desktop tile on the Start screen; if the desktop has been previously displayed, you can jump back to it quickly by pressing Esc.

- ✓ **The Charms bar is new in Windows 8.** To access it, move the mouse to the lower-right corner of the screen or swipe from the right edge.

- ✓ **Basic mouse operations in Windows 8 are the same as in earlier Windows versions.** Point, click, double-click, right-click, drag, and right-drag.

- ✓ **Touchscreen navigation commands are new in Windows 8.** They include tap, press and hold, pinch, stretch, slide, and swipe.

Know This Tech Talk

Charms bar: A vertical bar in Windows 8 that appears when you swipe in from the right side or move the mouse pointer to the bottom-right corner of the screen. It contains icons called *charms,* which act as shortcuts to some commonly used parts of Windows 8, including the Search feature and the Start screen.

charms: Icons on the Charms bar.

click: To press and release the left mouse button once.

desktop: The main interface of Windows 8, consisting of a colored or graphical background, a taskbar, and one or more shortcut icons.

double-click: To press and release the left mouse button twice in quick succession.

drag: To press and hold down the left mouse button on an item, and then move the mouse.

lock: To password-protect a computer when you step away from it.

Microsoft account: A free Microsoft service on the Internet for authenticating computer users.

notification area: The area of the taskbar just to the left of the clock, holding icons for programs running in the background.

pinch: On a touchscreen, to touch two fingers in different spots and then drag the fingers together.

point: To move the mouse pointer over an item without touching any of the mouse's buttons.

right-click: To press and release the right mouse button once.

right-drag: To press and hold down the right mouse button on an item, and then move the mouse.

sign in: To log onto the computer.

sign out: To log off of the computer.

Sleep mode: A low-power mode that shuts off power to all components except RAM.

slide: On a touchscreen, to touch down your finger or stylus and then slide it.

Start screen: The opening screen in Windows 8, consisting of a set of rectangular tiles representing programs and locations.

Start screen app interface: The part of the Windows 8 interface designed for tablet and touchscreen PC use. The Start screen uses the app interface, as do some of the new apps that come with Windows 8.

stretch: On a touchscreen, to touch two fingers to the screen together and then drag the fingers apart.

swipe: On a touchscreen, to slide a short distance in a certain direction.

system tray: See *notification area.*

tap: On a touchscreen, to press and release your finger or stylus once on an item.

Lesson 2

Running and Managing Applications

✔ Start and exit applications.

✔ Search for an application.

✔ Manage application windows.

✔ Install, repair, and remove applications.

omputers exist for one basic reason: to run applications. An *application* is a program that performs some useful function. For example, there are applications that create spreadsheets, play games, edit photos, and access e-mail, to name only a few. The applications installed on your PC determine the down-to-business tasks you can perform with it, as well as the entertainment options you have available (games, movies, music, and so on).

In this lesson, you'll learn how to run applications on your Windows 8 computer, as well as how to find out what applications you have available to you. You'll also see how to control application windows, and how to install and remove applications.

Running Applications

After successfully signing into Windows (which you learned about in Lesson 1), you'll probably want to run an application. Windows 8 supports two different types of applications.

✔ **Desktop applications:** Those that use the Windows desktop as their basis. These are the applications that you may have used in earlier Windows versions, such as Microsoft Word or Quicken. They have resizable windows (usually) and run with the desktop behind them. You can control them from the taskbar. Figure 2-1 shows an example of a desktop application.

LINGO

Desktop applications are traditional-style applications designed to run on Windows 8 or earlier versions of Windows; they run on the Windows desktop in windows that are typically resizable. **Windows 8 apps** are tablet-style applications designed specifically for Windows 8.

Application window

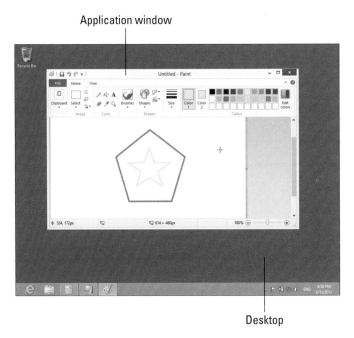

Desktop

Figure 2-1

- **Windows 8 apps:** Those that are designed specifically for the new tablet-style interface. (Microsoft calls them *apps,* rather than applications.) Windows 8 applications run only under Windows 8. They run full-screen (usually); if your display resolution is at least 1366 x 768, you can option-ally snap them into taking up either one-third or two-thirds of the screen area, so multiple Windows 8 apps can be run side by side. Figure 2-2 shows an example of a Windows 8 app.

Although the applications are different once you get into them, they all start the same way. If a shortcut for the application appears on the Start screen, you can start the program from there. If a shortcut for the application appears on the desktop or the taskbar, you can start from there. And you can always find and start an application from the Apps list. The following sections walk you through each of those possibilities.

Figure 2-2

Starting an application

The Start screen provides shortcuts for some of the applications installed on your computer. The default set of shortcuts on the Start screen is just a jumping-off point, though; you can customize the Start screen to show shortcuts for whatever applications you like. (See Lesson 3 to learn how to do that.) If the application you want to start appears on the Start screen, you just click or tap its shortcut. A single-click is fine; you don't need to double-click to activate a shortcut on the Start screen.

The taskbar can also potentially hold shortcut icons for programs you want to run. Shortcuts that are attached to a location are *pinned* there. For example, as you saw in Lesson 1, the taskbar has shortcuts for Internet Explorer and File Explorer pinned to it. You can pin your own favorite apps there, too, if you like. (Again, see Lesson 3.) To start a program that's pinned to the taskbar, click or tap its icon there.

LINGO

A **pinned** shortcut is one that is attached to a certain location, such as the taskbar or desktop.

The desktop can also have shortcuts on it that open applications, or that open File Explorer to specific folder locations (like Recycle Bin, for instance). Double-click an icon on the desktop to activate it. Note that, in this case, double-clicking (or double-tapping) is required.

Lesson 2

Finally, if none of the aforementioned apply to the program you want to run, you can resort to using the Apps list, which is a more-or-less complete list of all the applications installed on your PC. In earlier Windows versions, this function was handled by the All Programs list on the Start menu. To access the Apps list, open the Charms bar (by pointing to the bottom-right corner of the screen or swiping in from the right side) and click the Search icon. Alternatively, you can display the Start screen, right-click, and click All Apps.

In the following exercise, you will open four different applications, each using a different method.

1. **Press the Windows key to open the Start screen if it doesn't already appear.**

2. **Click the People tile (shown in Figure 2-3).**

   The People app opens. Leave it open for now.

3. **Press the Windows key again to return to the Start screen.**

4. **Click the Desktop tile on the Start screen.**

   The Desktop appears.

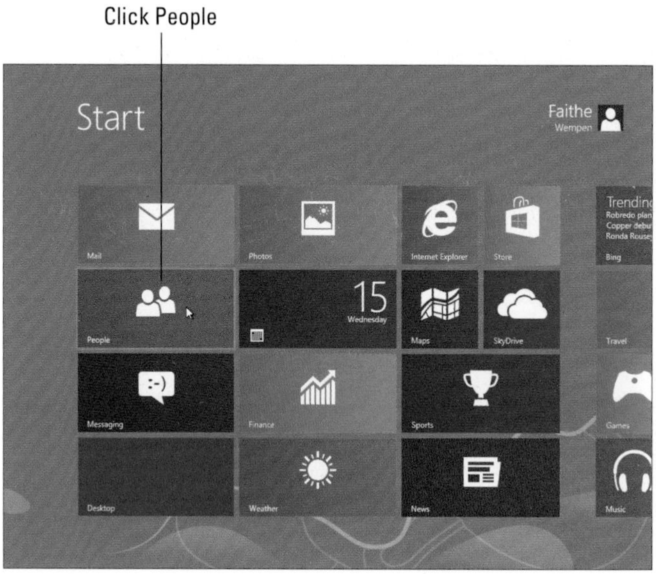

Click People

Figure 2-3

5. **In the taskbar, click the Internet Explorer icon shown in Figure 2-4.**

   Internet Explorer opens in its own window. The window may or may not be *maximized* (that is, fill the whole screen).

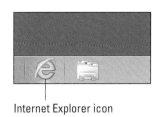

Internet Explorer icon

Figure 2-4

6. **If the window is maximized, double-click its title bar to *restore* (unmaximize) it.**

   The *title bar* is the bar across the top edge of a window. In most desktop applications, the title bar contains the application title, but in Internet Explorer, it doesn't. See Figure 2-5.

7. **Double-click the Recycle Bin icon on the desktop.**

   If you can't see the Recycle Bin icon, drag the Internet Explorer window's title bar to move the window. The Recycle Bin opens in its own window, which may partially or completely obscure the Internet Explorer window.

8. **Move the mouse pointer to the bottom-right corner of the screen.**

   The Charms bar appears.

Figure 2-5

9. **Click the Search charm.**

   The Apps screen appears, with a search box in the upper-right corner.

10. **In the search box, type** C.

The list of apps narrows to show only applications that contain a word that starts with the letter *C,* as shown in Figure 2-6.

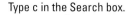

Type c in the Search box.

Apps list is filtered to show only items where a word begins with c.

Figure 2-6

11. **Click Calculator.**

Now, three applications are open on the desktop; plus a Windows 8 app (People) is open in the background that you don't see.

Leave all applications open for the next exercise.

Note: It's okay that the windows overlap. If you want to adjust them so they don't, see "Controlling Application Windows" later in this lesson.

Switching among applications

When you have multiple applications open at once, you can switch between them freely. There are many ways to do this, depending on the types of applications and whether you prefer to work with the keyboard, mouse, or touchscreen.

For desktop applications, you can switch to an application's window by clicking any visible part of the window, or by clicking the application's icon on the taskbar. You can point the mouse pointer at an icon to see a thumbnail preview of the application, as shown in Figure 2-7.

For Windows 8 apps, you can swipe the touchscreen from the left to switch to a different app. (The Windows 8 interface considers the desktop to be an app, so you can toggle between your Windows 8 apps and the desktop this way, but not between specific open desktop apps.)

EXTRA INFO

As you learned in Lesson 1, you can tell which icons in the taskbar represent open apps (versus pinned shortcuts) by looking at the icon background. If the background is lighter than the taskbar, it's an open app. If the background blends in with the taskbar, it's a pinned shortcut.

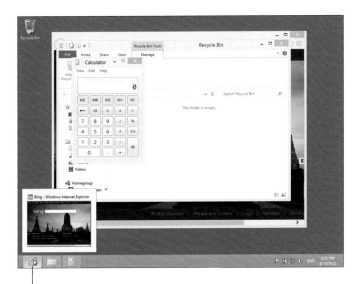

Point to an icon to see a thumbnail of the window the icon represents.

Figure 2-7

You can manage Windows 8 apps using your mouse by moving the pointer to the upper-left corner. When you see a thumbnail image appear there, move the mouse pointer down the left edge of the screen until a bar appears with thumbnails of all your running apps, as shown in Figure 2-8. From there, you can click the app you want to switch to. On a touchscreen, you can swipe in from the left to open the bar showing the running apps.

For all types of apps, you can hold down the Alt key and tap the Tab key. A bar appears in the center of the screen with thumbnail images of the open apps. Each time you tap Tab, a different one is selected. When the desired app is selected, release the Alt key.

Move pointer to the upper-left corner.

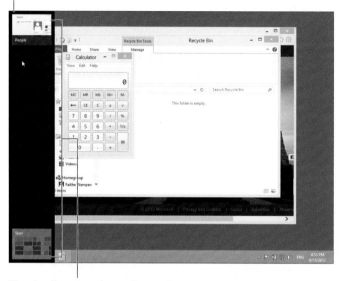

Thumbnails appear for each open Start screen app.

Figure 2-8

In the following exercise, you will switch among the open application windows using several different techniques.

1. **With the applications still open from the previous exercise, display the desktop if it isn't already displayed.**

   To display the desktop, press Escape. If that doesn't work, return to the Start screen (press the Windows key) and click the Desktop tile.

   The desktop shows three open application windows, similar to what you see earlier in Figure 2-7. The windows may be different sizes or in different positions on your screen.

2. **In the taskbar, click the Calculator icon.**

   The Calculator window becomes active if it wasn't already. If it was hidden behind another window before, it now appears at the top of the stack.

3. **Click any visible area of the Internet Explorer window.**

   The Internet Explorer window becomes active, and moves to the foreground.

4. **Hold down the Alt key and tap the Tab key.**

5. **Keep tapping the Tab key until the Recycle Bin thumbnail is selected; then release the Alt key.**

   See Figure 2-9. The Recycle Bin window becomes active.

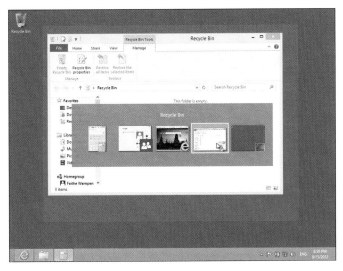

Figure 2-9

6. **Move the mouse pointer to the upper-left corner of the screen.**

   A thumbnail image of the People app appears in the top-left corner.

7. **Slide the mouse pointer down along the left edge of the screen.**

   A black bar appears with thumbnails for the People app and for the Start screen. Refer to Figure 2-8.

8. **Click the thumbnail for the People app.**

   The People app becomes active.

9. **Hold down the Alt key and tap the Tab key until the Calculator thumbnail is selected; then release the Alt key.**

   Leave the applications open for the next exercise.

PRACTICE

For more practice, open several other Windows 8 apps, and switch between them using the procedure from Steps 6-8. Or if you have a touchscreen, practice switching Windows 8 apps by swiping in from the left side of the screen.

Closing an application

For traditional desktop apps, you can easily close the application window by clicking the Close (X) button in the upper-right corner of the window. You can also right-click the app's icon on the taskbar and choose Close Window from the menu that appears. If the application has a menu system, there is probably also an Exit or Close command on the leftmost menu.

For Windows 8 apps, if you have a touch-screen, you can drag from the top of the window all the way down to the bottom of the screen to close the app. You can do the same thing with a mouse by dragging (with the left mouse button held down) from the top of the app window to the bottom of it.

Pressing Alt+F4 also closes the active app or window (and that method works for all types of apps and windows).

In the following exercise, you'll close all the applications that you left open in the previous exercise.

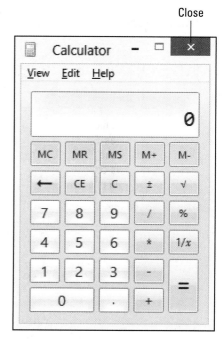

Close

Figure 2-10

1. **Click the red X button in the upper-right corner of the Calculator window, as shown in Figure 2-10.**

   The Calculator application closes.

2. **Right-click the Recycle Bin icon on the taskbar.**

   A menu appears, as shown in Figure 2-11.

3. **Click Close Window.**

   The Recycle Bin window closes.

4. **Click Internet Explorer's title bar to make sure that the window is active.**

5. **(Optional) If you don't see the menu bar for Internet Explorer, press the Alt key to make it appear.**

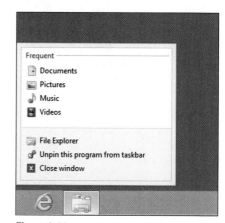

Figure 2-11

6. **Click File on the menu bar.**

   The File menu opens. See Figure 2-12.

7. **Choose Exit from the File menu, as shown in Figure 2-12.**

   Internet Explorer closes.

Figure 2-12

8. **Move the mouse pointer to the upper-left corner of the screen and click.**

   If you have just one open Windows 8 app, you can switch to it by clicking in the upper-left corner. If you have more than one app open, you must point to the upper-left corner and then click the thumbnail for the app you want to make active.

   The People app becomes active.

9. **Move the mouse pointer to the top of the screen, so the pointer becomes a grabbing hand.**

10. **Drag downward to the bottom of the screen.**

    The People app window gets smaller, and then closes. The Start screen displays.

Working in an Application

LINGO

A **menu bar** is a thin bar near the top of the window that contains a series of words. Each word represents a menu name. A **ribbon** is a multitabbed toolbar containing buttons for the commands you can run.

Earlier in this lesson, you saw how the two types of applications that Windows 8 supports are very different in terms of how you start them, switch to them, and exit them. The fun doesn't stop there, though: They go right on being very different from one another in terms of how you use them too.

Working in a desktop application

Desktop applications, as a general rule, have a menu bar or a ribbon. On a menu bar, click a menu name to open a menu, and then click a command on the menu. Some menu-based applications also have one or more toolbars, which are rows of graphical icons that represent common commands. Figure 2-13 shows an application with both a menu bar and a toolbar. In some applications, the menu bar is hidden by default; you can make it appear by pressing the Alt key.

Figure 2-13

In applications that use a ribbon instead of a menu bar, click a tab to display the desired set of buttons, and then click the button that represents the command you want to execute. See Figure 2-14.

Figure 2-14

In this exercise, you'll practice using a ribbon and the menu bar in two desktop applications.

1. **Display the Charms bar and click Search.**

To display the Charms bar, you can point the mouse pointer to the lower-right corner of the screen, or on a touchscreen, you can swipe in from the right side.

A list of the installed applications appears, with a search bar overlaid on the right side.

2. **Click away from the Search bar to see the full Apps list.**

3. **On the Apps list, click WordPad.**

The WordPad application opens. This is a desktop application, so it appears in its own window with the desktop behind it.

WordPad is an example of a desktop application that uses a ribbon. See Figure 2-14.

4. **Click View.**

The View tab on the Ribbon appears.

5. **Click the Ruler check box in the Show or Hide section of the View tab, and then click it again.**

See Figure 2-15. The ruler disappears, and then reappears.

Figure 2-15

6. **Click the Word Wrap button in the Settings section of the View tab.**

   A menu opens, showing the current Word Wrap setting.

7. **If Wrap to Ruler isn't already selected, click Wrap to Ruler.**

   See Figure 2-16.

Figure 2-16

8. **Open the Notepad app in the same way you opened WordPad in Steps 1-3.**

Display the Charms bar and click Search. Click away from the Search bar to see the full list of apps, and then click Notepad.

Notepad opens. Notepad is an example of an application that uses a menu bar.

Close button

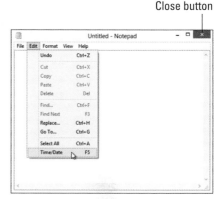

9. **Click Edit and then select Time/ Date from the menu that appears.**

See Figure 2-17. A code that shows the current date and time is inserted.

10. **Click the Close button in the window's upper-right corner to close Notepad.**

11. **Click Don't Save when asked if you want to save changes.**

Figure 2-17

Working in a Windows 8 app

Windows 8 applications have their own unique control methods. At first, new users may be taken aback by a Windows 8 app because it lacks any of the familiar components of a Windows desktop application. For example, it's not in a resizable window, there are no window controls in the upper-right corner, and there is no ribbon or menu system. It's not obvious how to proceed.

Here's a giant clue when it comes to Windows 8 apps: *When in doubt, right-click.* Right-clicking usually brings up a command bar with buttons for issuing commands such as starting a new data file, saving your work, or setting options.

In the following exercise, you will perform some basic activities in a few Windows 8 apps.

1. **Display the Start screen, and click the Calendar tile.**

The Calendar app opens.

2. Right-click anywhere within the Calendar.

A command bar appears across the bottom of the screen. See Figure 2-18.

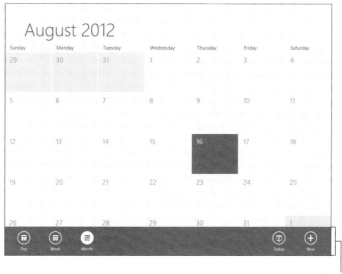

Command bar

Figure 2-18

3. Click Week on the command bar.

The view of the calendar changes to weekly view.

4. Right-click again, and click New on the command bar.

Fields appear in which you can create a new calendar event. The default date is today.

5. Type Mike's Birthday Party.

6. Change the When date to tomorrow, and change the Start time to 2:30 p.m.

Click the arrow to use the pop-up associated with each field. See Figure 2-19.

Each arrow opens a pop-up list.

Save button

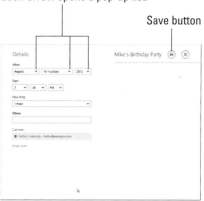

Figure 2-19

7. **Click the Save button — the one that sports a floppy disk as an icon — in the upper-right corner.**

   The event is saved to the calendar.

New contact

8. **Drag from the top of the Calendar app down to the bottom of the screen to close the app.**

9. **On the Start screen, click People.**

   The People app opens.

Figure 2-20

10. **Right-click and then click New on the command bar that appears.**

    Fields appear for creating a new contact.

11. **Fill in the fields shown in Figure 2-20 to create the contact.**

12. **Click the plus sign under the Other Info heading.**

    A pop-up list appears. See Figure 2-21.

Job title

Significant other

Website

Notes

Other info

13. **Click Significant Other.**

    The Significant Other field appears.

14. **In the Significant Other field, type** Duncan.

15. **In the command bar at the bottom of the screen, click Save.**

    The contact info is saved and the information appears onscreen, as shown in Figure 2-22.

Figure 2-21

Fiona Colvin

Email
fiona12914@hotmail.com

Phone
317-555-1411

Other info
Duncan

16. **Click the left-pointing arrow to the left of the contact's name.**

    The list of all stored contacts appears.

17. **Drag the top of the People app down to the bottom of the screen to close the app.**

Figure 2-22

Controlling Application Windows

Application windows are different depending on whether you're working with a desktop app or a Windows 8 app. (Sensing a pattern yet? Windows 8 apps are very different from anything else you've probably encountered in the Windows world.)

For desktop applications, all the window-control commands and buttons are the same as they've been for the last decade's worth of Windows versions. You can minimize a window so that it shrinks to just an icon on the taskbar, maximize a window to fill the screen, or restore a window to a resizable rectangular area that can be moved around on the desktop and resized as needed.

For Windows 8 applications, there are no windows in the traditional sense. Each app fills the entire screen when it is active. However, if you have a high-resolution display, you have the option of snapping open Windows 8 applications to take up either one-third or two-thirds of the screen, so you can run two apps side by side.

LINGO

A **window** is a rectangular area onscreen that contains a particular application, file listing, or message. A window has a title bar, window-control buttons in the upper-right corner, and usually a border that you can drag to resize the window.

Managing desktop windows

Windows that appear on the desktop can have any of three states:

- ✔ **Maximized:** The window fills the entire desktop. Maximize a window when you want to concentrate on the program or document in that window and nothing else.

- ✔ **Restored:** The window is open but not inflated to full-screen size.

- ✔ **Minimized:** The window is still open, but it's hidden from view. An icon for the application appears on the taskbar.

You choose the window's state with the buttons in the window's upper-right corner, as shown in Figure 2-23 and described here.

Minimize button

Maximize/Restore Down

Close button

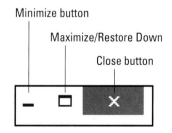

Figure 2-23

- ✔ **Leftmost button:** This is Minimize.

- ✔ **Center button:** This is called either Restore Down or Maximize, depending on the window's current state. (When the window is already maximized, the button is Restore Down; when the window is already restored, the button is Maximize.)

You can also switch between Restored and Maximized by double-clicking the window's title bar.

✔ **Rightmost button (X):** This is Close. This button closes the window, and closes the application, too.

EXTRA INFO

You can minimize all the windows at once with the Show the desktop command. Right-click the taskbar and choose Show the Desktop from the menu that appears.

When a window isn't maximized, you can move and resize it on the desktop. To move a window, drag its title bar. To resize a window, drag anywhere on its border (except at the top, because that's where the title bar is). Dragging a corner enables you to resize both dimensions at once.

In the following exercise, you work with a desktop application's window.

1. **From the desktop, click the Internet Explorer button on the taskbar.**

   Internet Explorer opens.

2. **Click the Maximize/Restore button on the window several times to toggle between maximized and restored sizes. Leave the window restored (nonmaximized).**

   This is the middle of the three window-control buttons in the upper-right corner of the window. Refer to Figure 2-23.

3. **Position the mouse pointer over the right edge of the window.**

   The mouse pointer changes to a two-headed arrow. See Figure 2-24.

4. **Drag inward until the window is about 1" narrower than it was before.**

5. **Drag the window's title bar to move the window to a different location on the desktop.**

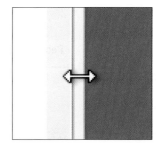

Figure 2-24

6. **Click the Minimize button to minimize the window.**

   The Minimize button is the leftmost of the three buttons shown in Figure 2-23.

7. **On the taskbar, click the Internet Explorer icon to restore the application window.**

8. **Click the Internet Explorer icon on the taskbar again to minimize the window, and then again to restore it.**

   Note that when a window is already open, clicking its icon on the taskbar minimizes it.

9. **Click the Close button.**

   Internet Explorer closes.

Arranging Windows 8 Apps

Windows 8 apps are designed to run full-screen. They can't be windowed like the traditional desktop applications.

However, if your screen resolution is at least 1366 x 768, you can use the Snap feature to make a Windows 8 app occupy either one-third or two-thirds of the screen, rather than filling it completely. You can then do the same to another Windows 8 app, so that the two of them are side by side and you can see them both at once. Figure 2-25 shows the People app in the left one-third of the screen and the Calendar app in the right two-thirds.

People app   Calendar app

Figure 2-25

To snap an app, start dragging the top of it downward, as if you were going to close it, but instead of dragging all the way to the bottom, pause in the center of the screen. The app appears as a thumbnail image, and a vertical bar appears onscreen. Still holding down the mouse button, drag to the left to make the vertical bar appear on the left, or drag to the right to make the vertical bar appear on the right. Then release the mouse button to drop the app into the space between the vertical bar and the edge of the screen. If you don't see the vertical bar, your screen resolution may not be high enough to support the feature.

Once you've got one Windows 8 app snapped into place, go back to the Start screen and open another. The second app nestles itself into the remaining space next to the first app.

You can drag the divider line between the two apps to change their respective shares of the screen space. You can't make them evenly balanced, but you can choose which one has the one-third section and which one has the two-thirds section.

In the following exercise, you arrange two Windows 8 apps side by side.

EXTRA INFO

The desktop itself is seen as an app in the eyes of the Windows 8 interface, so you can place it side by side with a Windows 8 app if you like. Just drag down from the top of the desktop until the desktop turns into a thumbnail image, and then drag it left or right to snap it into place, just like you would a Windows 8 app.

1. **From the Start screen, open the Weather app.**

2. **Position the mouse pointer at the top of the screen.**

   The pointer becomes a hand.

3. **Drag downward until the app becomes a thumbnail image that moves as you drag.**

   See Figure 2-26.

4. **Drag to the right until a vertical divider appears.**

5. **Release the mouse button.**

   The Weather app snaps into the rightmost one-third of the screen.

6. **Press the Windows key to redisplay the Start screen, and click the Calendar tile.**

   The Calendar app opens in the remaining two-thirds of the screen, to the left of the Weather app. See Figure 2-27.

Drag thumbnail to right to snap into place.

Figure 2-26

Calendar app   Weather app

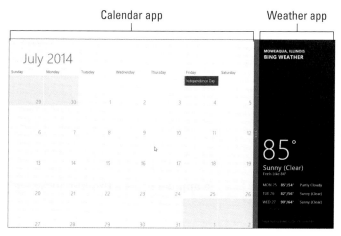

Figure 2-27

7. **Press the Windows key to redisplay the Start screen, and click the Desktop tile.**

   The desktop appears in the left two-thirds of the screen, replacing the Calendar app there.

8. **Move the mouse pointer to the upper-left corner of the screen, and when you see the thumbnail of the Calendar app, click it. Or if you have a touchscreen, swipe in from the left.**

   The Calendar app appears again in the left two-thirds of the screen.

9. **Close the Calendar app, and then close the Weather app.**

   The Start screen reappears.

Installing, Repairing, and Removing Applications

Windows has some great apps included with it, but for maximum productivity (and fun), you'll probably want to install additional apps. You can download new apps from the Windows Store, download apps from websites, buy apps on CD or DVD from stores, or acquire apps from your friends and relatives (providing, of course, that you aren't breaking any copyright laws in the process). In the following sections, I show you how to install, repair, and remove various types of applications.

Installing Windows 8 apps

The Windows Store is an online store you can use to acquire new apps. Some of them are free; others require you to pay by credit card. You access the Windows Store via the Store app.

The Windows Store, like other online stores, is constantly changing and offering different products, so it may look different on the day you visit it than what's shown here. That's to be expected.

LINGO

The **Windows Store** is an app in Windows 8 that enables you to easily browse, select, and install new apps.

The Windows Store's format is very much like that of the Start screen on your Windows 8 PC: It's a series of tiles. You can scroll to the right to see additional offerings. (Use the scroll bar at the bottom of the screen, or if you have a touchscreen, drag to the right.) When you see an app you want to check out, click (or tap) its tile.

In the following exercise, you'll download a new app from the Windows store.

1. **From the Start screen, click Store.**

    The Store app opens. See Figure 2-28.

Figure 2-28

2. **Click the Top Free tile.**

    A list of free apps appears.

3. **Click one of the apps that interests you.**

    For example, you could click the USA Today app.

    A screen appears telling you about the app you chose, and displaying an Install button.

4. **Click Install.**

    The app is installed in the background, and the list of free apps appears again. In the upper-right corner of the screen is a message saying that the app is being installed. When the installation is finished, a sound plays.

5. **Press the Windows key to return to the Start screen.**

6. **On the Start screen, locate and click the new app's tile.**

    It will probably appear at the far right, as shown in Figure 2-29.

7. **Explore the new app, and then close it.**

New app

Figure 2-29

Updating Windows 8 apps

Windows 8 app developers release bug fixes and new versions periodically to keep up with customer requests. You can install updates for the apps you have on your system through a simple point-and-click interface in the Windows Store.

In this exercise, you'll install all available updates for your Windows 8 apps.

1. **From the Start screen, notice the number in the bottom-right corner of the Store tile.**

   The number represents how many app updates are available to install. For example, in Figure 2-30 there is 1 update available. If you don't see a number there, no updates are available, so you can't do this exercise.

2. **Click the Store tile.**

   The Windows Store opens.

Number of updates available

Figure 2-30

3. Click the Update(s) hyperlink in the upper-right corner of the Windows Store screen.

A list of available app updates appears. By default, all the app updates are selected; you can tell because each one has a check mark in its upper-right corner. There's one update available in Figure 2-31. (Your list will be different.)

4. Click the Install icon.

All the updates are installed in the background.

5. When the updates are finished, close the Windows Store app.

Check mark

Install icon

Figure 2-31

Removing Windows 8 apps

Windows 8 apps are extremely easy to remove. Right-click the app's tile on the Start screen and choose Uninstall from the command bar that appears. Nothing to it!

In this very quick exercise, you'll remove the app that you installed earlier in the lesson.

1. From the Start screen, right-click the app that you want to remove.

A command bar appears at the bottom of the screen. One of the options on it is Uninstall. See Figure 2-32.

Uninstall icon

Figure 2-32

2. **Click Uninstall on the command bar.**

   A warning appears that the app will be removed from the PC. See Figure 2-33.

3. **Click the Uninstall button in the warning message.**

   The app is removed.

Figure 2-33

Installing a new desktop application

Even though Windows 8 apps are all the rage, desktop applications are still very much alive and well. Most of the business productivity tools you use will probably still be desktop applications for many years to come. Desktop applications include Microsoft Office, financial programs like Quicken, and photo-editing software like Photoshop. Desktop applications that were created for earlier versions of Windows should run just fine on Windows 8 in most cases.

If you bought your new application on CD or DVD, you may be able to just pop it into the drive, and the Setup utility will start automatically. If it doesn't, you can open up File Explorer, click Computer, and then double-click the drive icon for the CD/DVD drive. If Setup starts at that point — great. If it doesn't, then a list of files on the disc appears. Locate Setup. exe on that list and double-click Setup.exe to get the ball rolling.

If you downloaded the new application, the file you downloaded is probably a Setup package. Just double-click it to run it, and follow the prompts.

Repairing or uninstalling desktop applications

Sometimes an application may start acting funny. Not funny ha-ha, but funny like it got bonked in the head and is staggering around. Maybe it locks up or crashes, for example. Maybe it won't open files anymore, or it won't shut down.

Whatever the problem, you may be able to solve it by repairing the application. Repairing an application consults the original setup log file and checks to see what files should be present and what their file sizes should be. If anything's not right, the setup program recopies the altered or missing files.

Repairing is available only for desktop apps, not Windows 8 apps. With a Windows 8 app, it's so fast and easy to uninstall and reinstall that there's no real advantage to repairing it.

Uninstalling an application removes it completely from your computer. It deletes all the files needed to run the application, and it lets Windows know that the app is no longer available so that it won't appear on the Apps list.

To repair or uninstall a desktop application, you have to go into the Control Panel, which is a suite of utilities for adjusting settings and making changes to how Windows functions.

In the following exercise, you'll repair an application.

1. **From the desktop, display the Charms bar, and click Settings.**

   A Settings panel appears on the right side of the screen. See Figure 2-34.

Figure 2-34

2. **Click Control Panel.**

   A Control Panel window opens.

   The Control Panel is one thing that's fairly similar to Windows 7, once you get into it. So if you've used the Control Panel in the past, these steps should start seeming familiar at this point. See Figure 2-35.

Click Uninstall a Program

Figure 2-35

3. **Under the Programs heading, click Uninstall a Program.**

   The Uninstall or Change a Program screen appears.

4. **Click one of the applications on the list, and note the options available on the command bar above the list. Click several others, and compare the options.**

   Some applications will have only an Uninstall command there; others will have additional commands, perhaps Change and/or Repair. In Figure 2-36, the selected application has a single button labeled Uninstall/Change.

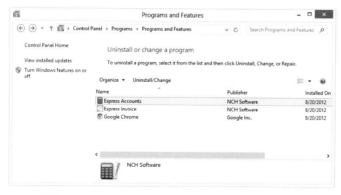

Figure 2-36

5. **Select one of the apps that has a Repair or a Change option, and click the Repair or Change command.**

If you wanted to uninstall a program, you'd click Uninstall in Step 5 instead of Repair.

The Windows Installer runs.

6. **If a User Account Control box appears, click Yes.**

This is a security warning designed to prevent viruses and other malware from modifying your system without your permission.

7. **Follow the prompts to check the application and repair or change it if necessary.**

From this point on, the steps are different depending on what application it is.

 Summing Up

In this lesson, you learned how to run and manage applications, both the traditional desktop apps and the newer Windows 8 apps. Here's a quick review:

✔ Desktop applications are the traditional Windows apps that run on the desktop, in their own windows; Windows 8 apps are the tablet-style apps.

✔ To start an app, click its shortcut on the desktop or taskbar, or on the Start screen. If there's no shortcut, you display the Apps list and select the app from there.

✔ To switch between apps, you can us Alt+Tab for desktop apps. For Windows 8 apps, move the mouse pointer to the upper-left corner of the screen and then click the thumbnail of the app to switch to, or swipe the touchscreen from the left.

✔ To close a Windows 8 app, drag from the top of the screen to the bottom. To close a desktop app, click the Close (X) button in its upper-right corner.

✔ Desktop apps use a menu system or a ribbon, depending on the program. Windows 8 apps have a command bar, which you can display by right-clicking.

🗸 You can minimize, maximize, restore, or close a desktop application window with the window controls in the upper-right corner of the window.

🗸 Windows 8 apps run full-screen by default, but if your screen resolution is at least 1366 x 768, you can snap an app to fill one-third or two-thirds of the screen by dragging from the top of the app to the center of the screen and then dragging right or left.

🗸 To install new Windows 8 apps, choose them from the Windows Store. Use the Store icon on the Start screen to enter the store.

🗸 To install desktop apps, insert the disc for the app and follow the prompts, or double-click the Setup file for the app.

🗸 To uninstall a Windows 8 app, right-click its tile in the Start screen and click Uninstall on the command bar. To uninstall a desktop app, display the Programs section of the Control Panel and then select the application and click Uninstall (or Uninstall/Change).

Know This Tech Talk

desktop application: A traditional-style application designed to run on Windows 8 or earlier, running on the Windows desktop in a resizable window.

maximized: A window that fills the entire desktop.

menu bar: The thin bar near the top of the window that contains a series of words. Each word represents a menu name.

minimized: An open window that doesn't appear on the desktop except for an icon on the taskbar.

restored: A window that isn't maximized.

ribbon: A multitabbed toolbar containing buttons for the commands you can run.

snap: A feature that enables you to tile two Windows 8 apps side by side.

window: A rectangular area onscreen that contains a particular application, file listing, or message.

Windows 8 app: A tablet-style application designed specifically for Windows 8.

Windows Store: An app that enables you to browse, select, and install new Windows 8 apps.

Customizing the Start Screen and the Desktop

✔ Customize the Start screen.

✔ Work with desktop shortcuts.

✔ Customize the taskbar.

✔ Set display options.

*W*indows 8 works pretty well right off the shelf, but to take full advantage of it, you'll probably want to make some adjustments. These may include pinning shortcuts for your favorite programs and locations to convenient spots like the Start screen and the taskbar, and adjusting display options to make the desktop easier to see and more fun to look at. In this lesson, you'll learn how to customize Windows 8 in a variety of ways to make it your own.

Customizing the Start Screen

The Start screen (ideally) provides quick access shortcuts to the applications and locations you use the most. In its default configuration, it contains shortcuts to things that Microsoft *thinks* you'll use the most, but that's not really the same thing, is it? Therefore, you'll probably want to ditch some of the tiles on the Start screen and add some others. You may want to resize some of the tiles too, and rearrange them.

Pinning and unpinning an app

Do you find yourself constantly browsing to a certain folder, or running a certain app that's not already on the Start screen? Give yourself a break. You can pin a tile to the Start screen for any installed application or any folder and then use that tile to jump right to that folder or application.

To pin an app to the Start screen, first locate the app on the Apps list. (To get to the Apps list, start at the Start screen, right-click, and click the All Apps icon on the command bar that

LINGO

To **pin** an item to the Start screen is to create a tile for it there. You can also pin items to the taskbar on the desktop, as you will learn later in this chapter. To **unpin** an item means to remove its tile or shortcut.

appears.) Then right-click the desired app and choose Pin to Start from the command bar. To unpin an app from the Start screen, right-click the app's existing tile and click Unpin from Start from the same command bar.

In the following exercise, you will pin a shortcut for Notepad to the Start screen, and then unpin it.

1. **From the Start screen, right-click in an empty area.**

   The command bar appears at the bottom of the screen, containing a single icon: All Apps. See Figure 3-1.

2. **Click All Apps.**

   A list of all the installed apps appears.

Figure 3-1

3. **Right-click the Notepad app.**

   A command bar appears at the bottom of the screen, containing several icons. See Figure 3-2.

4. **Click Pin to Start.**

   The command bar goes away, but the Apps list stays open.

5. **Press the Windows key to return to the Start screen.**

Figure 3-2

6. **Scroll the Start screen to the right to locate the new Notepad tile.**

7. **Right-click the Notepad tile.**

   A command bar appears at the bottom of the screen. See Figure 3-3.

Figure 3-3

8. **Click Unpin from Start.**

The Notepad tile is removed from the Start screen.

For more practice on your own, pin several other apps to the Start screen. Choose apps that you frequently use but that aren't already on the Start screen. For example, you might want Calculator or WordPad.

Pinning and unpinning a folder

As you saw in Lesson 1, you can access File Explorer from a tile on the Start screen. When you do so, it opens with the list of various Libraries displays. You can create your own shortcuts to other locations, too, for quick access to the folders you use most often.

To pin a folder to the Start screen, locate the folder in File Explorer, and then right-click it and select Pin to Start from the shortcut menu that appears. (Remember, since you're in File Explorer and not the Start screen, right-clicking brings up the shortcut menu, not the command bar.)

In the following exercise, you'll pin a shortcut to the Computer window (that is, the File Explorer location that shows all the drives on your computer) to the Start screen.

1. **From File Explorer, locate the Computer icon in the Navigation pane, and right-click it.**

   See Figure 3-4.

2. **Choose Pin to Start.**

3. **Press the Windows key.**

   The Start screen displays.

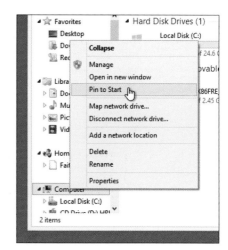

Figure 3-4

4. Scroll to the right to locate the new Computer tile.

See Figure 3-5.

Figure 3-5

Changing a tile size

Most tiles on the Start screen are squares, but some of the Windows 8 app tiles are larger rectangles that take up two squares' worth of space. You can adjust a tile's size by right-clicking it and then choosing Larger or Smaller from its command bar, whichever is not already in effect. If you don't see either of those options available, that tile can't be resized.

In the following exercise, you'll resize the tile for the Calendar app, and then put it back to its original size.

1. From the Start screen, right-click the Calendar app tile.

A command bar appears. See Figure 3-6. The Calendar app is currently at Larger size, so it appears as a rectangle.

2. Click Smaller.

The Calendar app's tile appears as a small square. See Figure 3-7.

3. Right-click the Calendar app tile again.

A command bar appears.

Figure 3-6

Figure 3-7

4. Click Larger.

The Calendar app's tile appears as a large rectangle again.

For more practice, resize all the app tiles to represent the size that's most appropriate for your usage. Make the tiles for apps you don't use very much smaller, and make the tiles for apps you use frequently larger.

Rearranging the tiles

You can move the tiles around on the Start screen so that the tiles you use the most appear in the leftmost positions (so you don't have to scroll to see them). To move a tile, drag and drop it.

Drag and drop gets a little tricky, though, when you're dealing with a touch-screen. When you drag in the direction that the display scrolls (which, for the Start screen, is left and right), Windows scrolls the display rather than moving the tile. Therefore, when you want to move a tile using a touchscreen interface, you must start by dragging it up or down to get it started; then you can drag left or right to position it as needed.

In the following exercise, you'll rearrange some icons on the Start screen using a mouse. You can do this exercise with a touchpad, too (or instead), if you have one.

1. On the Start screen, click and hold down the mouse button on the Calendar app's tile.

Don't release the mouse button — or the Calendar app will start, and that's not what you want right now.

2. Drag the Calendar app's tile up one position (or if the tile is already on the top row, drag it down one position).

See Figure 3-8.

3. Release the mouse button when the tile is in the desired spot.

Figure 3-8

For more practice, move all the tiles for the apps you use most frequently to the leftmost positions of the Start screen.

Working with Desktop Shortcuts

The Start screen is only one of several places where you can stash shortcuts to your most frequently used apps and locations. The desktop can also serve as a holding area for shortcuts, too.

Whereas the Start screen holds tiles only for apps and locations, the desktop is a bit more versatile. You can create a shortcut for *any* type of file, folder, or drive on the desktop.

LINGO

A **shortcut** is a pointer to a file or location. Shortcuts allow a single file to be in two places at once — or at least to seem so. For example, you could store the original of a file in your Documents library, and keep a shortcut to it on your desktop.

Make sure you understand the difference between a file and its shortcut before you go any further. (Both files and shortcuts can be placed on the desktop, so you can't go by location.) Each file has a unique storage location where it resides. A shortcut is a pointer to the file's actual location. When you double-click a shortcut, the original file to which it refers opens. The shortcut icon looks similar to the file's regular icon. It may have the word *shortcut* in its name, but don't count on that 100 percent. It may also have an arrow in the lower-left corner of the icon, as shown on the right in Figure 3-9.

Figure 3-9

Creating and deleting desktop shortcuts

To create a shortcut for any file or folder on the desktop, right-drag the item out of a File Explorer window and onto the desktop. When you release the mouse button, a menu appears. From that menu, select Create Shortcuts Here.

To delete a shortcut, you can do any of the following:

✔ **Drag the shortcut to the Recycle Bin.**

✔ **Right-click the shortcut and click Delete from the menu that appears.**

✔ **Click the shortcut to select it and then press the Delete key.**

In the following exercise, you'll create a desktop shortcut for the C drive and then delete it.

1. **In File Explorer, click Computer in the Navigation pane.**

   A list of the drives appears.

2. **Right-drag the C drive's icon to the desktop.**

   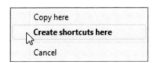

   To right-drag, click and hold down the right mouse button as you drag the icon to the desktop. When you release the mouse button, a menu appears. See Figure 3-10.

   Figure 3-10

3. **Click Create Shortcuts Here.**

   A shortcut is created on the desktop for the C drive.

4. **Double-click the C drive shortcut to open the C drive's contents in File Explorer.**

5. **Close all open File Explorer windows.**

6. **Drag the C drive shortcut to the Recycle Bin.**

The shortcut is deleted. Deleting a shortcut doesn't affect the original file or the location that it represents.

For more practice, create other shortcuts on your desktop to locations you access frequently. For example, create a desktop shortcut to your Pictures library by right-dragging the Pictures icon from the Libraries list in the Navigation pane in File Explorer to the desktop.

Sizing and arranging desktop shortcuts

By default, the icons on the desktop appear in medium size. You can make them larger or smaller by right-clicking the desktop, pointing to View, and then clicking Large icons, Medium icons, or Small icons. See Figure 3-11. This setting affects all icons on the desktop; you can't resize individual icons. Icon size is a matter of individual preference; you might want to display them at the larger size for easier touchscreen access, or smaller so you can fit more of them on the desktop at once.

Figure 3-11

Notice in Figure 3-11 that the View submenu has several other options on it, including these:

- ✔ **Auto Arrange Icons:** When this option is on, the icons line up in an orderly fashion along the left side of the desktop, and you can't move them around freely by dragging them.

- ✔ **Align Icons to Grid:** When this option is on and you drag an icon to move it, it drops into place in an invisible grid when you release it, so that icons that are approximately aligned with each other will be exactly aligned with each other. It makes the desktop look a bit more tidy.

- ✔ **Show Desktop Icons:** When this option is on, desktop icons display. When this is off, they're hidden.

You can also sort and arrange the desktop icons by name, size, item type, or date modified. To do that, right-click the desktop, point to Sort By, and then click one of those attributes. See Figure 3-12.

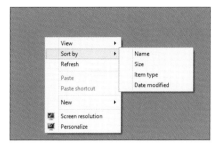

In this exercise, you'll create three desktop shortcut icons and then size and arrange them in several ways.

Figure 3-12

1. **From File Explorer, create a shortcut for the Documents library on the desktop.**

   To do so, right-drag the Documents icon from the Navigation pane to the desktop, and then select Create Shortcut Here from the menu that appears.

2. **Create shortcuts for the Music and Pictures libraries on the desktop.**

   Use the same technique as in Step 1.

3. **Close File Explorer.**

4. **Right-click a blank area of the desktop, point to View, and then click Large Icons.**

   The icons enlarge. See Figure 3-13.

5. **Right-click a blank area of the desktop, point to Sort By, and then click Name.**

   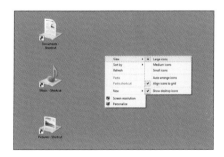

   The icons arrange themselves in a single column on the left side of the desktop, in alphabetical order. The Recycle Bin icon isn't affected by this sorting because it's a special-purpose icon.

   Figure 3-13

6. **Drag the Documents icon to the center of the desktop.**

7. **Right-click a blank area of the desktop, point to View, and then click Auto Arrange Icons.**

   The Documents shortcut snaps back into its previous location.

8. **Try dragging the Documents icon back to the center of the desktop.**

   This time it won't drag because Auto Arrange is on.

9. **Right-click a blank area of the desktop, point to View, and then click Auto Arrange Icons.**

   Auto Arrange is now turned off.

10. **Right-click a blank area of the desktop, point to View, and then click Medium Icons.**

    The icons are now back to the way they were originally.

Customizing the Taskbar

The taskbar can be customized in a variety of ways. For example, you can pin and unpin shortcuts to it, change its size, and change where it appears onscreen. In the following sections, you'll learn how to change the taskbar to meet your needs.

Pinning shortcuts to the taskbar

You probably noticed already that the taskbar has a couple of icons pinned to it by default: one for Internet Explorer and one for File Explorer. These are a good start.

You can pin a shortcut to almost any desktop application to the taskbar. (You can't pin shortcuts to Windows 8 apps there.) The left end of the taskbar can become your own personal app-launching toolbar, so you never have to leave the desktop (well, almost never) if you use Windows mostly to run desktop apps.

To pin an app to the taskbar, find it on the Start screen or on the Apps list, right-click it, and then click the Pin to Taskbar icon on the command bar or shortcut menu that appears. (Yep, it's nearly identical to the procedure for pinning to the Start screen, which you learned earlier in this lesson.)

In the following exercise, you'll pin a shortcut for the Calculator application to the taskbar.

1. **From the Start screen, right-click any blank area.**

   The command bar appears.

2. **Click All Apps.**

   A list of all installed applications appears.

3. Right-click the Calculator app.

Commands for that app appear in the command bar. See Figure 3-14.

Figure 3-14

4. Click Pin to Taskbar.

5. Press the Esc key to display the desktop.

A shortcut for Calculator appears on the task-bar. See Figure 3-15.

Figure 3-15

6. Click the Calculator shortcut.

The Calculator app opens.

7. Click the Close button in the upper-right corner of the Calculator window.

The Calculator app closes.

Autohiding the taskbar

Even though the taskbar doesn't take up very much space onscreen, some-times it still gets in the way. Fortunately, there's an Auto-hide option you can enable, which hides the taskbar when you're not using it. When you want the taskbar, you can just move the mouse pointer to the bottom of the screen, and the taskbar pops right into view.

In the following exercise, you'll enable the Auto-hide feature for the taskbar, experiment with it, and then disable it again.

1. **From the desktop, right-click the taskbar.**

   A menu appears.

2. **Click Properties.**

   The Taskbar Properties dialog box appears.

3. **Select the Auto-hide the Taskbar check box.**

   See Figure 3-16.

4. **Click OK.**

   The dialog box closes, and the task-bar disappears.

5. **Move the mouse pointer to the bottom of the screen.**

   The taskbar reappears.

6. **Move the mouse pointer to the center of the screen.**

   The taskbar disappears again.

7. **Move the mouse pointer to the bottom of the screen, and right-click the taskbar.**

Figure 3-16

8. **Click Properties.**

   The Taskbar Properties dialog box reappears.

9. **Deselect the Auto-hide the Taskbar check box.**

10. **Click OK.**

    The taskbar displays again.

Controlling taskbar options

Besides the autohide behavior, which you just learned about, there are also a variety of other taskbar options you can control from the Taskbar Properties dialog box. (Refer to Figure 3-16.) Here's a quick rundown:

✔ **Lock the Taskbar:** On by default, this option prevents accidental changes to the taskbar, such as accidentally dragging its border to change its size. You can also access this option by right-clicking the taskbar and choosing Lock the Taskbar.

PRACTICE

Try out the taskbar locking/unlocking now if you want: Unlock the taskbar, and then position the mouse pointer on the taskbar's top border and drag upward. Notice how you just made the taskbar taller? Drag it back to normal size, and then lock the taskbar again. Now try resizing it. Doesn't work — does it?

✔ **Use Small Taskbar Buttons:** This option makes the taskbar icons smaller.

✔ **Taskbar Location on Screen:** Bottom is the default, but you can place the taskbar at the Top, Left, or Right if you prefer.

✔ **Taskbar buttons:** The default is Always Combine, Hide Labels.

- *Always Combine* means that if you have multiple instances of the same app open, such as multiple documents in the same word processor, they'll appear as a single button on the taskbar.

- *Hide Labels* means that each icon appears as a small graphic without any text on it.

  The other available options are Combine When Taskbar is Full, which combines icons only when necessary, and Never Combine.

✔ **Notification area:** Click the Customize button here to open the Notification Area Icons page of the Control Panel, where you can choose which icons appear in the Notification area and under what circumstances.

LINGO

The **Control Panel** is the interface you use in Windows to change various system settings.

✔ **Use Peek to Preview the Desktop When You Move Your Mouse to the Show Desktop Button at the End of the Taskbar:** This rather self-explanatorily named check box turns the Peek feature on or off. The Show Desktop Button that's referenced here is at the far right end of the taskbar. There's no "button" there per se, but if you hover your mouse there, you can see Peek in action.

In the following exercise, you'll experiment with some taskbar settings.

1. **From the desktop, right-click the taskbar and choose Properties from the menu that appears.**

   The Taskbar Properties dialog box opens. (Refer to Figure 3-16.)

2. **Select the Use Small Taskbar Buttons check box.**

3. **Choose Never Combine from the Taskbar Buttons drop-down list.**

4. Click OK.

The buttons change on the taskbar to look more like earlier versions of Windows.

5. Click the File Explorer icon to open File Explorer.

Notice that when File Explorer is running, its taskbar button changes to show the name of the location being displayed (Libraries). With the current taskbar options, the difference between a pinned shortcut and an open window is more dramatic. See Figure 3-17.

Figure 3-17

6. Right-click the taskbar and note whether the taskbar is currently locked. If it's locked, click the Lock the Taskbar command to unlock it.

7. Position the mouse pointer at the top edge of the taskbar so that the pointer becomes a double-headed arrow, and drag upward to increase the size of the taskbar.

See Figure 3-18.

Figure 3-18

8. Drag the top border of the taskbar back down again so the taskbar is at its original height again.

9. Right-click the taskbar and choose Properties from the menu that appears.

The Taskbar Properties dialog box reopens.

10. Deselect the Use Small Taskbar Buttons check box and then click Apply to see the result.

Clicking Apply applies the new setting without closing the dialog box. If you had clicked OK instead, the dialog box would've closed.

The taskbar grows in height to accommodate larger icons. The names of the open windows still appear next to the icons.

11. Choose Always Combine, Hide Labels from the Taskbar Buttons drop-down list.

12. **Select the Lock the Taskbar check box.**

13. **Click OK.**

The taskbar returns to its original appearance.

Adding toolbars to the taskbar

The taskbar is very versatile. It doesn't seem like much in its default state — what's up with that immense empty space in the center? — but you can add toolbars to it to increase its functionality.

Windows 8 offers these toolbars for your use on the taskbar:

- ✓ **Address:** Adds an Address bar to the taskbar, into which you can type web addresses. When you do so, an Internet Explorer window opens to show the page.

- ✓ **Links:** Adds a button for Internet Explorer's Links toolbar to the taskbar. In Internet Explorer, you can customize the Links toolbar to contain buttons for the sites you visit most often; you can have those same buttons available to you on the desktop by adding the Links toolbar to the taskbar.

- ✓ **Touch Keyboard:** Adds a shortcut link to a pop-up onscreen keyboard, which may come in handy if you're using Windows 8 on a touchscreen tablet that doesn't have its own physical keyboard.

- ✓ **Desktop:** Adds a button for a Desktop menu to the taskbar. This Desktop menu contains buttons for all the icons on your desktop, plus a standard set of commonly accessed places, like Libraries, HomeGroup, Computer, Control Panel, and so on.

In this exercise, you'll turn on each of the optional toolbars on the taskbar, and then experiment with using them before turning them off again.

1. **From the desktop, right-click the task-bar, point to Toolbars in the menu that appears, and note which toolbars already have check marks next to them.**

   The ones with the check marks (if any) are already on.

EXTRA INFO

You can also create your own new toolbars using content from a folder you specify. That's useful because it enables you to create a toolbar that changes as the folder content changes. To create your own toolbar, first create a new folder and create shortcuts in it to all the items you want to reference. Then right-click the taskbar, point to Toolbars, click New toolbar, and specify the folder to use.

2. **Click one of the toolbars that isn't already on, to turn it on.**

3. **Repeat Step 1 until all four of the toolbars are on.**

4. **In the Address bar, type** www.wiley.com **and press Enter.**

   Internet Explorer opens and displays the Wiley website.

5. **Close Internet Explorer.**

6. **Click the double right-pointing arrow to the right of Links.**

   A pop-up list of links appears. (See Figure 3-19.) The items on the list depend on the Links toolbar content on your computer.

Figure 3-19

7. **Click away from the menu to close it.**

8. **Click the double right-pointing arrow to the right of Desktop.**

   A pop-up list of local locations appears. Besides the basic set shown in Figure 3-20, any desktop icons also appear on the list.

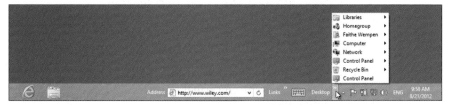

Figure 3-20

9. **Click away from the menu to close it.**

10. **Click the Touch Keyboard icon.**

    The Touch Keyboard icon looks like a keyboard.

    A keyboard opens onscreen.

11. **Click the Close button (X) in its upper-right corner of the keyboard window to close the keyboard.**

12. **Right-click the taskbar, point to Toolbars, and click one of the toolbars to turn it off.**

13. **Repeat Step 12 until all toolbars are off.**

    Exception: If you're using a touchscreen computer, you may want to leave the Touch Keyboard enabled in the taskbar.

Setting Display Options

Display settings can make a huge difference in your Windows experience. You can make items in the display larger and more readable, choose different desktop appearance themes, change the wallpaper picture on your desktop, and much more. In this section, you'll learn how to make some of the most common display changes.

Changing the display resolution

Changing the display resolution has several consequences. The most obvious of these is size: The higher the resolution, the smaller everything looks onscreen (text, icons, and so on).

In "Sizing and arranging desktop shortcuts" earlier in this lesson, you learn how to change the icon size on the desktop. Resolution indirectly affects icon size because the operating system describes each icon and each character of text as a certain number of pixels at a certain setting. For example, a typical icon at the Medium Icons size might be 30 x 30 pixels. On a low-resolution screen, 30 pixels might be 1/20th of the screen width, but at a higher resolution, 30 pixels might be only 1/40th of the screen width. Assuming that your monitor doesn't physically change size, the same icon in a high-resolution display mode could be only half the size it would be in a low-resolution mode.

Another consequence of resolution change is a differing amount of display sharpness. At the monitor's highest resolution (also called its *native resolution*), the display is the sharpest. At lower resolutions, the display may appear fuzzy, especially when displaying text. (This wasn't a problem on the older-style CRT monitors, the big boxy kind of monitor that was popular 10+ years ago. It's a big problem on flat-screen LCD monitors used today, though.)

LINGO

The **display resolution** is the number of individual pixels (colored dots) that comprise the display you see onscreen. It's expressed as a horizontal measurement and a vertical measurement, like this: 1366 x 768.

EXTRA INFO

Everyone wants their monitor image to be the sharpest it can be, but some people have trouble seeing text and icons at a tiny size. You can partly counteract the effect of using a high resolution by increasing the desktop's and taskbar's icon sizes (as you learned in "Sizing and arranging desktop shortcuts" and "Controlling taskbar options" earlier in the chapter) and by changing the text size of Windows system fonts (covered in "Adjusting screen font size" later in this chapter).

In this exercise, you'll change the display resolution.

1. **Right-click the desktop and choose Screen Resolution from the menu that appears.**

   The Screen Resolution dialog box opens. It's part of the Control Panel.

2. **Open the Resolution drop-down list to reveal a Resolution slider, then drag the slider to the desired resolution.**

   The resolutions available on your PC depend on your display adapter and your monitor, and may not be the same as shown in Figure 3-21.

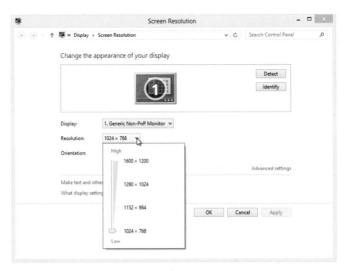

Figure 3-21

3. **Click OK.**

   A message appears, asking if you want to keep the changes.

4. **Click Keep Changes.**

   The display shows the new resolution. If you decreased the resolution, the display may appear slightly fuzzy. If you chose a resolution that has a different ratio of width to height, buttons and text on the screen may appear stretched or squashed.

Adjusting screen font size

After changing the display resolution, you may find that the onscreen text needs adjustment also. For example, the text in dialog boxes, under desktop icons, and in file listings may be too small or too large for your reading comfort. Fortunately, you aren't stuck with the default font size in a given resolution; you can adjust font size separately. Changing the font size may be a more satisfactory solution than lowering the resolution if you're having a hard time reading text onscreen, because lowering the resolution may make the display fuzzy, as mentioned previously.

The exact size choices available depend on the monitor and the display adapter, but a 125% option is almost always available. This size makes everything a little bit more readable and easy to see without going overboard and making text too large and obtrusive.

EXTRA INFO

Some apps rely on the screen font being a certain size in order to display certain dialog boxes properly. If you're using a large screen font size and some text is truncated in some apps, try decreasing the screen font size when running that app.

In the following exercise, you'll choose a larger screen font size.

1. **Right-click the desktop and choose Personalize from the menu that appears.**

   The Personalization screen appears. It's part of the Control Panel. See Figure 3-22.

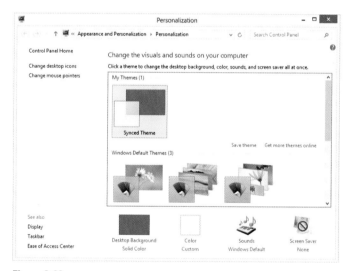

Figure 3-22

2. **In the lower-left corner of the screen, click Display.**

   The Display screen appears.

3. Click Medium – 125%.

See Figure 3-23. Depending on your display adapter and monitor resolution, you may have other font size choices than the ones shown here.

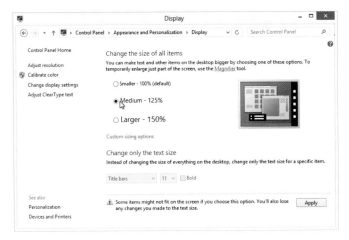

Figure 3-23

4. Click Apply.

A message appears, notifying you that you must sign out of your computer to make these changes.

5. Click Sign out Now.

You are signed out of Windows.

6. Press the spacebar to open the login prompt.

7. Type your password and press Enter to log back in.

8. Click the Desktop tile to redisplay the desktop.

The fonts and icons are now 25 percent larger.

For more practice, return the desktop to the smaller font size.

Changing the desktop wallpaper and window color

Wallpaper provides the image that you see on your desktop. Windows 8 comes with a variety of images suitable for use as wallpaper; you can also use pictures of your own, such as photos you've taken with your digital camera, or if you'd rather not use a picture, you can make the desktop a solid color, as shown in the figures in this book.

You can also affect the desktop appearance by changing the window color. In the figures in this book, I've set the window color to pale gray for maximum readability, but you may prefer something a bit more cheerful.

In this exercise, you'll choose a different desktop wallpaper image and a different window color.

1. **Right-click the desktop and click Personalize.**

   The Personalization screen appears. (Refer to Figure 3-22.)

2. **Click Desktop Background.**

   Options appear for changing the desktop background.

3. **From the Picture location drop-down list, select Windows Desktop Backgrounds.**

   A selection of background images appears.

4. **Click Clear all, and then click any picture that appeals to you.**

   See Figure 3-24. The background behind the dialog box changes immediately to that image.

5. **Hold down the Ctrl key and click a second picture.**

   Windows will switch among the chosen pictures for desktop backgrounds because of the selection you made in Step 3.

   Now both pictures are selected; each has a check mark in its upper-left corner. The Change Picture Every drop-down list also becomes active.

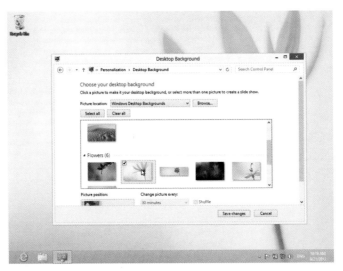

Figure 3-24

You can change the Change Picture Every interval if you want to, so the picture(s) change more or less frequently.

If you'd rather use one of your own pictures as wallpaper, you can instead choose Pictures Library from the Picture Location drop-down menu and select a picture that's saved in your Pictures library.

You might instead opt to select a solid background color, perhaps so that the desktop icons are easy to identify. In that case, choose Solid Colors from the Picture Location drop-down list, as shown in Figure 3-25 and click a square to select a color.

Figure 3-25

6. Click Save Changes.

The Personalization screen reappears.

7. Near the bottom, click Window Color.

A palette of window colors appears. See Figure 3-26.

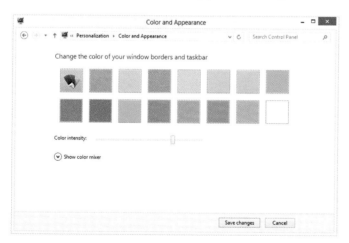

Figure 3-26

8. Click a color swatch.

The window color changes immediately to that color.

9. **Click the first swatch in the top row (Automatic).**

   This swatch represents Automatic, which allows the theme to choose the window color. Since you'll be applying a theme later in this lesson, leaving the window color set to Automatic is a good idea for now.

10. **Click Save Changes.**

    The choice of Automatic is saved, and the Personalization screen reappears.

11. **Click the Close button to close the Personalization screen.**

Changing the screen saver

Employing a screen saver was important back in the days when a monitor could "burn in" an image if the image were displayed on it for too long. Nowadays, most people don't use the kind of monitor that burns in an image easily anymore, so a screen saver is no longer a must. However, some people still enjoy using one because they like seeing the moving image onscreen.

LINGO

A **screen saver** is a moving graphic that appears onscreen after a specified period of inactivity.

In addition, a screen saver can provide a rudimentary form of local privacy on your computer. While you're away from the computer, a screen saver obscures what you're working on onscreen, so passers-by can't snoop on your activity. If you set up the screen saver to prompt for a password on wake-up, no one without your Windows password can sit down at your computer while you're gone and access your work.

In this exercise, you'll enable a screen saver and set it up to require a password upon wake-up.

1. **Right-click the desktop and click Personalize.**

   The Personalization screen appears. (Refer to Figure 3-22.)

2. **Near the bottom, click Screen Saver.**

   The Screen Saver Settings dialog box opens.

3. **Choose a screen saver from the Screen Saver drop-down menu.**

   For example, choose Ribbons. A sample of the screen saver you chose appears in the Preview area.

4. **Set the Wait value to 10 minutes by clicking the up arrow on the Wait box.**

5. **Select the On Resume, Display Logon Screen check box.**

Selecting this check box means that your computer will require a password to log on after the screen saver is displayed. Figure 3-27 shows the dialog box at this point.

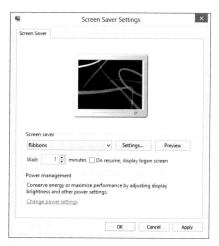

Figure 3-27

PRACTICE

For more practice, try selecting the 3-D Text screen saver and clicking Settings to experiment with its many options. For example, change its text to wording of your choice. and change other settings such as the rotation type, surface style, rotation speed, size, and resolution.

6. **Click Preview.**

A preview of the screen saver appears.

7. **Move the mouse to return to the Screen Saver Settings dialog box.**

8. **Click OK to close the dialog box.**

9. **Close the Personalization screen.**

Choosing a different desktop theme

Applying a desktop theme is an easy way of changing several settings all at once. Windows comes with a variety of basic and high-contrast themes. (People who have limited vision may find the high-contrast themes easier to read.) You can also download more themes online and create your own themes.

In the following exercise, you'll save your current settings as a theme, and then switch to a different theme. You'll go online to download a new theme and apply it, and then finally return to your original settings by applying the theme you created based on those settings.

LINGO

A **desktop theme** is a set of formatting specifications saved under a single name. A theme includes a desktop background, window color, sounds, and a screen saver.

1. **Right-click the desktop and choose Personalize.**

The Personalization screen appears. (Refer to Figure 3-22.)

2. **Click the Save theme hyperlink.**

   The Save Theme As dialog box opens.

3. **Type** Original — **if that's what you'd like to call your theme — in the Theme Name text box and click Save.**

   Your current settings are saved as a theme. The Personalization screen is still open.

4. **Click Get More Themes Online.**

   A web page appears, showing many themes you can download.

5. **Locate the Dark Skies theme (in the Nature category), for example, and click its Download hyperlink, shown in Figure 3-28.**

   A security warning appears at the bottom of your browser window. This warning lets you know that a file is going to be downloaded to your PC. This is okay, because you initiated it yourself.

Figure 3-28

6. **In the security warning, click Open.**

   The theme is downloaded and installed on your PC, and applied automatically.

7. **Close the web browser window.**

   The new theme is active. The Personalization screen is still open.

8. **In the My Themes section of the list, click Original, if that's what you named your theme in Step 3.**

The theme changes to your original settings.

9. **Close the Personalization screen.**

 Summing Up

In this lesson, you learned how to customize the Windows 8 interface, including the Start screen and the desktop. Here is a quick synopsis of the skills you learned:

- To pin or unpin an app, right-click it and then choose the Pin or Unpin command. You can pin apps to the Start screen and/or the desktop depending on the app. You can also pin folders.

- For some tiles on the Start screen, you can change the tile size. Right-click a tile and click Larger or Smaller.

- To rearrange the tiles on the Start screen, drag a tile where you want it.

- You can create a desktop shortcut by right-dragging an icon to the desktop. Click Create Shortcut Here in the menu that appears.

- To change how icons appear on the desktop, right-click the desktop, point to View, and click the desired setting.

- Autohiding the taskbar gets it out of the way until you need it. Right-click the taskbar and click Properties, and then select or deselect the Auto-hide the Taskbar check box. In that same dialog box, you can also set many other taskbar options.

- To enable additional toolbars on the taskbar, right-click the taskbar, point to Toolbars, and click the desired toolbar.

- To change the display resolution in Windows, right-click the desktop and choose Screen Resolution.

- To change many other display options, right-click the desktop and click Personalize. You can change the desktop background window color, screen saver, and so on. Applying a theme changes several display features at once.

Know This Tech Talk

desktop theme: A set of formatting specifications saved under a single name, including a background, window color, sounds, and a screen saver.

display resolution: The number of individual pixels that comprise the display you see onscreen, expressed as a horizontal measurement and a vertical measurement, like this: 1366 x 768.

pin: To create a tile or shortcut for an item on the Start screen or taskbar.

screen saver: A moving graphic that appears onscreen after a specified period of inactivity.

shortcut: A pointer to a file or location.

unpin: To remove a pinned tile or shortcut from the Start screen or task-bar, respectively.

wallpaper: The background on the desktop.

window color: The tint of the title bar and border around a window.

Lesson 4

Storing and Managing Files and Folders

✔ Understand your storage options.

✔ Organize local files and folders.

✔ Manage libraries.

✔ Access your SkyDrive.

✔ Work with file properties

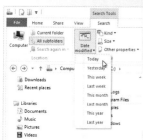

✔ Change the File Explorer layout.

✔ Customize how Explorer displays files and folders.

*B*esides running apps, managing files and folders is the most important must-have Windows skill. You need to know how to create, modify, and delete files so you can take control of your saved data on your computer, from financial spreadsheets to art projects.

In this very important lesson, you'll learn how to work with files and folders both on your local disk drives and on your SkyDrive online. You'll find out how to organize file locations via libraries, and how to customize File Explorer to better suit your preferences.

Understanding File Storage

Maybe you store and access files every day, but do you really understand the ins and outs of what's going on? Most people don't realize what file storage options they have, and how the file system really works. Take a few minutes to review the following sections, and you'll be able to approach the rest of this lesson with more confidence.

Types of storage available in Windows 8

Your computer has hundreds, maybe even thousands, of files on it. They're nicely organized into folders to keep track of them. For example, you have a Windows folder that holds the system files needed to keep Windows up and running, and you have a Program Files folder that stores the files you need to run your installed apps.

LINGO

Folders are electronic locations on a drive in which you can store electronic files.

Your *hard drive* is the main storage unit. It holds the operating system files, the files for the installed apps, and probably a lot of your own personal files too, such as your word processing documents and spreadsheets. Your main hard drive is probably internal, meaning it's inside the computer box. You can also have other hard drives besides the main one, and the other drives can be either internal or external.

In addition to hard drives, you can also store and retrieve files from optical discs (like CDs and DVDs) and flash RAM drives that you connect to your computer's USB port, as well as flash card readers that accept storage cards from digital cameras and smartphones.

LINGO

Local storage is storage that's in the same place as you and your computer. In contrast, **network** (or remote) **storage** is located somewhere else, and accessed via a network or the Internet.

The types of storage I just enumerated are all local storage. That means they are storage devices that are physically present at the same place as you. Local storage relies on nobody and nothing other than your own local equipment, so you always have access to it.

Remote storage, or network storage, is located somewhere away from you and your computer. For example, you might store certain files for your job on a file server that your company hosts on equipment in another room or even in another building, and you might share your music collection on your home network by placing all the music on a network-enabled storage device.

You can also store data on the Internet. Microsoft provides a free SkyDrive service that enables users to store data in a secure and reliable cloud system online. You don't have to take advantage of Microsoft's cloud-based applications (such as Office 365) in order to enjoy the convenience of storing files on SkyDrive; you can simply access your files through a web browser, an application, or Windows 8 itself (via File Explorer). Best of all, every Windows 8 user can have her own SkyDrive account for free.

LINGO

When people talk about the **cloud**, they mean a nonlocal location that is accessed via the Internet. **Cloud computing** delivers computer data and services online as a service. For example, in a cloud computing environment, you might access an online word processor and save your work to an online server. Your own computer is just a doorway to the main services and storage areas on the Internet.

So, as you see, you have quite a large variety of storage options when it comes to your files. In the rest of this lesson, I explain the mechanics of storing and retrieving files from these media.

Folders and paths: How storage is organized

A file can be stored directly at the top level of a drive's organizational system, or it can be stored in a folder on that drive. The top level of a drive is called the root directory; it's like the lobby of a building. It's the entryway to the disk. On a small-capacity drive, such as a USB flash drive, you might be able to get away with storing most (or all) files in the root directory, because you're working with a limited number of files. The list isn't unmanageable to browse. However, when you start getting into higher-capacity drives, including your main hard drive, folders are a necessity because they help you keep things sorted.

File locations on a drive are described as *paths*. A path begins with the drive letter and a colon (:), followed by a backslash (\). If the file is in the root directory, the filename appears immediately after the backslash, like this: C:\ myfile.txt. If the file is in a folder on the disk, the path shows the folder name, then another backslash, and then the filename, like this: C:\school-work\myfile.txt.

You can have folders within folders, to further organize and segment your file storage. For example, within the C:\Windows folder on your hard drive, you'll find a Help folder, and within that folder there's a Windows folder, and within that folder there's a ContentStore folder, and within that folder is an en-US folder (or some other folder, if you are using a non-USA version of Windows), and within that folder is a file called art.mshc. The path to this file is written as follows:

    C:\Windows\Help\Windows\ContentStore\en-US\art.mshc

Notice that two different folders in that path — Windows and Windows — have the same name. They're completely different folders; the name similarity is coincidental.

Paths are represented in Windows 8 in several different ways. You may see a path in an address bar shown with right-pointing triangle arrows between each folder, as in Figure 4-1.

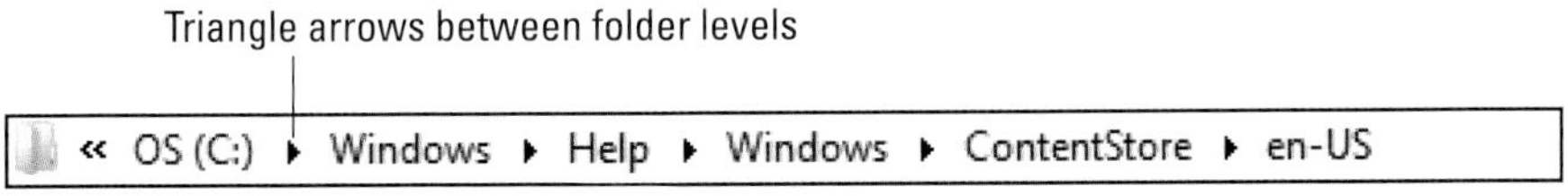

Triangle arrows between folder levels

« OS (C:) ▸ Windows ▸ Help ▸ Windows ▸ ContentStore ▸ en-US

Figure 4-1

Paths are also sometimes represented by *folder trees,* which are visual representations of the hierarchy of the folder system. Figure 4-2 shows how the Navigation pane displays a partial folder tree of the path discussed previously. Notice how the folders directly involved in the path being illustrated have black triangles next to them, indicating those levels of folders are expanded in view at the moment. The white triangles indicate a collapsed folder.

Expanded folder

Collapsed folder

Figure 4-2

Organizing Local Files and Folders

Now that you understand the concepts behind file storage, let's get practical. In the following sections, you'll learn how to view and manage the files and folders on your local PC.

Browsing drives and folders

File Explorer is the primary tool for working with files in Windows. No matter which folder or drive you're viewing at the moment, the same basic File Explorer interface is in effect. (You'll learn how to customize it in some minor ways at the end of this lesson.)

107

The File Explorer interface consists of two main panes. On the left is the Navigation pane, which provides shortcut links to various locations you can browse in addition to a collapsible folder tree of the entire local drive system (under Computer). On the right is the content pane, which shows the names of the files and folders in the currently selected location. At the top is an address bar, which shows the current location's path. See Figure 4-3.

Navigation pane   Address bar

Content pane

Figure 4-3

To browse to a certain location, click the shortcut for it in the Navigation pane. The Favorites section of the Navigation pane contains shortcuts for the most common destinations; you can add your own shortcuts there, too, by dragging and dropping a folder onto that list.

If there's no shortcut readily available for the location you want to browse to, start by clicking Computer in the Navigation pane, and then choose the drive, and then choose the folder, and so on, until you arrive at your destination.

You can also move between locations by using the triangle arrows on the address bar. Clicking one of them opens a drop-down list of other

EXTRA INFO

You can optionally add more location shortcuts to the navigation bar, such as for the Control Panel and Recycle Bin, by turning on the Show all folders feature. To do so, click the View tab, click Navigation pane, and click Show all folders. Doing so can save you time in later lessons, because it provides a quick shortcut method of accessing the Control Panel. If you turn on Show all folders, you will have more locations in the Navigation pane than shown in this lesson, and the locations may appear in a somewhat different order than shown.

locations at that same level in the folder hierarchy. For example, in Figure 4-4, I'm clicking the arrow that follows the C: drive, and I'm seeing a list of other folders that are on that drive.

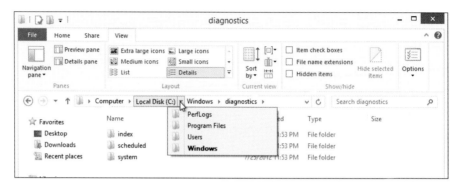

Figure 4-4

In the following exercise, you'll browse to several different locations using a variety of methods.

1. **Open File Explorer.**

   You can do so by clicking the File Explorer button on the taskbar or by clicking the File Explorer tile on the Start screen.

   File Explorer opens to the list of libraries by default.

2. **Double-click the Documents icon in the content pane.**

   The content of the Documents library appears. You will learn more about libraries later in this lesson.

3. **In the Navigation pane, click Computer.**

   A list of the local drives on your computer appears. There may be only one local drive, or there may be more. In Figure 4-5 there is a hard disk drive and a CD drive.

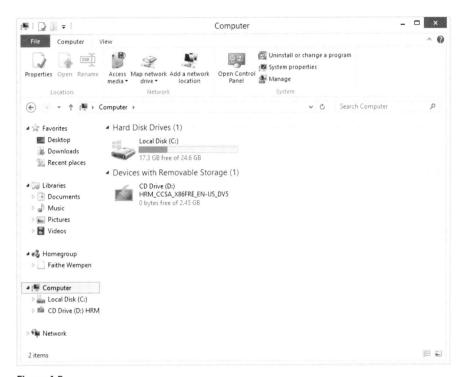

Figure 4-5

4. In the content pane, double-click the C: drive.

A list of the folders and files in the root directory of the C: drive appears.

5. Double-click the Windows folder.

A list of the folders within the Windows folder appears. There are also some files on the list, too; these files are contained within the Windows folder itself (not within a subfolder). You may need to scroll down in the content pane to see the files if there are a lot of folders.

6. Double-click the security folder.

A list of the folders within the security folder appears.

7. On the address bar, click the triangle arrow to the right of Windows.

A menu of all the other folders in the Windows folder appears. See Figure 4-6. Your folders might be different.

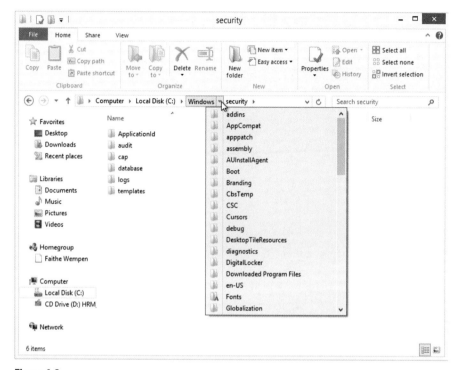

Figure 4-6

8. **Click the Boot folder.**

   The content of the `C:\Windows\Boot` folder appears.

9. **In the address bar, click the triangle arrow to the left of Computer.**

   A menu appears containing shortcuts to several common locations, as shown in Figure 4-7.

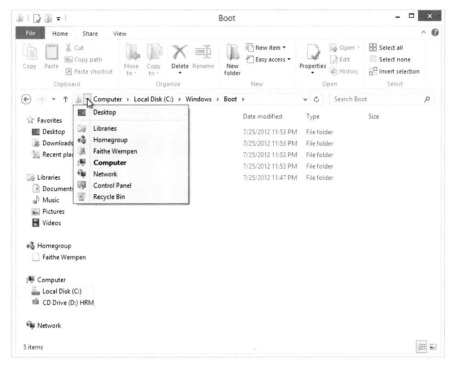

Figure 4-7

10. **Click Libraries.**

    The list of libraries reappears. Now you're back where you started in Step 1.

11. **In the Navigation pane, click to expand the folder tree to show the C: drive, and the Windows\System32 folder within it.**

    A list of folders in the System32 folder appears below the System32 folder in the Navigation pane. See Figure 4-8. The content pane doesn't change.

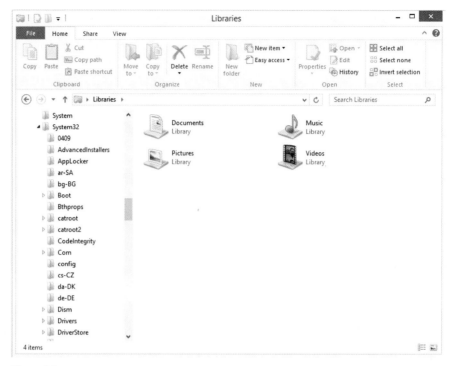

Figure 4-8

12. **Click the black arrow to the left of the System32 folder.**

    The folder collapses again.

13. **Using the Navigation pane, navigate to the C:\Users folder, and double-click your user name.**

    A list of folders that are specific to your Windows user account appears. See Figure 4-9. These are the folders that hold your personal data. For example, My Documents is the default storage location for the work you create in most applications, and Favorites is a list of the stored web shortcuts from Internet Explorer. You may not have the same set of folders shown in Figure 4-9.

14. **Close File Explorer, or leave it open for the next exercise.**

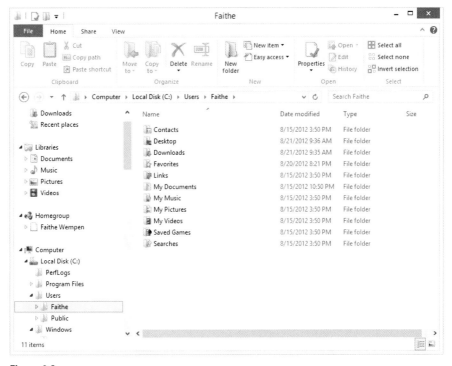

Figure 4-9

Creating a new folder

Besides the folders already on your hard drive, you can also create your own folders. For example, you might create a folder called *Books* to store the data files for the books you're writing, or you might create a folder called *Finances* to store the data files from your financial management software.

You can create the new folders anywhere you like. You might want to create them in the root directory of the C: drive, for example, so that they will appear on the top-level list of folders when you browse the C: drive's content. Alternatively, you might create them in the My Documents folder, or on some other drive, such as a USB flash drive you plan to share with others or take to another computer.

Note: If you store your personal files within your Documents library, those files will not be accessible to other people who log into the local computer with their own Windows IDs. On the other hand, if you store your personal files in some other location, such as a folder you create in the root directory of the C: drive, other local users will have access to them.

To create a new folder, use any of these methods:

✔ Click the New Folder button in the Quick Access Toolbar of the File Explorer window.

The Quick Access Toolbar is the set of icons at the left end of the File Explorer window's title bar. Figure 4-10 points them out.

✔ Press Ctrl+Shift+N.

✔ Right-click an empty area of the content pane, point to New, and click Folder.

New Folder button

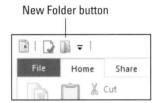

Figure 4-10

In the following exercise, you will create two new folders.

1. **In File Explorer, navigate to the Documents library.**

   Use any of the methods you learned in the previous exercise.

2. **Click the New Folder button on the Quick Access Toolbar.**

   Refer to Figure 4-10. A new folder appears. Its default name is New Folder, but that name is selected, ready to be replaced by your typing. See Figure 4-11.

3. **Type** Experiments **and press Enter.**

   The new folder's name is now Experiments.

4. **Navigate to the root directory of the C: drive.**

5. **Right-click an empty area of the content pane.**

6. **In the contextual menu that appears, point to New, and then click Folder.**

   A new folder appears.

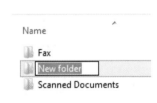

Figure 4-11

7. **Type** Samples **and press Enter.**

The new folder's name is now *Samples*. (You'll use this folder later in the "Copying or moving a file or folder" and in other sections in this lesson.)

8. **Close File Explorer, or leave it open for the next exercise.**

Selecting files and folders

Windows has many commands you can issue to do things to files and folders, but first you must select the file(s) or folder(s) you want the commands to affect.

Selecting a single file or folder is simple: Just click it. The file or folder name is highlighted, indicating that it's selected.

To select a group of contiguous items, click the first one, hold down the Shift key, and click the last one. Everything in between is selected, too, as well as the two items you clicked. To select a group of noncontiguous items, click the first one, hold down the Ctrl key, and click each individual item you want included in the selection; then release the Ctrl key.

In File Explorer, you can select items only in the content pane, and only from the currently displayed location. So, for example, you can select three files at once that are in the same folder, but you can't select three files that are in three different folders.

In the following exercise, you will practice selecting groups of files and folders.

LINGO

Contiguous means adjacent. For example, in an alphabetical list, A, B, and C are contiguous. **Noncontiguous** means not adjacent; for example, in an alphabetical list, A, P, and Z are noncontiguous.

EXTRA INFO

To quickly select everything in the current location (all files and folders), press Ctrl+A, or click the Home tab and click Select All.

1. **In File Explorer, navigate to the Windows folder.**

2. **Click the first folder on the list in the content pane.**

It's highlighted.

3. **Hold down the Shift key and click the fourth folder on the list.**

The first, second, third, and fourth folders on the list are all highlighted. See Figure 4-12. (Your first four folders on the list may be different from the ones shown.)

Contiguous folders selected

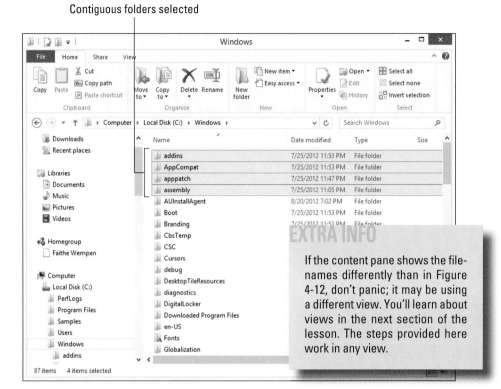

> **EXTRA INFO**
>
> If the content pane shows the file-names differently than in Figure 4-12, don't panic; it may be using a different view. You'll learn about views in the next section of the lesson. The steps provided here work in any view.

Figure 4-12

4. **Click away from the selected folders.**

   The selection is cleared.

5. **Click the second folder on the list.**

6. **Hold down the Ctrl key and click the fourth folder on the list.**

7. **Hold down the Ctrl key and click the sixth folder on the list.**

   The second, fourth, and sixth folders are selected. See Figure 4-13. (Again, the folders may be different on your PC.)

Non-contiguous files selected

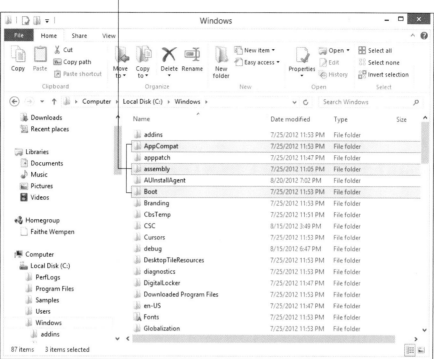

Figure 4-13

8. Still holding down the Ctrl key, click the sixth folder again.

It's deselected. Ctrl+clicking a folder toggles its selection on and off each time you click.

9. Click away from the selected folders.

The selection is cleared.

10. Close File Explorer, or leave it open for the next exercise.

Changing the file listing view

You can change the way the files and folders appear in the content pane of File Explorer by selecting a different view. The Details view (refer to Figures 4-11 and 4-12) shows the file's name, its date modified, its type, and its size (files only, not folders). You can also choose to show them in List view (which is nearly the same as Detail but without the details), or as Small, Medium, Large, or Extra Large icons.

In the lower-right corner of File Explorer are two icons for quickly switching to Details and Large Icons views. If you want some other view, click the View tab, and then select the desired view from the Layout group. See Figure 4-14, which shows Medium icons view.

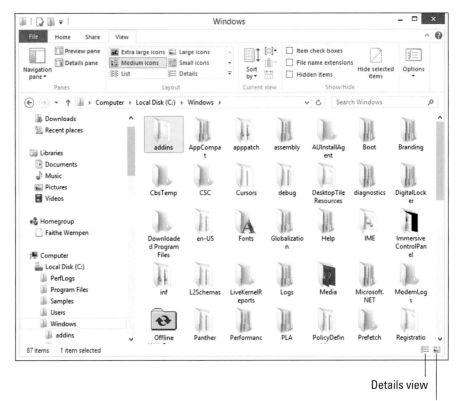

Details view

Large Icons view

Figure 4-14

In the following exercise, you will experiment with the available views in File Explorer.

1. **In File Explorer, navigate to the** `C:\Windows` **folder.**

2. **Click the View tab.**

   The View tab of the ribbon appears.

3. **In the Layout group, click Details.**

   The file listing switches to Details view if it wasn't so already.

4. **Click Large Icons.**

   The file listing switches to Large Icons view.

5. **Click Extra Large Icons.**

The icon size increases for each item.

6. **Click Medium Icons.**

The icon size decreases for each item.

7. **Click List.**

The items appear in a multicolumn list.

8. **Close File Explorer, or leave it open for the next exercise.**

Sorting and grouping file listings

When you're looking for files of a specific name, type, or other specification in a long list, it can be difficult to see what you want at a glance. To help with this problem, Windows 8 enables you to sort and/or group a file listing. Sorting arranges the items in ascending or descending order according to a criterion you specify, such as name, size, or creation date. Grouping does the same thing, except it restructures the listing into groups according to the chosen criteria. Figure 4-15 shows the Windows folder grouped by Type, for example.

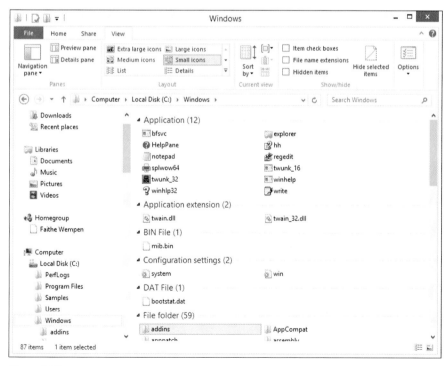

Figure 4-15

In the following exercise, you will group and sort files in File Explorer.

1. **In File Explorer, navigate to the** C:\program Files\Internet Explorer **folder.**

2. **Click the View tab, click the Group button, and then click Type.**

   See Figure 4-16.

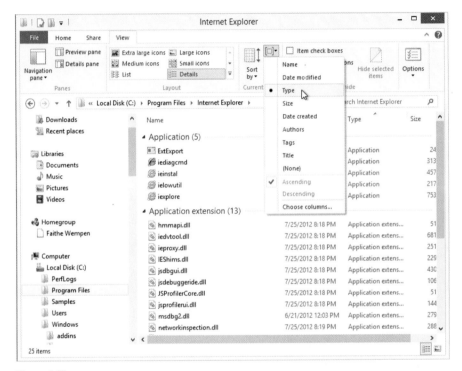

Figure 4-16

3. **If the files aren't already displayed in Details view, click the View tab and then click Details in the Layout group.**

4. **On the View tab, click Sort By, and click Date Modified.**

   The files remain grouped by type, but within each group, the listing is sorted by the date modified. See Figure 4-17.

5. **On the View tab, click Sort by, and then choose either Ascending or Descending — whichever wasn't previously selected.**

   Within the groups, the sort order changes to the opposite of what it was before. Ascending is A to Z, and Descending is Z to A.

Sorted within group by Date Modified

Grouped by type

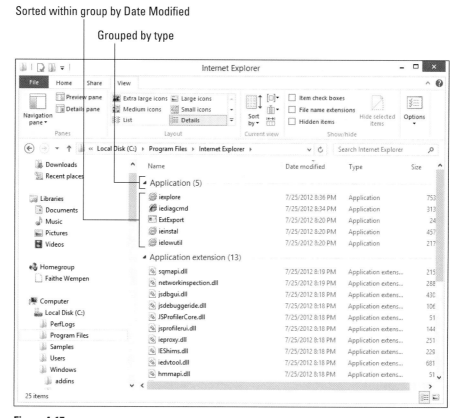

Figure 4-17

6. **On the View tab, click Group By to open a menu and then click (None).**

   Grouping is removed.

7. **Close File Explorer, or leave it open for the next exercise.**

Searching for files

If you can't easily locate the file(s) you seek by sorting and grouping, you might want to try searching for them. Searching creates a filter, and displays only files that meet the filter criteria.

You can perform a quick keyword search by clicking in the Search box (in the upper-right corner of File Explorer) and typing the word there that you want to find. Windows will search not only the file and folder names, but also within files, and if you have a Microsoft e-mail program like Outlook, it will search within e-mail messages and contacts, too.

If you want more control over the search, click in the Search box and then click the Search tab. (The Search tab becomes available when you click in the Search box.) On the Search tab, you'll find options for specifying where to search and what properties the found content must have (such as date modified, size, or type of file).

In the following exercise, you'll search for files using several different search criteria.

1. **In File Explorer, display the root directory of the C: drive.**

2. **In the Search box, type** DOS **and press Enter.**

   In a minute or so, search results appear. Some of the files found have *DOS* in their names; in those cases, the *DOS* in the name is highlighted in yellow. Other files contain *DOS* somewhere inside them; their names don't appear with any highlighting. Figure 4-18 shows an example of the kinds of search results you can get; your results may differ.

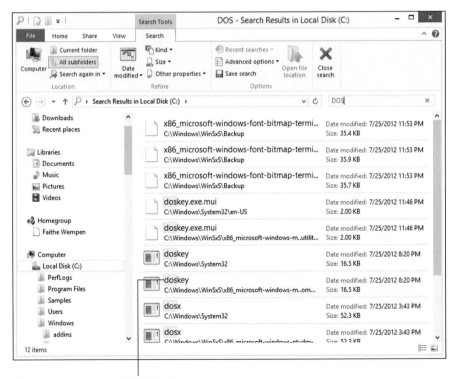

Search text in names is highlighted.

Figure 4-18

3. **Click the X at the right end of the Search box to clear the search results.**

All the content of the C: drive appears again.

4. **Click the Search tab.**

Search tools appear on the Ribbon.

5. **In the Refine group of the Search tab, click date Modified, and choose Today.**

See Figure 4-19. The file listing changes to show only files and folders that were modified today. Your list will have different files and folders than shown here.

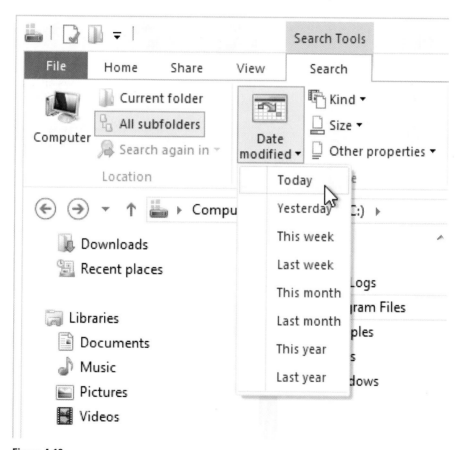

Figure 4-19

6. **Click the X at the right end of the Search box to clear the search results.**

7. **Click the Search tab, click the Recent Searches button, and click DOS from its drop-down list.**

   The DOS search you did in Step 2 reruns.

8. **Click the X at the right end of the Search box to clear the search results.**

9. **Close File Explorer, or leave it open for the next exercise.**

Copying or moving a file or folder

You can move and copy files freely from location to location. However, be careful in doing so, because if you move the files that an app needs to run, the app won't work anymore. That includes Windows itself as well; if you move any files out of the Windows folder, Windows might just decide not to work anymore. When you aren't sure whether a file is needed in its current location in order for something to function, your best bet is to copy it rather than move it.

Data files, on the other hand, are generally safe to either move or copy. Any files that you've created yourself in an app can be moved or copied anywhere you like without any adverse effects to the program.

There are many different ways to move or copy files and folders in Windows 8. The simplest is to just drag and drop the item(s) where you want them.

You have to have two File Explorer windows open at the same time to drag and drop between locations — one window for the original location and one for the destination. To open an additional copy of File Explorer, hold down Shift as you click the File Explorer icon in the taskbar, or hold down Shift as you double-click a folder in an existing File Explorer window. For some locations, you can also right-click a shortcut to the location and choose Open in New Window.

Does drag and drop move, or does it copy? That all depends on where you're dragging and dropping to and from. If you're going from one location to another on the same drive (that is, the same drive letter, such as C:), drag and drop moves. If you're going to a different drive (for instance, from the C: drive to an external storage device such as a USB flash drive) drag and drop copies. If you want something other than the default behavior, you can get it, though:

- ✔ **Move:** To ensure a move, hold down Shift as you drag.
- ✔ **Copy:** To ensure a copy, hold down Ctrl as you drag.

You can also use the Clipboard to move and copy. The Windows Clipboard is a temporary storage area in memory. When you issue a Cut command, you move the selection to the Clipboard; when you issue a Copy command, you copy the selection to the Clipboard. Then you can display the destination location and issue the Paste command to either move or copy the file to the new location.

Yet another way to move and copy is with the Move To and Copy To buttons in the Organize group of the Home tab. Select the items to be moved or copied, and then either choose a destination location from among recently viewed locations from the appropriate button's drop-down menu or select the menu's Choose Location option to select a location not on the list.

In the following exercise, you'll start by moving and copying the folders you created in the previous exercise, and you'll then move and copy some files in them.

1. **In File Explorer, navigate to the** C:\Windows\Media **folder, and select** chimes.wav, chord.wav, **and** ding.wav.

   If you need to review how to select multiple files, return to the "Selecting files and folders" section earlier in this lesson.

2. **Press Ctrl+C to copy those three files to the Clipboard.**

3. **Navigate to the** C:\Samples **folder.**

   You created this folder in the "Creating a new folder" section earlier in this lesson.

4. **Press Ctrl+V to paste the copied files into** C:\Samples.

5. **In the Navigation pane, right-click the Music library and choose Open in New Window.**

6. **Size and arrange the two windows so that both are visible at once side by side.**

   See Figure 4-20. Your Music folder might or might not already have files in it.

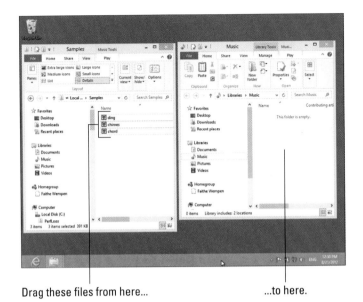

Drag these files from here...   ...to here.

Figure 4-20

7. **Select the three files in the Samples folder.**

8. **Drag the files from Samples to the Music library in the other window.**

   By default, the files are *moved* to the new location (as opposed to being *copied* to the new location) because the two locations are on the same drive.

   To practice forcing Windows to copy the files, move on to the next step.

9. **Hold down the Ctrl key and drag the files from the Music folder in the destination window to the Samples folder in the original window.**

   The files are copied there because the Ctrl key forces a copy.

10. **In the window that displays the Samples folder, with the files still selected, click the Home tab, and click Move To.**

   A menu of locations appears. See Figure 4-21.

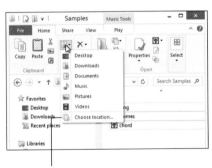

Click here to choose a location not on the list.

Figure 4-21

11. Click Choose Location.

The Move Items dialog box opens.

12. Using the folder tree in the dialog box, navigate to the Experiments folder you created earlier.

You can access this location by selecting `Libraries\Documents\ My Documents` in the folder tree. See Figure 4-22.

13. Click Move.

The three files are moved from Samples to Experiments.

14. Close File Explorer, or leave it open for the next exercise.

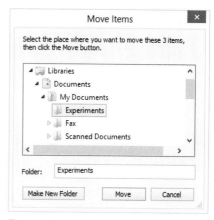

Figure 4-22

Deleting and recovering files

Here are some ways to delete a file or folder you've selected (or a group of them, if you've selected multiples):

✔ **Press the Delete key.**

✔ **Drag the selection to the Recycle Bin icon on the desktop.**

✔ **Right-click the selection and choose Delete from the contextual menu that appears.**

✔ **Click the Delete command on the Home tab.**

Deleting a file removes it from the location where it's stored. Depending on your system settings, it may not be gone forever, though; by default, deleted files on the hard drive go to the Recycle Bin, a temporary holding area. You can retrieve deleted files from the Recycle Bin at any time. The Recycle Bin retains deleted files until you empty the bin, delete specific files from the bin, or run out of room on your hard drive.

LINGO

The **Recycle Bin** is a storage location that holds the files you delete. It's a safety measure, in case you want any of the files back that you deleted.

EXTRA INFO

To completely delete a file, bypassing the Recycle Bin, hold down the Shift key as you delete it.

In the following exercise, you will delete the file copies you created in the previous exercise, then retrieve some of them from the Recycle Bin and empty the Recycle Bin.

1. **In File Explorer, navigate to the Documents library, and then to the Experiments folder in the library.**

   You created this folder, and placed three files in it, in earlier exercises in this lesson.

2. **Click to select** chimes.wav **and then press Delete.**

   The file is deleted (moved to the Recycle Bin).

   Note: You might not see the .wav extension for chimes.wav or the other two files here, depending on your current File Explorer settings.

3. **Click to select** ding.wav **and then drag it to the Recycle Bin.**

4. **Right-click** chord.wav **and then choose Delete from the contextual menu that appears.**

5. **Double-click the Recycle Bin icon on the desktop.**

   The Recycle Bin opens. There are at least the three files in it that you deleted; there may be other files there as well.

6. **Select** chimes.wav.

7. **In the Restore group of the Manage tab, click the Restore the Selected Items button.**

   See Figure 4-23. The file disappears from the Recycle Bin; it has moved back to the Experiments folder.

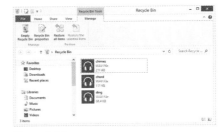

8. **Right-click** chord.wav **and then choose Restore from the contextual menu that appears.**

Figure 4-23

   The file disappears from the Recycle Bin; it has moved back to the Experiments folder.

9. **In the Manage group of the Manage tab, click the Empty Recycle Bin button.**

   A warning appears asking if you're sure you want to permanently delete this file.

10. **Click Yes.**

11. **Close the Recycle Bin window.**

12. **Reopen the Experiments folder to confirm that the files are restored; then close File Explorer.**

Managing Libraries

Windows 8 helps you work with your data
files by providing a library system. Shortcuts
to the various libraries are available from
the Navigation pane in File Explorer, as
shown in Figure 4-24. You work with libraries
earlier in this book, although I haven't made
a big deal out of it yet.

It's important to know that each library *isn't* a specific folder location on
your hard drive. Instead, a library is a combined view of a number of different locations, all in one window, so it looks like the files are all stored
in the same place.

Libraries make it possible for you to view all of your files of a certain type in
one window, regardless of their actual locations. For example, in the Music
library in Figure 4-24, you see three files and four folders in the content pane,
and in the Navigation pane you see the individual folders in which they're
stored: My Music and Public Music.

Libraries

Figure 4-24

Each of the four libraries has a Public folder included in it. These folders have less restrictive sharing permissions than their "My" counterparts, so you might put content in them that you wanted to share with other people on your network.

Windows 8 provides four libraries by default: Documents, Pictures, Music, and Videos. Each of those libraries, in turn, has default folders that it pulls content from. Table 4-1 summarizes the default folders contained in each library. In each of the folder paths, *username* is your actual Windows username that you are logged in as.

Table 4-1	Libraries and Their Default Folders
Library	*Default Folders*
Documents	`C:\Users\`*username*`\My Documents`
	`C:\Users\Public\Public Documents`
Music	`C:\Users\`*username*`\My Music`
	`C:\Users\Public\Public Music`
Pictures	`C:\Users\`*username*`\My Pictures`
	`C:\Users\Public\Public Pictures`
Videos	`C:\Users\`*username*`\My Videos`
	`C:\Users\Public\Public Videos`

Adding a folder to an existing library

If you already have a lot of data files in some other location besides one of the library locations, you may want to add that folder to one of your libraries. That way, you can easily access its files without having to move or copy anything.

In this exercise, you will create a new folder on your hard drive, create a new file in it, and then add it to the Documents library.

1. **In File Explorer, navigate to the root directory of the** C: **drive.**

2. **In the New group on the Home tab, click New Folder.**

   A new folder appears named New folder. Its name is highlighted, so you can type a different name to rename it.

3. **Type a name for your folder and press Enter. For example, you could name it Extra, as shown in Figure 4-25.**

   The folder you created gets a new name.

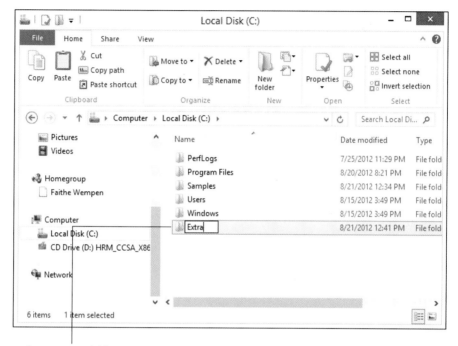

Create a new folder.

Figure 4-25

4. **Double-click the Extra folder to open it.**

   Now you're ready to create a new document and save it in this folder.

5. **Right-click an empty area in the content pane, hover your mouse over New in the contextual menu that appears, then choose Text Document from its submenu, as shown in Figure 4-26.**

   A new document appears, with the generic name highlighted so you can type a new name for it.

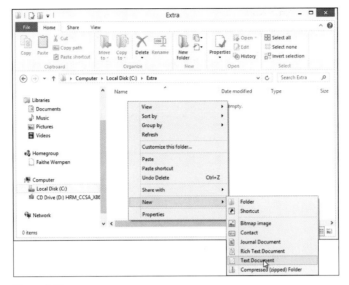

Figure 4-26

6. **Type a name for your new document, such as** Extra Credit **for the purpose of this exercise, and press Enter.**

Now you see a new file named Extra Credit in the `C:\Extra` folder.

Next you will add this folder to your Documents library, so that the Extra Credit file is included in the Documents library's file listing.

7. **In the Navigation pane, click Documents.**

The content of the Documents library appears in the content pane.

8. **In the Navigation pane, right-click Documents and choose Properties from the contextual menu that appears.**

The Documents Properties dialog box opens. The two folders that the Documents library already references appear on the list. See Figure 4-27.

Folders in Documents library

Figure 4-27

9. **Click the Add button.**

   The Include Folder in Documents dialog box opens.

10. **Navigate to the** C: **drive and select the Extra folder.**

    See Figure 4-28.

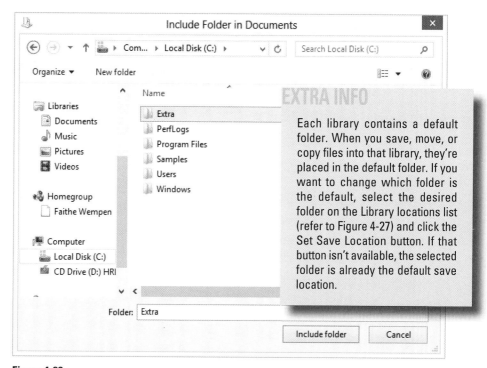

Figure 4-28

11. **Click the Include Folder button.**

    The Extra folder now appears on the Library locations list in the Documents Properties dialog box.

12. **Click OK.**

    Now the Extra Credit.txt file appears in the Documents library window, because the Document library now includes the content of the Extra folder.

Creating a new library

The default libraries— Documents, Music, Pictures, and Videos — may not provide enough flexibility for some users. If that's the case, you may want to create additional libraries for specific types of documents, or you might create libraries for different customers, or for business and personal files.

In the following exercise, you will create a new library called *Business*.

1. **From File Explorer's Navigation pane, right-click Libraries, hover your mouse over New in the contextual menu that appears, then choose Library from its submenu.**

   A new library appears in the Navigation pane. Its default name is New Library, and its name is highlighted, ready for you to rename it.

2. **Type the name you want to assign to your new library, such as** Business **for the purpose of this exercise, and press Enter.**

   The new library's name changes to Business. That's it! Now you have a new library, which works the same in every way as other libraries.

3. **Right-click the Business library and choose Properties from the contextual menu that appears.**

   The Business Properties dialog box opens.

4. **Open the Optimize this Library For drop-down menu and choose Documents.**

   See Figure 4-29. By optimizing a library for a particular type of content, you enable tabs in the ribbon for that type of content.

5. **Still in the Business Properties dialog box, click the Change Library Icon button.**

   The Change Icon dialog box opens.

6. **Scroll through the icons and pick one you like.**

   For example, in Figure 4-30, I've selected an icon that shows a projector screen.

Figure 4-29

7. Click OK.

The icon change is applied to the library. If you want to keep the new library, stop here. Otherwise, keep going and you'll delete the new library next. If you were going to keep it, you would need to add one or more folders to it, as you added folders in the previous exercise.

8. Right-click the Business library and choose Delete from the contextual menu that appears.

The Business library is deleted.

Figure 4-30

Working with Your SkyDrive

SkyDrive is a free online file storage service that enables you to securely store files in a Microsoft-sponsored cloud. Your SkyDrive is your personal storage area within the Microsoft cloud, tied to your Microsoft ID. Windows 8 enables you to tie your local login on your PC to your Microsoft ID so that whenever you're logged into your PC, you're also logged into SkyDrive, giving you seamless access to any files that you have stored on your SkyDrive.

You can work with your SkyDrive in a variety of ways, including a Start screen SkyDrive app, via File Explorer (with the SkyDrive utility loaded, which I'll explain shortly), and the www.skydrive.com website. You'll sample all three of those methods in this lesson.

Accessing Your SkyDrive with the Windows 8 App

The SkyDrive Windows 8 app provides a very simple interface for working with your SkyDrive content. It has some limitations, such as not allowing you to create new folders, rename items, or delete items, but it provides a quick and easy interface that is ideal for showing someone a few pictures on your tablet PC or looking up a quick fact in a stored document.

In this exercise, you will access your SkyDrive using the SkyDrive app. You'll upload a file, and then download it to a different location on your hard drive.

1. **From the Start screen, click the SkyDrive tile.**

   Your SkyDrive account opens. If you have any documents that you've already saved there, they appear. The default folders are Documents, Pictures, and Public, as shown in Figure 4-31.

Figure 4-31

2. **Click the Documents tile.**

   If you have any files stored in the Documents folder on your SkyDrive, icons for them appear. If you don't, the folder appears empty.

3. **Right-click any blank area.**

   A command bar appears. See Figure 4-32.

Figure 4-32

4. **Click the Upload button.**

   A list of the folders and files on your computer appears. Folders are represented by tiles, and files by icons. The location it starts at depends on
   what folder location you have previously browsed, so it may not be the
   location shown in Figure 4-33 (which shows the Documents library), and
   you will likely have different files and folders.

5. **Browse to a location that contains a file you want to upload.**

   To go up one level in the folder tree, click Go up. To go into one of the
   folders shown, click the folder's tile.

6. **Click the file you want to upload to SkyDrive, and click Add to
   SkyDrive.**

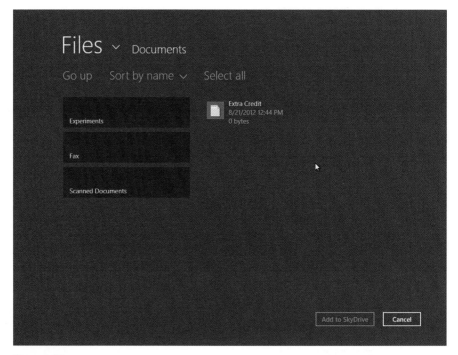

Figure 4-33

7. **Wait for the file to be uploaded.**

   The file appears as an icon when it has finished uploading.

   Next, you'll save a local copy (that is, download) the file to your hard drive again. Yes, it's already there, because you just uploaded it from there, but this is for practice.

8. **In the SkyDrive app, right-click the file you uploaded.**

   A command bar appears. See Figure 4-34.

9. **On the command bar, click the Download button.**

   A file interface appears, similar to the one you worked with in Step 5.

10. **Browse to a location where you want to download a copy.**

    Choose a different location than the one from which you uploaded. Remember, to go up one level in the folder tree, click Go up. To go into one of the folders shown, click the folder's tile.

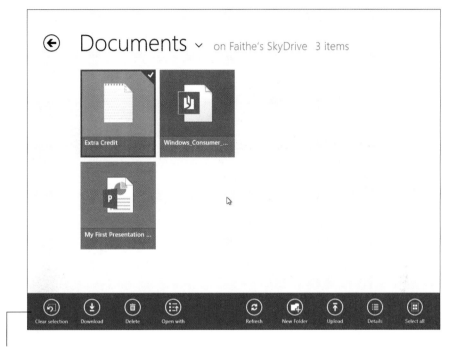

Command bar

Figure 4-34

11. **Click the Choose this folder button.**

The folder name appears on a small tile in the lower-left corner of the screen.

12. **Click OK.**

The file is downloaded to the chosen folder on your hard drive. You may want to delete the extra copy using File Explorer after you finish the exercise, just to keep things tidy; that's up to you.

13. **Close the SkyDrive app.**

Remember, to close a Windows 8 app, drag from the top of the screen down to the bottom.

Accessing Your SkyDrive via the Web

Another way to manage your SkyDrive content is to open your web browser (such as Internet Explorer) and navigate to www.skydrive.com. From there you can browse and manage files and folders, including adding and deleting content, renaming it, moving it, and more.

In the following exercise, you will access SkyDrive via the web, and use the Web interface to create a folder and upload a file. Then you'll save a local copy of it to another folder on your hard drive—basically the same thing you did in the previous exercise, but using the Web interface.

1. **From the desktop, click the Internet Explorer icon on the taskbar, and then navigate to** www.skydrive.com.

   To display the desktop, click the Desktop tile on the Start screen.

   A SkyDrive file-management interface appears in the web browser.

2. **Click the Create button, and on the menu that appears, click Folder.**

   See Figure 4-35. A new folder appears.

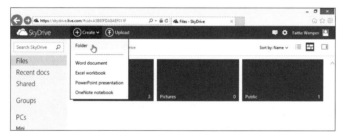

Figure 4-35

3. **Type a name for your folder, such as** Business, **and press Enter.**

   The new folder is now named Business.

4. **Click to select the Business folder.**

   The Business folder is now the active location. The folder is empty.

5. **Click the File Explorer icon in the taskbar.**

   File Explorer opens, showing your Libraries.

6. **Navigate to the Documents library.**

   You should still have the file Extra Credit.txt there from the "Adding a folder to an existing library" section earlier in this lesson.

7. **Double-click** Extra Credit.txt **to open the file in Notepad. Type your name in it, and then save and close it.**

   This step is necessary because you can't upload empty files to SkyDrive, and the file didn't have anything in it before this step.

8. **Arrange the windows so that File Explorer and Internet Explorer are both visible. Then drag-and-drop** `Extra Credit.txt` **into the Business folder.**

   As you drag, the mouse pointer indicates that you're moving the file, but that's misleading; you're actually copying the file to the SkyDrive. See Figure 4-36. The file appears in the Internet Explorer window after you drag it there, and it also continues to appear in the Documents library.

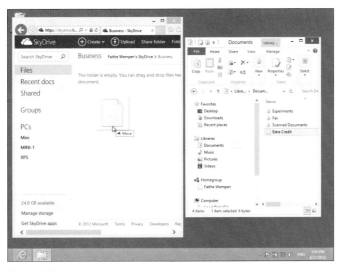

Figure 4-36

9. **Select the newly uploaded file.**

   A security box appears at the bottom of the screen asking whether you want to Open or Save it. See Figure 4-37.

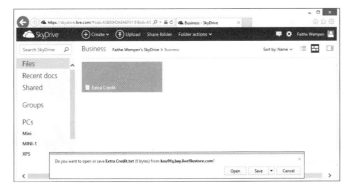

Figure 4-37

10. **Click Save.**

   The file is saved to your default folder for Internet Explorer downloads. (That's the `C:\Users\username\Downloads` folder.)

11. **Click the Open Folder button in the information bar.**

   File Explorer opens, displaying the folder where the file was downloaded.

12. **Close Internet Explorer.**

13. **In File Explorer, locate the downloaded file, select it, and press Delete.**

   The downloaded file is deleted.

14. **Close all open windows and apps.**

Accessing Your SkyDrive the SkyDrive Desktop App

One final way to work with your SkyDrive files is to use the SkyDrive app that integrates with File Explorer. You'll need to download this app from Microsoft (which is free) in order to use it. This app is really cool because it enables you to treat your SkyDrive just like any other folder location.

To download the SkyDrive for Windows app, go to `https://apps.live.com/skydrive`, and under the Windows Desktop heading, click Download the app. Go through the prompts to download and install it. (If given a choice between Run and Save, pick Run.) Accept the defaults during the setup process if you aren't sure what settings to choose.

After you go that that (one-time) setup process, you will find a SkyDrive shortcut in the Favorites list of File Explorer's navigation pane, as shown in Figure 4-38. It opens a local folder named SkyDrive that automatically syncs with your online SkyDrive via the Internet, so you never have to manually upload or download SkyDrive files. The green check marks in Figure 4-38 indicate that the local folders and the online ones are fully synchronized and up-to-date.

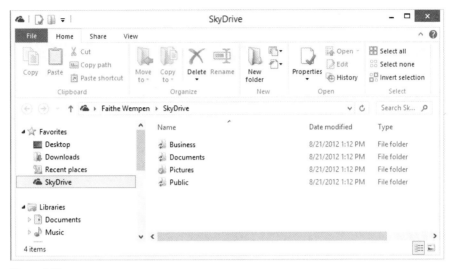

Figure 4-38

Working with File Properties

File properties are information about a file or attached to a file. Properties include two types of information:

- ✔ **Metadata:** Information attached to a file that states something about that file, such as author name or keywords. Metadata is most often associated with data files.

- ✔ **Attributes:** On/off flags set for a file that determine such things as whether the file is read-only, indexed, hidden, compressed, or encrypted. All files have attributes, not just data files.

LINGO

File properties provide information about a file. That information can include **metadata** (such as author name and keywords) and **attributes** (such as Read-Only or Hidden).

Adding and editing metadata

Depending on the file type, a Details tab might be available in a file's Properties dialog box. On the Details tab, shown in Figure 4-39, you can define values for various metadata properties.

Some of the metadata isn't editable, such as the date the file was created, the file size, and so on. For other items, however, you can double-click to select the item and then type a new value.

In this exercise, you will view and change the metadata for a Microsoft Word file. You can use any Word file you happen to have on your hard drive. If you don't have one, you can use the file `Research.docx` provided in the data files for this lesson.

Move mouse here to display text box.

Figure 4-39

1. **In File Explorer, right-click the `Research.docx` file, or any Word file of your choosing, and choose Properties from the contextual menu that appears.**

   The Properties dialog box for the file appears.

2. **Click the Details tab.**

   Metadata for the file appears.

3. **Move the mouse pointer to the blank area to the right of Title.**

   A text box appears there, as in Figure 4-39.

4. **Click to move the insertion point into that text box.**

5. **Type the title of your choosing. For the example shown here, I'm using Preliminary results.**

6. **Click OK.**

   The Properties box closes for the file.

Changing file attributes

A file's attributes define basic yes/no facts about it. Depending on the file system the drive is using, you might have access to some or all of these attributes:

 ✔ **Read-only:** The file can't be deleted or modified.

 ✔ **Hidden:** The file doesn't appear in File Explorer file listings (unless hidden files are set to be shown, as you'll learn how to configure later in this lesson).

✔ **Archive (File is ready for archiving):** The file has changed since it was backed up with a backup program, which sets the archive flag to off.

✔ **Indexed (Allow this file to have contents indexed in addition to file properties):** The content of the file is included in Windows 8's index of the disk's contents, so any searches for words it contains will find the file.

✔ **Compressed (Compress contents to save disk space):** The file has been compressed with NTFS compression. This is available only on drives that use the NTFS file system. When you apply this to a folder, rather than a file, you're prompted to choose whether to apply the change to the selected folder only or all its subfolders and files as well.

✔ **Encrypted (Encrypt contents to secure data):** This file has been encrypted with NTFS encryption. This is available only on drives that use the NTFS file system.

Read-only and Hidden attributes can be turned on or off from the General tab of the file's Properties dialog box. For other properties, you must click the Advanced button on the General tab to open the Advanced Attributes dialog box.

In this exercise, you will change several properties of a file. Feel free to use any file you like, including the `Extra Credit.txt` file you created earlier in the lesson or the `Research.docx` file you worked with in the previous exercise.

1. **In File Explorer, right-click the `Extra Credit.txt` file, or any other file of your choosing, and then choose Properties from the contextual menu that appears.**

   If you don't use `Extra Credit.txt` or `Research.docx`, use one of your own data files for this exercise, and not a Windows system or application file.

2. **On the General tab, select the Read-only check box.**

   See Figure 4-40. Making a file read-only prevents it from being modified or deleted. You might make a data file read-only to protect it from being accidentally changed.

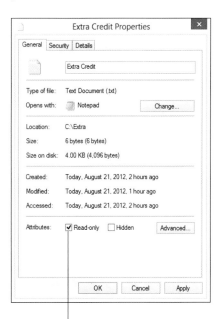

Read-only check box

Figure 4-40

3. **Click the Advanced button.**

   The Advanced Attributes dialog box opens.

4. **Deselect the File is Ready for Archiving check box.**

   Doing so clears the archive attribute from the file, so that it will not be backed up the next time a backup program runs that looks for files to back up that have this attribute set.

5. **Select the Compress Contents to Save Disk Space check box.**

   Doing so sets the compression attribute for the file, so that it takes up slightly less disk space.

   See Figure 4-41.

6. **Click OK to close the Advanced Attributes dialog box.**

7. **Click OK to close the Properties dialog box.**

8. **Close File Explorer.**

Clear this check box.

Figure 4-41

Changing the File Explorer Layout

You can set up File Explorer to display or hide several types of listings and information. For example, you can show or hide the Preview and Details panes and you can choose what appears in the Navigation pane as well as how large the Navigation pane is.

On the right side of File Explorer, you can optionally display either of two special panes:

- ✔ **Details pane:** Provides information about the selected file(s), folder(s), or drive(s). For a file, this information includes Date Created, Date Modified, and Size. For some types of files — Microsoft Office documents, for instance — many more details appear as well, such as author names, total editing time, and tags or keywords.

- ✔ **Preview pane:** Shows a preview of certain types of data files when they're selected. If the selected item can't be previewed, a *No preview available* message appears here instead.

These two panes are mutually exclusive — you can show either or neither of them, but not both at once. To display or hide one of these panes, click the View tab and then, in the Panes group, click the Preview Pane or Details Pane button. See Figure 4-42, which shows the Details pane.

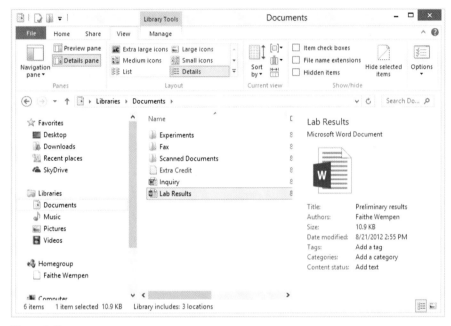

Figure 4-42

The Navigation pane is the pane on the left side of File Explorer, providing shortcuts in such categories as Favorites, Libraries, and so on. As you found out earlier in this lesson, you can use the Navigation pane to quickly jump to a variety of locations. In the Panes group of the View tab, you can click the Navigation pane button for access to the following menu of on/off toggles:

✓ **Navigation Pane:** Turns the Navigation pane on or off.

✓ **Expand to Open Folder:** Ensures that the Navigation pane always shows the complete folder hierarchy expanded down to the level of the currently displayed folder. (It may do this anyway, depending on how you navigated there.)

✓ **Show All Folders:** Makes the shortcuts in the navigation bar (other than Favorites) appear as a single hierarchical list organized under the Desktop heading. When this option is off, shortcuts in the Navigation pane are grouped into the categories such as Libraries, HomeGroup,

Computer, and Network. Figure 4-43 compares these two views: Regular (left) and Show All Folders (right).

✔ **Show Favorites:** Shows or hides the Favorites section of the Navigation pane.

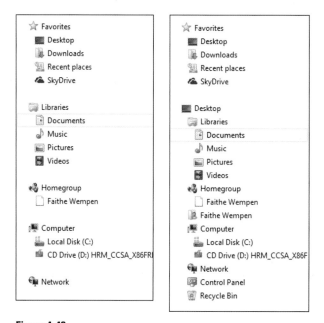

Figure 4-43

Several of the panes in File Explorer can be resized. To resize a pane, drag the divider between two panes. Resizing a pane doesn't change the overall size of the window, so space added to one pane means space subtracted from the adjacent one. Resizing panes can be useful when you need to see more of one pane's content than is currently displayed and you don't mind if the adjacent pane's content has less room. If you need to see a larger portion of both panes, you must resize the entire window instead.

In this exercise, you will customize File Explorer's layout in several ways.

1. **In File Explorer, click the View tab.**

2. **In the Panes group, click the Details Pane button.**

   The Details pane appears. If the Preview pane was previously displayed, it's now hidden.

3. **On the View tab, click to open the Navigation Pane button to open its drop-down menu.**

   Note which options are already enabled (with a check mark next to them). See Figure 4-44.

4. **Click Show All Folders to either toggle that check box on or off, depending on its current setting.**

   Note the change in the layout of the Navigation pane.

5. **Drag the right border of the Navigation pane to the right to expand the size of the Navigation pane. Then drag it back to the left again to restore the Navigation pane's original size.**

Figure 4-44

Customizing How Explorer Displays Files and Folders

In addition to modifying the look of File Explorer itself, you can also modify how the file and folder listings appear within it. The following sections explain a few of the modifications you can make.

Displaying or hiding extensions for known file types

By default, Windows 8 hides file extensions for known file types. When a file's extension doesn't appear, the file's type can sometimes be deduced by looking at its icon. For example, a Word document's icon has a *W* on it for *Word*. However, if you haven't memorized the icons for all the applications you have on your system, that might not be useful. Instead, you might prefer to turn on the display of file extensions for all files. (See the upcoming instructions.)

LINGO

An **extension** is a code that follows the filename, separated from it by a period. Windows 8 determines a file's type by its extension. For example, the file Memo.docx is a Word file because it uses the .docx extension.

Another benefit of turning on file extensions is that they make it more noticeable when a file has a double extension, such as graphic.gif.vbs. An executable extension on the end like that (.vbs is a Visual Basic Script) often indicates a virus-carrying file.

In earlier versions of Windows, the process for displaying or hiding extensions was a laborious multistep affair, but in Windows 8, it's a simple File Name Extensions check box in the Show/Hide group of the View tab. See Figure 4-45.

Figure 4-45

Displaying hidden files and folders

As you learned earlier in the lesson, one of the attributes that a file or folder can have is Hidden. When the Hidden attribute is turned on for a file or folder, that file or folder doesn't appear in the File Explorer window — that is, unless you've specified that hidden files and folders be visible there. When you choose to turn on the display of hidden files, folders, and drives, hidden items appear with their icons slightly faded to distinguish them from unhidden ones.

As with the file extensions, in earlier Windows versions it took several steps to change the setting for displaying or hiding hidden files, but in Windows 8, there's a Hidden Items check box for it on the View tab. Refer to Figure 4-45.

You'll probably want to leave the hidden files hidden most of the time, because otherwise there isn't much point in having hidden files and folders. Files and folders are hidden to prevent others from knowing they exist. However, whenever you need to work with a hidden file or folder, you must temporarily turn on the display so you can access it. There are also occasionally situations where you may need to browse a hidden folder in order to make a system change. For example, if you want to work with Microsoft Office templates, you must have access to a folder called AppData in your Users folders, which by default is hidden.

Showing and hiding OS files

Windows 8 requires operating system (OS) files to operate. These files are hidden by default from normal File Explorer listings so that they aren't accidentally moved or deleted. At some point, you might need to see these files.

For example, you might need to check a date on one of them as you're troubleshooting a problem.

Unfortunately, there's no easy check box for this setting like there is for the previous two; you must delve into the File Options dialog box to adjust the setting.

In this exercise, you will turn on the display of OS files.

1. **Click the View tab on the Ribbon, and then click Options.**

   The Folder Options dialog box opens.

2. **Click the View tab of the dialog box.**

   On this tab, you can adjust many aspects of how files appear in File Explorer. The one you adjust in this exercise is only one of many. See Figure 4-46.

3. **Deselect the Hide Protected Operating System Files (Recommended) check box.**

   A warning appears letting you know that these files are required to start and run Windows and you shouldn't delete or edit them.

4. **Click Yes.**

5. **Click OK to apply the new setting.**

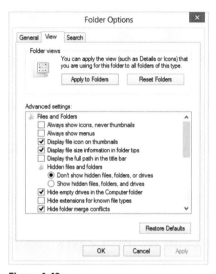

Figure 4-46

   You probably don't want to leave this setting as is it now, because it's safer to keep OS files hidden unless you have a specific reason for needing to show them. So now let's put the setting back the way it was.

6. **Click View, and click Options.**

7. **Click the View tab.**

8. **Select the Hide Protected Operating System Files (Recommended) check box.**

9. **Click OK.**

10. **Close File Explorer.**

Summing Up

In this lesson, you learned how to store and manage files and folders in Windows 8. Here are the highlights:

✔ You can store files locally on your own computer, in a network location, or in the cloud (online).

✔ A path is the complete specification that describes where a file is stored. It includes the drive letter, folder name, and filename, like this: `C:\books\myfile.xls`.

✔ The root directory is the top level of the drive's file storage system. Another name for it is *top-level folder*.

✔ To create a new folder, click the New Folder button at the left end of the File Explorer window's title bar. That area is known as the Quick Access Toolbar.

✔ To select contiguous files and folders, hold down Shift as you click the first and last one; to select noncontiguous ones, hold down Ctrl as you click each one.

✔ Use the Search box in the upper-right corner of File Explorer to search for files and folders.

✔ You can move or copy files with the Clipboard or with drag and drop. Hold down Shift (to ensure a move) or hold down Ctrl (to ensure a copy) when dragging.

✔ To delete a file, press Delete, or drag the file to the Recycle Bin. You can retrieve deleted files from the Recycle Bin.

✔ Libraries are combined views of a number of different locations; they provide a convenient way of viewing content from many places at once.

✔ Your SkyDrive is your personal storage area in Microsoft's cloud. It's free, and you can store up to 25GB there. You can access it via the SkyDrive Start screen app or via `www.skydrive.com`.

✔ Each file has attributes such as Hidden and Read-only; set these from the file's Properties box. Some files also have meta tags — managed from the Details tab in the Properties dialog box — which contain extra information such as the name of the author.

✔ You can customize File Explorer's layout using commands on the View tab, including what to display in the Navigation pane.

✔ Use the check boxes on the View tab to choose whether to display hidden files and folders, and whether to display extensions for known file types.

Know This Tech Talk

attribute: An on/off toggle property for a file, such as Hidden or Read-Only.

cloud: An Internet-accessible, file-storage location.

cloud computing: Delivering computer data and services online as a service.

contiguous: Adjacent in a listing.

extension: A code that follows the filename, separated from it by a period, describing its file type.

File Explorer: A feature of Windows that provides file and folder browsing and navigation capabilities.

file properties: Information about a file, including both attributes and metadata.

folder: An electronic location on a drive, in which you can store files.

folder tree: A visual representation of the hierarchy of the folder system. Lower level items appear below and indented from the folders or drives that contain them.

library: A combined view of a number of different locations in a single window.

local storage: Storage that's in the same place as you and your computer.

metadata: Information about a file such as author name, title, and keywords.

network storage: Storage located somewhere else and accessed via a network or the Internet.

noncontiguous: Adjacent in a listing.

path: The complete specification that describes where a file is stored.

Quick Access Toolbar (QAT): A small customizable toolbar in the left corner of the title bar in File Explorer.

Recycle Bin: A storage location that holds the files you delete.

remote storage: Storage that isn't in the same place as you and your computer.

root directory: The top level of a drive's file storage system, not in any particular folder. Also called the top-level folder.

SkyDrive: A free Microsoft-sponsored cloud storage system.

Lesson 5

Using Internet Explorer 10

✔ Browse and search for websites.

✔ Store and recall the addresses of websites you visit frequently.

✔ Browse a list of sites you have recently visited.

✔ Use tabs to enable multiple browsing sessions.

✔ Manage your security and privacy online.

*W*hen most people hear the word Internet, the first thing they think of is the World Wide Web (WWW), or *web,* for short. The web is an interconnected network of millions of documents available on the Internet. Chances are very good that if you need some information or need to find out how to contact a certain person or business, you'll be able to get the required info on the web.

In this lesson, I'll show you how to get around the web using Internet Explorer (also known as IE), the web browser software that comes with Windows 8. You'll learn how to browse and search for pages, how to get back to pages you have previously visited and enjoyed, and how to protect your privacy and security online.

Navigating the Web with Internet Explorer 10

To browse the web, you need browsing software, such as Internet Explorer. A web browser enables you to view web pages, download files from websites, watch online videos, listen to streaming music from a web server, participate in discussion forums, and much more.

Making sense of the interface

Two different versions of Internet Explorer 10 are included with Windows 8: The standard desktop version and the Windows 8 version. To open the desktop version, click the Internet Explorer icon on the taskbar. To open the Windows 8 version, click the Internet Explorer tile on the Start screen. This book primarily covers the desktop version, but an exercise later in this lesson — "Exploring the IE Windows 8 App" — familiarizes you with the Windows 8 version, too.

The Internet Explorer window consists of these components, pointed out in Figure 5-1:

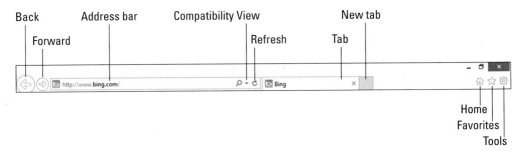

Back   Address bar   Compatibility View   New tab

Forward   Refresh   Tab

Home
Favorites
Tools

Figure 5-1

✔ **Address bar:** Enter the address (the URL) of the page you want to display here. If you click a link to visit a page, the address of the link you clicked appears here.

✔ **Refresh:** Click here if the page doesn't load correctly, to force it to reload.

✔ **Compatibility View:** Toggles a backward-compatible display mode on or off, disabling advanced features of the web content you're displaying in order to make a page load that otherwise doesn't. Use this in the event that a page doesn't load correctly after repeated refresh attempts. The icon is blue when enabled and gray when disabled.

✔ **Tab:** You can open multiple pages at once, each on its own tab. In Figure 5-1, the tab represents the open page Bing.com.

✔ **New tab:** This small blank square to the right of the existing tab opens a new tab when you click it.

✔ **Home:** Click this icon to return to your home page. (You'll learn how to set your home page later in this lesson.)

✔ **Favorites:** Click here to open the Favorites Center, from which you can manage stored shortcuts to web pages and browse your usage history.

✔ **Tools:** Click here to open a menu of tools and settings you can adjust.

✔ **Menu bar:** Provides access to several standard menus. If the menu bar doesn't appear (and it isn't shown in Figure 5-1), press Alt to display it.

LINGO

The term **URL** is short for Uniform Resource Locator. It's a web address.

Moving from page to page

One way to move to a specific web page is to type its address (its URL) into the Address bar. Another is to click a hyperlink on an already-displayed web page.

In Figure 5-1, notice the big arrow buttons on the left. The left-pointing arrow is the Back button, and the right-pointing arrow is the Forward button. After you've moved from one page to another, the Back button becomes active (blue rather than gray). You can click Back to return to the previous page.

After you've used the Back button, the Forward button becomes active (blue). You can click Forward to return to the page you were on before you clicked Back.

In the following exercise, you will use the desktop version of Internet Explorer to view several web pages.

1. **From the desktop, click the Internet Explorer icon in the taskbar.**

   Internet Explorer opens and displays whatever page is set as your home page. It may be MSN.com, or it may be something else.

2. **Hover your mouse pointer over a picture or a text hyperlink.**

   When the mouse pointer is over a clickable hyperlink, the mouse pointer appears as a pointing hand. See Figure 5-2.

3. **Click the hyperlink you pointed at.**

   A different page displays.

4. **Click the Back button shown in Figure 5-3.**

   The previous page reappears.

5. **Click the Forward button.**

   The page from Step 3 reappears.

6. **Click the URL in the Address bar.**

   The URL is highlighted.

Mouse pointer

Figure 5-2

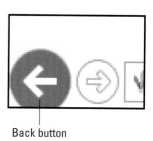

Back button

Figure 5-3

7. Type www.wiley.com **and press Enter.**

See Figure 5-4. Your typing replaces the highlighted URL. Pressing Enter activates the URL you just typed and opens the page for Wiley, the company that published this book.

8. Keep Internet Explorer open for the next exercise.

Figure 5-4

Setting your home page

By default, Internet Explorer sets MSN.com as the home page. That means that every time you open Internet Explorer, that page loads automatically. You can set up Internet Explorer to load some other page instead at startup, or multiple pages, or no page at all.

You can control which page(s) displays at startup on the General tab of the Internet Options dialog box, shown in Figure 5-5. To get there, click the Tools icon (pointed out in Figure 5-1) and then choose Internet Options from the menu that appears.

Type home page URL here.

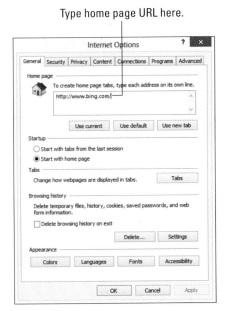

Figure 5-5

LINGO

The **home page** (sometimes called the **start page**) is the page that loads automatically each time you open your browser. The term *home page* can also refer to the main page of a multipage website.

On the General tab, in the Home Page section, you can enter the URLs you want. Here are some tips:

- **Single home page:** To specify a single page to use, enter its URL in the Home Page text box.
- **Multiple home pages:** To specify multiple pages to use (each on its own tab), enter the URLs in the Home Page text box, each on its own line.
- **Current page:** To set the current page as the home page, click Use Current.
- **Default:** To return the home page to the default, click Use Default.
- **Blank tab:** To display a blank tab as the home page, click Use New Tab. A blank tab isn't completely blank; it shows a page containing links to previously opened websites.

You can set up IE so that it opens the last pages you looked at in the browser. Go to the Startup section of the General tab and click the Start with Tabs from the Last Session radio button.

In the following exercise, you will set your Home page to show an additional tab at startup for a website of your choice.

1. **In Internet Explorer, click the Tools icon, and choose Internet Options from the menu that appears.**

   The Internet Options dialog box opens. Refer to Figure 5-5.

2. **In the Home Page box, click to move the insertion point to the end of the current URL there and then press Enter to start a new line.**

3. **On the new line, type the URL of a website of your choice.**

4. **Click OK.**

5. **Close Internet Explorer and reopen it.**

   This time, both pages appear, each in a separate tab. See Figure 5-6.

   In the next steps, you will set your home page to a blank page.

Figure 5-6

6. **Click the Tools icon and choose Internet Options from the menu that appears.**

The Internet Options dialog box reopens.

7. **Click Use New Tab.**

The address in the Home Page text box changes to about:Tabs. See Figure 5-7.

8. **Click OK to close the dialog box, and then close and reopen Internet Explorer.**

A blank tab appears at startup.

In the next steps, you will reset the home page back to the default.

9. **Click the Tools icon and choose Internet Options from the menu that appears.**

10. **Click Use Default.**

The URL in the Home page text box changes back to its original default setting.

11. **(Optional) Change the home page back to your preferred page if you don't want to keep it at the default.**

12. **Click OK to close the dialog box. Then close Internet Explorer.**

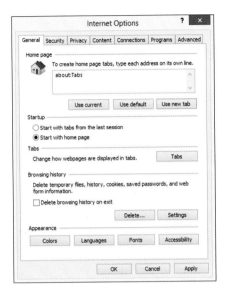

Figure 5-7

Working with multiple tabs

It's often useful to have multiple web pages open at once and jump back and forth between them. You can do this by opening two separate browser windows, but there's also another way. Internet Explorer enables you to open multiple tabbed pages in a single browser window, with each tab displaying a different site.

Tabs appear across the top of the browser window. Each tab shows the title of the page that's displayed on that tab. To open a new tab, click the New Tab square to the right of the existing tabs. To close a tab, right-click it and choose Close Tab from the menu that appears. You'll find some other useful commands on a tab's shortcut menu, such as Duplicate tab and Close other tabs. See Figure 5-8.

Figure 5-8

In this exercise, you will open several tabs, arrange them, and then close them.

1. **In Internet Explorer, click New Tab to open a new tab.**

   New Tab is the blank square to the right of the rightmost existing tab.

2. **With the new tab displayed, click in the Address bar, type a web address, say** www.wiley.com **for the purpose of this exercise, and press Enter.**

   The Wiley home page appears.

3. **Press Ctrl+T to open another new tab.**

4. **With the new tab displayed, click in the Address bar, type a web address, say** www.yahoo.com **for the purpose of this exercise, and press Enter.**

   The Yahoo! home page appears.

5. **Drag and drop the Yahoo! tab between the other two tabs.**

   You can rearrange tabs by dragging them into the order you want them.

6. **Display the Wiley page, and right-click any hyperlink on the page and choose Open in New Tab from the menu that appears.**

   The page opens in a new tab. This page and the Wiley home page are considered a *group* because they're from the same site. Grouped tabs are highlighted with the same tab color.

7. **Right-click the Wiley home page, and notice that the Ungroup This Tab command is available.**

   You have the option of removing this tab from the group that it's in.

8. **Choose Close This Tab Group from the displayed menu.**

   Both of the Wiley pages close.

9. **Right-click the Yahoo! tab and choose Close Tab from the menu that appears.**

Now you're back to a single tab. You can't close the last tab; there must always be at least one tab open.

10. **Keep Internet Explorer open for the next exercise.**

Finding and Refinding the Content You Want

There are two parts to content management in a web browser: The first is to find the content you want in the first place, and the second is to be able to find it again later. In the following sections, I show you how to do both of those things.

Searching for websites

If you don't know the URL of the site you want to visit, you must hunt for it online. Search engines can help with that. There are many search engines available online, including big hitters like Google, Yahoo!, and Bing. (Just add *.com* to each of those names to find the search engine.)

A single keyword search may not produce the most useful results, because there are so many pages on the web. The results will likely contain hundreds of unhelpful sites. You can get far better results by using multiple keywords. Here are some tips for using multiple keywords:

~ **Multiple keywords in no specific order:** If you specify multiple keywords with spaces between them and include no other punctuation, the search results will prefer pages that have all words, but will also show results that have only one of the words, further down on the list of results.

- ✔ **Phrases:** If you want to search for a multi-word phrase in which the words must be adjacent and in a certain order, put the entire phrase in quotation marks.

- ✔ **Including and excluding keywords:** You can use Boolean operators like AND, NOT, and OR to combine keywords. For example, you could use *Apple NOT computer* to find information about apples as a fruit and omit pages that mention Apple computers.

You access a search engine (such as Google) on its website (such as www.google.com), but there's also an easier way to search. Internet Explorer incorporates search engines into its Address bar, so you can type keywords into the address bar instead of typing a URL there. The search results then appear from Microsoft Bing (the default search engine in Internet Explorer) or from some other search engine you have chosen instead to be your default search provider. You will learn how to change the search provider later in this lesson.

In this exercise, you will perform some web searches using specific providers' sites and using the Address bar.

1. **In Internet Explorer, go to** www.google.com.

2. **In the blank text box in the center of the page, type** poodles **and press Enter.**

    A list of pages dealing with poodles appears.

3. **Click in the Address bar and press Delete to remove the existing URL there. Then type** poodles **and press Enter.**

    See Figure 5-9. This time, search suggestions appear from Bing, the default search provider in Internet Explorer. (That is, unless someone has changed the default on your PC already.)

Bing icon

Figure 5-9

4. **In the search box at the top of the page, type** "Standard poodles" (in quotes) **and press Enter.**

The results now show pages where the words *Standard poodles* appear together, in that order.

5. **In the search box, type** poodles NOT Standard **and press Enter.**

Make sure you type *NOT* in all caps. The results now show pages where the word *poodles* appears but the word *Standard* doesn't.

6. **Keep Internet Explorer open for the next exercise.**

Changing the default search provider

Microsoft of course sets the Microsoft search provider (Bing) as the default in its own product. However, you're free to set up any search engine as your preferred provider instead, so that when you type keywords into the Address bar, your favorite search provider is used.

In this exercise, you will add a new search provider to the Address bar and set it as the default.

1. **In Internet Explorer, click the down arrow in the Address bar to open its menu.**

See Figure 5-10. Notice the B icon at the bottom of the menu. B stands for Bing; you see only one icon here, meaning that only one search provider is set up so far in Internet Explorer.

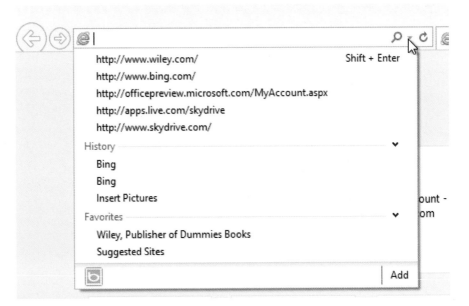

Figure 5-10

2. Click Add.

The Internet Explorer Gallery web page appears.

3. Click the Search hyperlink to narrow the add-ons displayed to only search providers.

In Figure 5-11, the Search hyperlink is in the bar at the left — but this page changes its look frequently, so it may not look like the figures shown in this book.

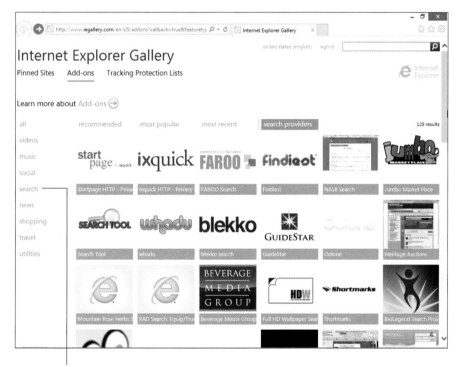

Search hyperlink

Figure 5-11

4. Locate your favorite search engine, such as Google Search, on the list and click it.

A page appears from which you can add the search engine to Internet Explorer. See Figure 5-12.

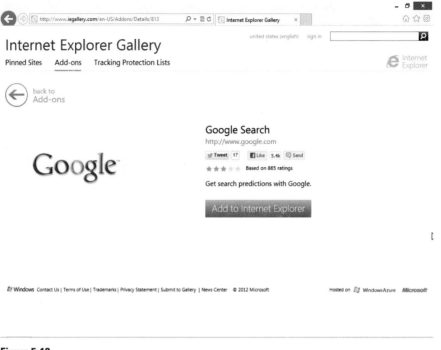

Figure 5-12

5. **Click Add to Internet Explorer.**

The Add Search Provider dialog box opens. See Figure 5-13.

6. **Click Add.**

The new search engine is added to your search provider list.

Figure 5-13

7. **Click the down arrow on the Address bar to reopen its menu.**

   Note that you now see the icon for your preferred search provider at the bottom of the menu. See Figure 5-14. However, note also the blue outline around the Bing icon, indicating that it's still the default.

8. **Click the icon of your preferred search provider.**

   That search provider is now the default.

Google icon

Figure 5-14

9. **Click away from the menu to close it.**

10. **(Optional) Perform another keyword search from the Address bar to make sure the results are delivered from your selected search provider, not Bing.**

11. **Keep Internet Explorer open for the next exercise.**

Working with favorites

Internet Explorer maintains a Favorites list, which is like an address book in which you store all the page addresses you want to remember on the web. You can add and remove items on your Favorites list and rearrange items on the list, including sorting them into folders for easier management.

To open the Favorites list, click the Favorites button (the star) in the upper-right corner of Internet Explorer's window. The panel that opens is called the Favorites Center. It has three tabbed sections in it: Favorites, Feeds, and History. In this section, you'll work with the Favorites tab.

LINGO

Favorites, also called **bookmarks**, are stored URL shortcuts. The **Favorites Center** is the section of Internet Explorer from which you can view and manage favorites, as well as news feeds and your browsing history.

In this exercise, you will add a page to the Favorites list. Then you'll create a new folder on the Favorites list and move the page into that folder.

1. **In Internet Explorer, navigate to a website.**

   I chose www.wiley.com.

2. **Click the Favorites button.**

   The Favorites Center opens. See Figure 5-15. Make sure the Favorites tab is active. It should already be active unless someone has used one of the other tabs more recently than the Favorites tab. You may have many URLs listed on the Favorites tab; Figure 5-15 shows a brand-new system with no saved favorites yet.

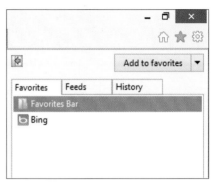

Figure 5-15

3. **Click Add to Favorites.**

   The Add a Favorite dialog box opens.

4. **In the Name box, change the page title.**

   Use whatever descriptive terms you prefer. As you can see in Figure 5-16, I changed the title for my favorite website to *Wiley, Publisher of Dummies Books.*

Figure 5-16

5. **Click Add.**

   The favorite is added to the Favorites list.

6. **Click the Favorites button.**

   The Favorites Center opens, and the favorite you just created appears on the list.

   Next you'll start creating folders for organizing your favorites.

7. **Click the down arrow to the right of the Add to Favorites button.**

   A menu appears.

8. Choose Organize Favorites from the menu.

The Organize Favorites dialog box opens.

9. Click the New Folder button.

A new folder appears on the list, named New Folder. Its name is highlighted so you can rename it. See Figure 5-17.

10. Type a name for your new folder, such as Book Info, **and then press Enter.**

The new folder now appears on the list in the Organize Favorites dialog box. Next you will move favorites into the new folder.

11. In the Organize Favorites dialog box, click the name of the website you recently added to the Favorites list to select it.

12. Click the Move button.

The Browse for Folder dialog box opens. See Figure 5-18.

13. Click the name of your new folder and click OK.

Doing so selects the folder as the new home for your favorite.

14. Click Close.

The Organize Favorites dialog box closes.

Figure 5-17

Figure 5-18

In the next steps, you will check the Favorites list to confirm that your new folder appears there and contains the shortcut you placed in it.

15. Click the Favorites button.

The Favorites list opens.

16. **Click your folder.**

    The shortcut appears there.

17. **Click away from the Favorites Center to close it. Keep Internet Explorer open for the next exercise.**

Accessing your history

The Back button's memory clears whenever you close Internet Explorer, so you can't use Back to access sites you visited during previous sessions. However, there are a couple of ways you can recall the sites you've visited. One is through the Address bar, and the other is through your History list.

LINGO

The **History list** is a record of all websites visited during a certain timeframe. Internet Explorer maintains the History list automatically.

The Address bar has a drop-down list from which you can select recently typed URLs. Click the down arrow at the right end of the Address bar to open it. Although this isn't a complete record of all the sites you've visited, the Address bar does list the URLs that you've manually typed or copied and pasted into the Address bar recently. This ability to recall previous addresses in the Address bar is called Address Bar AutoComplete.

If you require a more complete record of visited sites, check out the History list. It's one of the tabs in the Favorites Center, which you worked with earlier in this lesson. You can sort the History list by site, URL, date, or frequency of visits.

To protect your privacy, you may want to clear the History list at some point. Although this doesn't turn off the recording of future history, it removes previously viewed sites. You might consider this if you're using a public computer, for example, or if you allow other people to use your PC. You can use InPrivate browsing, which I tell you about later in the "Covering your Tracks with InPrivate Browsing" section, to prevent browser history recording in the first place.

In the following exercise, you will check out your own History list, clear it, and then visit a couple of sites to start adding to it again.

1. **In Internet Explorer, click the Favorites button, and click the History tab.**

    On the History tab, categories appear according to the way the list is sorted and the dates of your previous usage. For example, in Figure 5-19, View by Date is the sort order, and the categories are 3 Weeks Ago, 2 Weeks Ago, Last Week, Monday, and Today.

2. **Click Today.**

   A list of the sites you've visited today expands.

3. **Open the View By drop-down list and click View by Site.**

   The list re-sorts to show the sites in alphabetical order.

4. **Open the View By drop-down list and click View by Date.**

   The list re-sorts to show the sites by date, under categories for the date ranges, such as Last Week.

Figure 5-19

5. **Click the Favorites button again to close the Favorites Center panel.**

   Next you will clear your browsing history.

6. **Click the Tools button, and choose Internet Options from the menu that appears.**

   The Internet Options dialog box opens.

7. **On the General tab, under Browsing History, click Delete.**

   The Delete Browsing History dialog box opens. See Figure 5-20.

8. **Make sure the History check box is marked.**

   You can select or deselect any other check boxes as desired to clear other information.

9. **Click Delete.**

   A message appears on an information bar at the bottom of the browser window letting you know that the browsing history has been deleted.

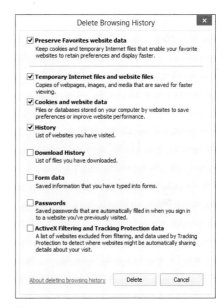

Figure 5-20

10. **Click OK in the Internet Options dialog box.**

    The Internet Options dialog box closes.

    Next you will check your browsing history for today. It will include only the sites you have visited since you cleared the history.

11. **In the Address bar, type a web address and press Enter.**

12. **Click the Favorites button.**

   The Favorites Center opens. The History tab is still active.

13. **Click Today.**

   A list of sites expands. The only site on the list is the one you typed in Step 10.

14. **Close Internet Explorer.**

Exploring the IE Windows 8 App

The Windows 8 Internet Explorer app is designed to be easy to use on tablet and touchscreen computers. As such, its interface is very different from the desktop version of IE.

As shown in Figure 5-21, the Address bar is across the bottom rather than the top. The Back and Forward buttons are separated: The Back button is on the far left and the Forward button is on the far right.

Sample callout Sample callout Refresh Forward

Pin to Start

Figure 5-21

In this exercise, you will try out the Windows 8 Internet Explorer app, using it to visit several websites.

1. **From the Start screen, click the Internet Explorer tile.**

    The Windows 8 version of Internet Explorer opens.

2. **Click in the Address bar.**

    A group of tiles appears, representing Frequent and Pinned pages you've visited. Your list will look different from the ones in Figure 5-22.

Figure 5-22

3. **Click one of the tiles in the Frequent section that represents a different page than the page that appeared in Step 1.**

    That page opens. The Frequent section holds links to pages that you've recently or frequently visited. If you haven't visited any other pages yet, the home page is the only tile that appears here (probably Bing or MSN), so you don't have any choice but to choose it.

4. **Click the Back button.**

    The previously displayed page appears. If the address bar (and the Back button) are hidden, click the left-arrow button on the left side of the screen.

5. **Click the Forward button.**

   The page appears that you chose from the Frequent section in Step 3.

   In the next steps, you will pin a shortcut to the current page to the Start screen.

6. **Click in the Address bar, type a web address into it, and press Enter.**

7. **Click the Pin to Start icon.**

   The icon looks like a pushpin. A pop-up appears for adding a link to the current page. See Figure 5-23.

Figure 5-23

8. **In the text box (which currently shows *Website*: Home), edit the text to read say something more meaningful to you.**

   For example, I changed the text to read, simply, *Wiley*.

9. **Click Pin to Start.**

   A tile for this page is pinned to the Start screen.

10. **Click the Address bar.**

    Notice that the new tile appears in the Pinned section.

    Next, I tell you how to remove that tile.

11. **Right-click the new tile and click Remove in the command bar.**

    A confirmation box appears.

12. **Click Remove Tile.**

13. **Drag the top of the app screen down to the bottom to close the app.**

Guarding Your Privacy

You're being watched. No, really. There are all kinds of ways that advertisers, pollsters, and criminals spy on Internet users, both individually and in aggregate. Furthermore, if you choose not to be watched, you may forfeit your ability to access certain types of content. The following sections can help you find the right balance between performance and privacy.

Controlling cookies

Cookies have many uses. A cookie can tell an advertiser that you've previously viewed a certain ad, for example, or can keep track of the items in your shopping cart at a store's site. Cookies are harmless 99.99 percent of the time, and can perform useful functions that you want. However, two risks are involved with cookies. One is a privacy threat, since a cookie can deliver personal information to a website. The other is a security threat, since a virus or Trojan Horse infection might copy a stored password from a cookie and deliver it to someone else. (That's really rare, but it can happen.)

LINGO

A **cookie** is a plain text file stored on your hard disk that contains information about previous interactions you may have had with a particular website. The information in the cookie is used to help the page remember who you are and what your preferences are.

Cookies can be categorized according to how they were created. A first-party cookie is one that a website places on your computer because you visited that site. For example, when you shop at www.amazon.com, a cookie provides your name so that the site can welcome you by name. In contrast, a third-party cookie is placed on your computer by an advertisement on a website you visit, where the ad's owner isn't related to the website's owner. For example, as you use Facebook, a third-party cookie might record which ads you click, indicating your interest in certain products.

LINGO

A **first-party cookie** is created by a website you visit. A **third-party cookie** is created by an advertiser.

Cookies can also be categorized according to how long they remain. A session cookie lasts only as long as the web browser is open. When you finish your browsing session, session cookies are deleted. For example, on some websites, shopping carts are set up with session cookies, so if you don't place the order, the next time you visit, the shopping cart is empty. Other sites with shopping carts use persistent cookies — so you can return to the site after you've ended your original session, and the items you placed in the cart are still there.

LINGO

A **session cookie** expires when you close the browser. A **persistent cookie** remains after the browser is closed.

In Internet Explorer, you can control how your system stores each type of cookie. You can create rules for handling cookies, identify sites from which to allow or deny cookies, and delete existing cookies.

In this exercise, you will experiment with IE's cookie settings to become aware of cookie handling behind the scenes.

1. **In the desktop version of Internet Explorer, click the Tools icon and then choose Internet Options from the menu that appears.**

   The Internet Options dialog box opens.

2. **Click the Privacy tab.**

   If you haven't already modified your cookie settings, a slider appears, as shown in Figure 5-24. If you don't see the slider, click the Default button to override your custom settings and make it appear.

3. **Drag the slider all the way to the top, so that Block All Cookies is selected. Read the description of what that setting entails.**

4. **Drag the slider a bit down so it lands on High, and then read the description.**

   The High setting blocks cookies from websites that don't have a compact privacy policy, as well as cookies that contain information that could be used to contact you.

   Figure 5-24

5. **Drag the slider down to Medium High, and read the description. Do the same for the Medium, Low, and Accept All Cookies settings.**

6. **Reset the slider to Medium, or to whatever level is most appropriate for your needs.**

   Next you will set policies for a specific site.

7. **Click the Sites button.**

   The Per Site Privacy Actions dialog box opens. See Figure 5-25.

8. **In the Address of Website text box, type a full web address, such as** http://www.dummies.com, **and click Allow.**

   Dummies.com is added to the Managed Websites list in the dialog box, meaning that it will be handled differently from the default when it comes to cookies.

9. **Click OK.**

10. **Back in the Privacy tab of the Internet Options dialog box, click the Advanced button.**

Figure 5-25

   The Advanced Privacy Settings dialog box opens, where you can override automatic cookie handling to specify different settings for first-party versus third-party cookies.

11. **Select the Override Automatic Cookie Handling check box.**

12. **Select the Prompt radio buttons in both First-Party Cookies and Third-Party Cookies columns.**

    See Figure 5-26.

13. **Click OK.**

    The Advanced Privacy Settings dialog box closes.

14. **Click OK.**

    The Internet Options dialog box closes.

15. **Type** www.msn.com **in the Address bar and press Enter.**

    The page loads, and multiple Privacy Alert boxes appear, one at a time, asking about each cookie. See Figure 5-27.

Figure 5-26

Figure 5-27

16. **For each Privacy Alert box, click Block Cookie.**

    The reason you're dealing with each one separately in this exercise is so you'll realize how many there are on a typical commercial website like MSN.

    After clicking the final one, the page may still appear, or the entire page may be blocked. Some content can't appear without a cookie being stored.

17. **Press F5 to reload the page.**

    The Privacy Alert boxes appear again.

18. **Click Allow Cookie for each prompt.**

    After you respond to all the prompts, the page appears.

19. **Click the Settings button and choose Internet Options from the menu that appears.**

20. **On the Privacy tab, click the Default button to restore the default cookie settings.**

21. **Click OK. Keep Internet Explorer open for the next exercise.**

Covering your Tracks with InPrivate Browsing

Concerned about the tracks you might leave behind as you surf the web? You can surf in complete privacy and anonymity with InPrivate Browsing, a special mode in Internet Explorer that saves nothing. Nada. Zilch. Like the browsing never happened.

Even though Internet Explorer doesn't track your usage, your employer or ISP might still track it in some way, so your usage may not be completely anonymous.

InPrivate Browsing opens a new browser window. To exit InPrivate mode, you close that browser window and open Internet Explorer again.

In this exercise, you will start an InPrivate browsing session.

1. **In Internet Explorer, click the Tools button, point to Safety, and then choose InPrivate Browsing from the submenu that appears.**

    See Figure 5-28. A new browser window opens. The Address bar shows "InPrivate" to the left of the address bar.

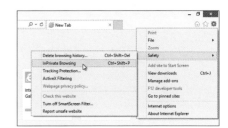

Figure 5-28

2. **In the Address bar, type a web address, such as** www.msn.com**, and press Enter.**

   The page loads, but no cookies are accepted, and no history of the visit is recorded. If you want to see for yourself, open the History list and confirm that there's no record there.

3. **Close the InPrivate browser window.**

Staying Secure

Security, in the context of Internet use, has a couple of different meanings. On one level, security means guarding your identity when using sites where you have to log in to access certain content. On another level, security means being protected from fake sites, viruses, and other malware as you surf the web. In the following sections, you'll learn about security in both of those ways.

Surfing secure sites with confidence

One way that criminals steal data online is by intercepting private data as it's sent over the Internet. For example, a criminal could gain access to the member's account number or balance when that person uses the bank's website. To prevent this from happening, sites that exchange important and sensitive data with users employ encryption. Even if the encrypted data is intercepted, the person intercepting it can't decode it. Encrypted data is unscrambled once it reaches its destination.

A secure site's URL typically begins with `https://` rather than `http://`, and Internet Explorer shows a lock icon in the Address bar and a green background in the Address bar when you're accessing this type of secure site.

Another way criminals operate is to simulate a secure site to trick users into logging in and sharing private information. (This is called *spoofing*, or *phishing*.) To minimize this risk,

LINGO

Encryption is the process of scrambling data before it's sent out on a network in order to prevent snooping. A **secure site** is a website that employs some type of encryption technology.

LINGO

A **security certificate** is a unique code that provides an assurance that the site you're communicating with is legitimate.

some sites employ security certificates to verify the connection. A security certificate includes a serial number, the identity of the person or organization that issued it, and the dates during which it's valid. A certificate is issued by an issuing authority, which is a company that maintains a server that tells your browser whether the certificate that a secure web page is presenting is valid. A warning message displays if the certificate doesn't match the expected information. Internet Explorer also has a SmartScreen Filter feature, which warns you if you visit any sites that are known to be fraudulent according to Microsoft's database.

In this exercise, you will visit a secure website, and you will check out the list of certificates that Internet Explorer maintains.

1. **In Internet Explorer, type** www.paypal.com **in the Address bar, and press Enter.**

   Notice that the background in the Address bar turns green, indicating that this site's security certificate is valid. A lock appears, indicating that it's a secure site, and the name of the certificate appears next to the lock. The prefix on the address is `https://` rather than `http://`. If you don't see the green background, try pressing F5 to refresh the page.

2. **Point at the certificate name in the Address bar.**

   A pop-up appears, showing the certificate information. See Figure 5-29. PayPal, Inc. [US] is the certificate name, and VeriSign is the certificate authority.

   Figure 5-29

3. **Click the certificate name in the Address bar.**

   A more detailed pop-up appears. See Figure 5-29. From this one, you can see that PayPal, Inc. is registered in San Jose, California, U.S.

   Figure 5-30

4. **In the pop-up, click View Certificates.**

   A Certificate dialog box opens, showing the complete security certificate for this site. See Figure 5-31.

5. **Click the Details and Certification Path tabs in the dialog box and review the information there. Then click OK to close the dialog box.**

6. **Click the Tools icon in Internet Explorer, point to Safety, and then choose Check This Website from the submenu that appears.**

   A SmartScreen Filter dialog box opens, showing that there are no reported threats associated with this site. (If this is the first time using SmartScreen Filter, a dialog box appears describing the feature before the results appear.)

7. **Click OK to close the SmartScreen Filter dialog box.**

   Next, you'll examine the certificates that Internet Explorer recognizes.

8. **Click the Tools icon and then choose Internet Options from the menu that appears.**

   The Internet Options dialog box opens.

9. **Click the dialog box's Content tab.**

   See Figure 5-32.

10. **In the Certificates section, click the Certificates button.**

    The Certificates dialog box opens.

11. **Click the Trusted Root Certification Authorities tab, and examine the list of certificate authorities that appear there.**

    These companies issue and verify certificates. One of the companies on this list is Verisign, the company that's responsible for the PayPal certificate you just viewed. See Figure 5-33.

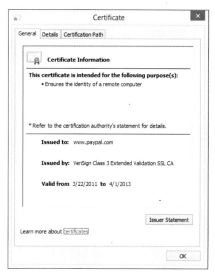

Figure 5-31

Figure 5-32

12. **Click Close to close the Certificates dialog box, and then click OK to close the Internet Options dialog box.**

13. **Keep Internet Explorer open for the next exercise.**

Avoiding malware

While most websites are safe to visit, some of them pose a security or privacy threat. Some sites (especially sites with adult or illegal content) try to transfer malware to your computer.

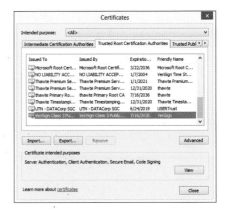

Figure 5-33

Internet Explorer has many safeguards in place to prevent a website from installing anything on your computer without your knowledge and permission. When a website tries to trigger a download, an information bar or box pops up in IE, and you must click a button to give it your permission to proceed.

LINGO

Malware is a very broad term meaning any kind of undesirable software that could compromise your privacy or security or damage your computer's software or hardware.

Internet Explorer enables you to fine-tune many different settings to specify how much protection you want, and you should keep in mind that some forms of protection may limit your ability to view and use certain types of content. Rather than making you understand and evaluate each setting, IE offers some easy presets to choose from.

You can choose a different security preset (such as Medium, Medium-High, or High) for each of four zones:

- ✔ **Internet:** All sites that aren't in one of the other zones fall into this zone.

- ✔ **Local Intranet:** This zone is for sites that are within your local intranet. An *intranet* is an internal web-based network within a company.

- ✔ **Trusted Sites:** You can define which sites are on this list, and then set more lenient permissions for them.

- ✔ **Restricted Sites:** You can define which sites are on this list, and then set more restrictive permissions for them.

In the following exercise, you will adjust the security permissions in Internet Explorer for the Trusted Sites list, and add a site to your Trusted Sites list.

1. **In Internet Explorer, click the Tools icon and choose Internet Options from the menu that appears.**

   The Internet Options dialog box opens.

2. **Click the dialog box's Security tab.**

   Icons for each of the four zones are displayed across the top of the dialog box.

3. **Click the Trusted Sites icon.**

   The current setting for trusted sites appears.

4. **If you don't see a slider in the Security Level for This Zone section, click the Default Level button to reset any custom settings.**

5. **Drag the slider to the Medium-Low setting.**

   See Figure 5-34. Note that the Low and Medium-Low settings are not available for the Internet or Restricted sites zones, as a safety precaution.

   Now you will add a site to the Trusted Sizes zone.

6. **Click the Sites button.**

   A Trusted Sites dialog box opens.

7. **Deselect the check box next to Require Server Verification (https://) for All Sites in This Zone.**

   If you don't do this step, you won't be able to enter any sites that don't begin with the https:// prefix.

EXTRA INFO

One of the greatest risks of malware infection comes from ActiveX controls. Normally, a website that runs interactive content, like a game, does so within a temporary environment such as a Java application. Nothing is transferred to your computer for that. However, some websites run interactive content by installing an ActiveX application on your PC and allowing the webpage to interact with it. Most ActiveX controls are harmless, but some of them contain viruses or other malware, such as *key loggers* that spy on your keystrokes to steal your passwords and other private information.

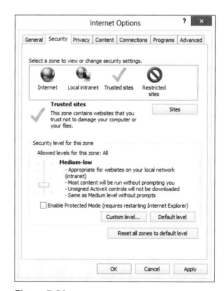

Figure 5-34

8. **In the Add This Website to the Zone text box, type** www.dummies.com, **and then click the Add button.**

   The site is added to the Trusted Sites list. See Figure 5-35.

9. **Click Close to close the Trusted Sites dialog box, and click OK to close the Internet Options dialog box.**

Figure 5-35

 *Summing Up*

In this lesson, you learned how to use Internet Explorer 10 to browse and search the web.

- ✔ To visit a certain website, type its URL (address) into the Address bar.

- ✔ Click a hyperlink to follow it to another page or to a different spot on the same page. Use the Back button to return to the previous page.

- ✔ To set your home page, open the Internet Options dialog box and specify the page on the General tab.

- ✔ To open a new tab, press Ctrl+T or click the small blank tab to the right of the existing tabs. To close a tab, right-click the tab and choose Close from the menu that appears.

- ✔ You can type keywords to search for directly into the Address bar; IE will use your default search provider.

- ✔ To save the current page as a favorite, click the Favorites button and then click Add to Favorites.

- ✔ The IE Windows 8 app, accessed from the Start screen, is different from the desktop version of IE accessed from the desktop's taskbar.

- ✔ Many pages save cookies to your hard disk. To control cookie policy, open the Internet Options dialog box and click the Privacy tab.

- ✔ An InPrivate browsing session saves no record of your surfing. To start one, click Tools, point to Safety, and click InPrivate Browsing.

- ✔ Set a security level for each of the four zones on the Security tab in the Internet Options dialog box.

Know This Tech Talk

compact privacy policy: Information about how a website uses cookies. The information is delivered along with the web page, in a format that the browser software can read and interpret.

cookie: A plain text file stored on your hard drive that contains information about previous interactions you had with a particular website.

encryption: The process of scrambling data before it's sent out on a network, in order to prevent snooping.

favorites: Stored URL shortcuts, also called *bookmarks*.

Favorites Center: The section of IE from which you can view and manage bookmarks, as well as news feeds and your browsing history.

first-party cookie: A cookie created by a website you visit. Compare to *third-party cookie.*

History list: A record of all websites visited during a certain time frame.

home page: The page that loads automatically each time you open your browser. Also called the start page. A second meaning is the main page of a multipage website.

hyperlink: An active link that, when clicked, opens a different web page or jumps to a different spot on the same page.

Internet: A network of millions of private, public, academic, business, and government networks.

keyword: A word that you search for to find specific content.

malware: A very broad term meaning any kind of undesirable software that could compromise your privacy or security or damage your computer's software or hardware.

persistent cookie: A cookie that remains after the browser is closed.

search engine: A website or utility that displays a list of matching websites from a computer-compiled database in response to a keyword search.

secure site: A website that employs some type of encryption technology.

security certificate: A unique code that provides an assurance that the site you're communicating with is legitimate.

session cookie: A cookie that expires when you close the browser.

third-party cookie: A cookie created by an advertiser on a website you visit. Compare to *first-party cookie.*

URL: Stands for uniform resource locator. A web address.

web page: An HTML-based document available at a given web address.

website: A collection of related web pages on the same server.

World Wide Web: A network of hyperlinked documents on the Internet. Also called the *web.*

Lesson 6

Networking Your PCs

✔ Determine whether you're already part of a network and what networking hardware you have.

✔ Set up the security features on a wireless router.

✔ Create a HomeGroup to simplify file and printer sharing on a small network.

✔ Browse the network resources that others have shared.

✔ Share libraries and other folders, and configure network sharing settings.

✔ Share a local printer with others, and set up your PC to use network-aware printers.

✔ Stream video or music to other PCs in your network.

*W*hen you install Windows 8, the setup utility does its best to configure a network connection for you automatically, including a connection to the Internet if one is available. That means you probably already have a network and Internet connection before you even start this chapter. If you don't — or if you aren't sure — don't sweat it. This chapter will help you get going with both your local area network and your Internet connection.

Assessing Your Existing Network

Networking: *it's a good thing*, to borrow a phrase from Martha Stewart. Networked computers can share files and printers with one another, and can share an Internet connection. You can also use your network to share music and video files between computers, transfer TV shows from your home theater system to your PC (with the right software to do so), and access your handheld and gaming devices from your computers.

Your computer may already be connected to a network. If you already have Internet connectivity on your PC, and there are multiple PCs in your household that all share that connection, then your network is already good to go.

Take a moment to identify your current networking and Internet equipment. Find your broadband modem, to start with: that's the box with the flashing lights that delivers your Internet service (via cable, DSL, satellite, or some other method). The broadband modem is probably connected to another box, also with flashing lights. That's the router. Sometimes the router and the broadband modem are a single, dual-purpose device, so you might not have two separate boxes.

LINGO

A **network** is a group of connected computers. When connected computers are in the same room, or the same building, they're part of a **local area network (LAN)**.

LINGO

A **broadband modem** is a device provided by your Internet provider (usually cable or DSL) that interfaces with your phone or cable line so you can use it for Internet connectivity.

Each of your computing devices connects to the router, either with a cable (wired access) or wirelessly. If you have a wired connection, then you have an Ethernet cable that plugs into your computer. An Ethernet cable, used for wired Ethernet connections, looks like a telephone cable but it's thicker, and the plug is slightly wider. See Figure 6-1. The other end of the cable looks the same, and plugs into your router.

Figure 6-1
(Photo by David Monniaux)

A wireless connection connects to a wireless router via radio waves. It may not be obvious from your computer's hardware whether it has wireless networking capability, so you have to look at Windows itself to determine this.

LINGO

Ethernet is the most common technology used for home and business networking. It can be wired or wireless, but the term is most often used to refer to wired connections.

A **router** is an intelligent traffic-routing box into which the computers in the network all connect.

LINGO

Wi-Fi is a shorthand way of referring to the type of wireless technology that computers commonly use for networking and Internet. The more precise name for the technology is IEEE 802.11. There are other types of wireless network connections besides Wi-Fi, such as infrared (IrDA) and Bluetooth, but they aren't usually used for Internet or for sharing files and printers with other computers.

Look in the notification area for a Network icon, and then point the mouse at it to see a pop-up message telling you your current connection status. If it's a wired network, it appears as shown in Figure 6-2; if it's a wireless network, it appears with five stair-stepped bars on it, as shown in Figure 6-3. The more white bars, the stronger the connection.

Figure 6-2

Figure 6-3

Point to the icon and read the tooltip, as in Figures 6-2 and 6-3. You may see one of these messages:

✔ **Internet Access:** You have an Internet connection.

✔ **No Internet Access:** You have local network access but no Internet. That probably means you don't have an Internet service hooked up to your router, or that the one you have isn't working.

✔ **Not connected – Connections are available:** There are wireless networks available, but you haven't connected to one yet. Along with this message, you may see a star on the network icon.

✔ **Not connected – No connections are available:** Your computer can't find any networks to connect to. There may not be any, or your computer's wireless network adapter may be disabled or malfunctioning. Along with this message, you may see a red X on the network icon.

For a wired connection, there's no need to do anything to enable the connection in Windows; the connection begins when you plug in the cable. For a wireless network, you must connect to the network — at least the first time. You can indicate that you want this connection to be reestablished automatically whenever you're in that network's range, so you have to manually connect only once.

In this exercise, you will connect to a wireless network. Connecting to a Wi-Fi router when a connection is available, and when your PC recognizes connections are available, is quite easy.

1. **Click the wireless network icon in the notification area.**

   The Networks panel opens, showing a list of available wireless networks. In Figure 6-4, there's only one: Sycamore_Knoll. If the network doesn't use security, a shield icon appears on its icon.

2. **Click the network you want to connect to.**

   Information about that network appears, along with a Connect automatically check box and a Connect button. See Figure 6-5.

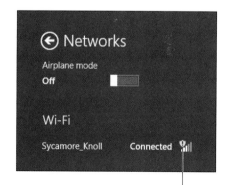

Shield indicates no security

Figure 6-4

TIP

An unsecure network is good in that you can connect to it without knowing the access key code for it, but it's bad in that other people can connect to it freely too, including people you might not want to be on the same network with (like hackers and other computer criminals).

Figure 6-5

3. **(Optional) Select the Connect Automatically check box.**

If you do so, Windows will reestablish this connection automatically in the future, so you won't have to go through these steps again.

4. **Click the Connect button.**

The computer attempts to connect to the network.

5. **If prompted, enter the access code and then click OK.**

Networks that use security require you to type an access code. This code is set up in the router's software. Ask the person who set up the network what the code is, if needed.

6. **Click away from the Networks panel to close it.**

Setting Up a Home Network

Let's assume for a moment that you came up empty in the previous section, and you don't already have a network. What do you need to get started with that, and what's the process for setting it up? The following sections get into those nitty-gritty details.

Checking out your network adapter

Need to create a network? First of all, find out what network adapter(s) you already have in your computer. Almost all portable computers (laptops, tablets, and so on) come with wireless networking built in, and almost all desktop computers come with a wired network adapter built in.

To create a home network, you need a network adapter (sometimes called a *network interface card*, NIC) for each computer or other device that will be participating in the network. Some devices have wired or wireless NICs (or both) built into them; others can accommodate NICs in internal expansion slots, or plugged into external ports.

You also need a *router,* which is a central gathering point for all the devices to communicate through. Routers can be either wired or wireless; most wireless routers have a few ports for wired connections too, so your network can consist of a combination of wired and wireless connections.

Examining the ports on a computer is one way to see what's available, but that won't tell you about any wireless networking devices in the computer. Therefore, the best way overall to check out what you've got is to look in Device Manager.

In this exercise, you will use Device Manager to browse the network adapters in your computer.

1. **Open the Control Panel.**

   To do so, start at the desktop. Display the Charms bar (by pointing the mouse at the lower right corner of the screen), click Settings, and then click Control Panel.

2. **Click the System and Security heading.**

   The System and Security section of the Control Panel appears.

3. **Click System.**

   The System section of the Control Panel appears.

4. **Click Device Manager.**

   The Device Manager window opens. Categories of hardware appear; each category can be expanded or collapsed by clicking the triangle arrow next to it. By default, cat-egories that have one or more devices in them that have a problem are expanded; categories in which everything is working normally appear collapsed. See Figure 6-6.

LINGO

A **network adapter** (or network interface card, **NIC** for short) is a communication interface that an individual device uses to connect with a network. It may be a an add-on device, or it may be built into the computer.

LINGO

Device Manager is a utility in Windows that provides a list of the installed hardware and enables you to access Properties boxes for configuring each of the devices and its driver. A **driver** is a file that contains instructions for translating between a device and the operating system.

Figure 6-6

5. **Click to expand the Network Adapters category if it isn't already expanded.**

A list expands of the networking hardware on your PC. See Figure 6-7. (Note that your list will probably have different items on it.)

EXTRA INFO

802.11n is the current standard for wireless Ethernet networks (Wi-Fi networks). Earlier standards included 802.11b and 802.11g. Most modern 802.11n equipment is backward-compatible with the earlier standards, so for example, if you have a router that is 802.11g and a NIC that is 802.11n, they will work together.

▲ ⛛ Network adapters

⛛ Bluetooth Device (Personal Area

⛛ Bluetooth Device (RFCOMM Pro

⛛ Microsoft Kernel Debug Networ

⛛ Qualcomm Atheros AR9285 802.11b/g/n WiFi Adapter

Figure 6-7

There may be other network adapters listed also, such as Bluetooth, but these aren't relevant to the task at hand. Bluetooth technology is used to connect nearby devices or printers to the computer, not to connect to a home computer network.

6. **Double-click the icon for the network adapter you identified in Step 5 as being the one to use for your home network.**

Its Properties dialog box opens.

7. **Check the Device Status section.**

It should report that "This device is working properly." See Figure 6-8.

Figure 6-8

TIP

If the device's status is anything other than working properly, you may need to install the software that came with the device (or download and install it from the Internet using a different computer). If that doesn't work, you could try removing the device's driver from Device Manager (by clicking Uninstall on Device Manager's toolbar) and then refreshing the hardware list (by clicking Scan for Hardware Changes on the toolbar) to allow Windows to redetect it.

8. **Click Cancel.**

   The Properties box closes.

9. **Close the Device Manager window.**

Setting up a wireless router

In addition to having a NIC in each device, you also need a router to connect your devices to one another. A router can be either wired or wireless. A wired router should work fine with its default settings, so you won't need this section if your router is wired-only. (If you do need to configure your wired router, check the instructions in the router's documentation.)

A router has several ports on it. The one that looks different from the other (different color, separated from the others, or in some other way, and possibly labeled WAN or Modem) is for your Internet connection. Run an Ethernet cable (which probably came with the router) from your broadband modem to the router to share the Internet connection with all the computers on the network. The other ports are for wired network connections; connect any computers that have wired network adapters to these ports. If it's a wireless router, it may also have an antenna on it, enabling wireless devices to connect with the router. See Figure 6-9.

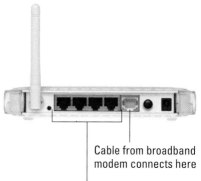

Cable from broadband modem connects here

Ports for computers that have wired Ethernet network adapters

Figure 6-9

A wireless router should work right out of the box, but by default wireless routers have no security encryption on them. That means that anyone in the vicinity can connect to your network without your permission unless you lock things down by configuring some type of security setting. To do that, you have to talk to the router. (Don't panic; it's not that hard.)

This isn't an issue for a wired-only router because in order to connect to one of those, you have to be physically able to access the router, so random people driving by your house can't do it.

To set up router security, you must use a web browser to access the router's configuration page.

First, get the network up and running without the security. Then Open your Web browser and type the router's IP address in the Address bar. If you don't know the IP address of the router, look in the router's documentation to find out what the default IP address for it is, or look in the properties for your existing network connection to it, and use the address that's listed as the default gateway. You'll learn to determine the router's IP address and set up router security in the following exercise.

Once you get into the router's configuration page, look for the security settings. It's different for different models. In the security settings, you'll find a Security Mode setting, set to Disabled or Off by default. You can set it to one of the available security modes and then create an access code for it. (WPA2 is the best mode to use, followed by WPA; WEP isn't as secure.) Then on each of the computers in the network, you enter that access code to allow the device to communicate with the router.

Figure 6-10

In this exercise, you will determine a router's IP address by looking at your network connection's properties; then you'll use that address to access your router's configuration, and set up security for it.

Figure 6-11

1. **Right-click the Network icon in the notification area and choose Open Network and Sharing Center from the menu that appears, as shown in Figure 6-10.**

   The Network and Sharing Center appears onscreen. (You can also get to the center via the Control Panel, if you prefer.)

2. **Next to Connections, click the hyperlink for your current network connection, as shown in Figure 6-11.**

   The Wi-Fi Status dialog box opens.

3. **Click the Details button.**

   The Network Connection Details dialog box opens.

4. **Make a note of the IPv4 Default Gateway setting, and then click Close twice to close both dialog boxes.**

   In Figure 6-12, the default gateway is 192.168.2.1, but yours may be different.

EXTRA INFO

IPv4 stands for Internet Protocol version 4. It's the current method of addressing computers on the Internet and on most networks. A newer addressing method, IPv6, isn't yet widely in use, but Windows supports it; in Figure 6-12, you can see an IPv6 address too next to Link-local IPv6 Address.

5. **Open Internet Explorer, and in the address bar, type** http:// **followed by the address you noted in Step 4, as shown in Figure 6-13. Then press Enter.**

   If all goes well, the configuration interface for your router opens. If it doesn't, you probably have the wrong IP address. Check the router documentation to troubleshoot. Some routers don't allow logging in using a wireless connection.

Different routers have very different interfaces from the one shown in this exercise, so if the option names don't correspond to what you see in these steps, don't panic; just poke around and find something equivalent if you can. If not, check the documentation for your router to get steps that are customized for that device.

IPv4 default gateway

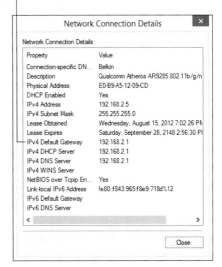

Figure 6-12

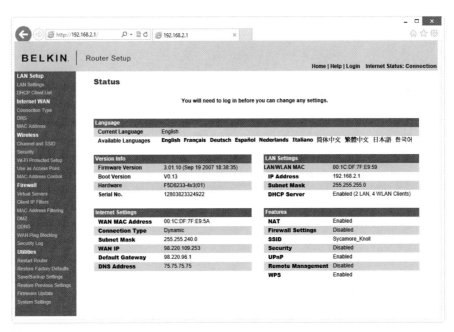

Figure 6-13

6. **Look for a Security hyperlink or category, and click it.**

7. **If you're prompted to log in with a password, enter the username and/or password specified in the router's documentation.**

Login

Before you can change any settings, you need to login with a password. If you have not yet set a custom password, then leave this field blank and click "Submit."

Password

Default = leave blank

Clear   Submit

Figure 6-14

Notice in Figure 6-14 that, on this particular router, the default is no password, and a hint to that effect appears onscreen. Your login prompt will probably look different from the one shown here.

8. **Change the security mode to WPA2 if it's available; otherwise choose WPA (the second-best choice) or WEP.**

Leave the Authentication method and Encryption Technique settings at their defaults unless you know enough about security to understand why you're changing them.

9. **Enter the access code you want to use for the router in the Pre-shared Key (PSK) box.**

The box for entering the key may have a different name in your program; it may be called a password or an access code rather than a key. Follow the rules for creating the key that are specified onscreen; the rules depend on the security mode and other settings you chose. In general, the key must be between 8 and 63 characters. See Figure 6-15.

Figure 6-15

10. **Click Apply Changes.**

    The button may be named differently in your program; it might be Save Changes, for example.

11. **Close the web browser window.**

    The next time a computer attempts to connect to the router wirelessly, the user will be prompted for the access code you entered in Step 9. You can also go in and configure the network connection with the access code proactively; to do so, continue to the next step.

12. **On the Windows 8 PC that you want to configure, right-click the Network icon in the notification area and choose Open Network and Sharing Center from the menu that appears.**

    The Network and Sharing Center appears (again) onscreen.

13. **Next to Connections, click the hyperlink for your current network connection.**

    The Properties dialog box opens for that connection.

14. **Click the Wireless Properties button.**

    The Wireless Network Properties dialog box opens.

15. **Click the Security tab.**

16. **Open the Security type drop-down list and select the type of security you chose for the router. Change the other settings to also match those for the router too.**

    The choices for the computer may not be exactly the same as the choices on the router. For example, you might choose WPA2-PSK on the router, but WPA2-Personal on the computer.

17. **In the Network Security Key box, type the access code you set up for the router.**

    See Figure 6-16.

18. **Click OK to close the dialog box.**

19. **Click Close to close the Wi-Fi Status dialog box.**

    Now your computer has automatic access to your router, and connects to it without any assistance, but other people can't connect to the router to piggyback on your Internet access or snoop your files without your permission.

Figure 6-16

Getting better wireless signal strength

A typical wireless router can transmit signals throughout a 100-meter radius when you set it up indoors. Walls and floors, especially thick ones like those in older homes, decrease that range significantly.

Here are some tips for wireless router placement to help optimize signal strength throughout your house:

- **Closer is better.** Place the router as close as possible to the rooms where you use computers with wireless network access the most often.

- **Don't put the router in a closet.** Remember, walls degrade signal strength, and a closet is just another layer of wall barrier.

- **Experiment with antenna positions.** If your router has antenna that rotate, try different angles to see which one works best. You can also buy an antenna booster kit to increase the effectiveness of your antenna.

- **Placing the router higher up may result in a better signal strength.** Try placing the router on a tall bookshelf or on top of your refrigerator.

- **Keep the router away from any other devices that also use RF (radio frequency) signals.** Cordless phones, baby monitors, and wireless stereo speakers are RF devices. Don't locate the router near a microwave oven because when the oven is operating, it can interfere with the RF signal.

Note: 802.11g routers are more susceptible to interference from other devices than 802.11n ones.

Building a HomeGroup

Windows 7 and Windows 8 computers that are part of a network can also be part of a HomeGroup. A HomeGroup can make file and printer sharing especially easy between computers because Windows contains some easy preset security permissions that apply to HomeGroup.

Being part of a HomeGroup is optional; you don't need a HomeGroup to share files and printers on your network. Only Windows 7 and Windows 8 computers can be part of a HomeGroup, and if you have both of those on the same network, you must create the HomeGroup from Windows 8.

LINGO

A **HomeGroup** is a grouping of networked computers that trust one another and therefore are allowed more simple and relaxed sharing permissions with one another than with the network at large.

In this exercise, you will create a HomeGroup on one computer, and then join the HomeGroup on another computer.

1. **From the Start screen, type** homegroup**, and then pause.**

   A search pane appears at the right.

2. **Click Settings in the listing on the right.**

   A list of settings that include the word *homegroup* appear in the main part of the screen. See Figure 6-17.

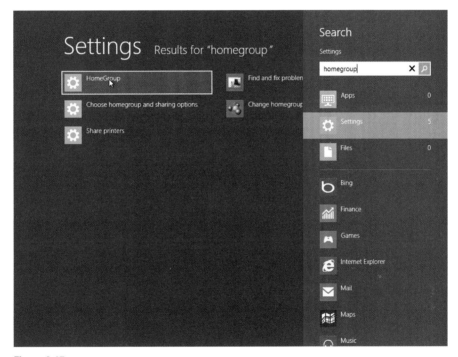

Figure 6-17

3. **Click the HomeGroup result.**

   The configuration screen for HomeGroups appears. If you haven't already created a HomeGroup, a Create button appears.

   If there's already a HomeGroup in place, you'll see a Libraries and Devices heading; skip to Step 5.

4. **Click the Create button.**

   The Libraries and Devices list of resources to share appears.

5. **Drag the Documents slider from Not Shared to Shared, as shown in Figure 6-18.**

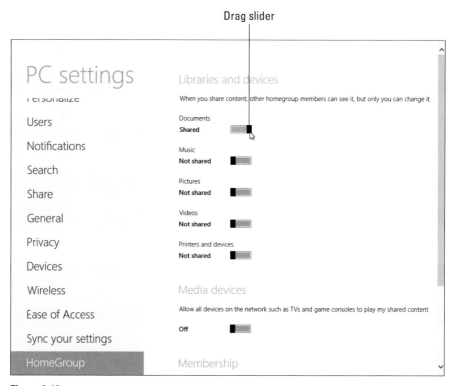

Figure 6-18

6. **Drag the Music, Pictures, Videos, and Printers and devices sliders to the Shared position.**

These sliders represent the libraries, not the specific file types. For example, if you put other types of content in the Music library besides music, it will also be shared.

7. **Scroll down to the Membership section and make a note of the access code there.**

See Figure 6-19. Your access code will be different.

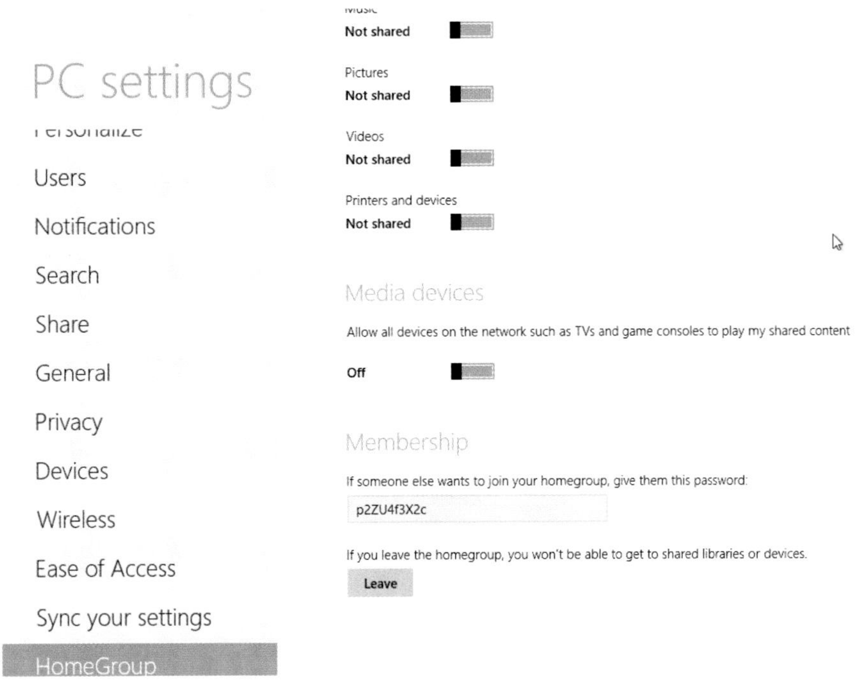

PC settings

Personalize

Users

Notifications

Search

Share

General

Privacy

Devices

Wireless

Ease of Access

Sync your settings

HomeGroup

Music
Not shared

Pictures
Not shared

Videos
Not shared

Printers and devices
Not shared

Media devices

Allow all devices on the network such as TVs and game consoles to play my shared content

Off

Membership

If someone else wants to join your homegroup, give them this password:

p2ZU4f3X2c

If you leave the homegroup, you won't be able to get to shared libraries or devices.

Leave

Figure 6-19

8. **Drag from the top of the screen to the bottom to close the PC Settings screen.**

9. **Go to the other PC that you want to include in the HomeGroup. Right-click the Network icon in the notification area, and choose Open Network and Sharing Center from the menu that appears.**

10. **In the Network and Sharing Center, click the Available to Join hyperlink shown in Figure 6-20. (It's next to the HomeGroup link.)**

    The Share with Other Home Computers screen appears.

11. **Click the Join Now button.**

    The Join a HomeGroup dialog box opens.

12. **Click Next.**

Click here.

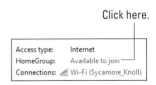

Access type:	Internet
HomeGroup:	Available to join
Connections:	Wi-Fi (Sycamore_Knoll)

Figure 6-20

13. Open the drop-down lists in the Permissions column for each resource type, as shown in Figure 6-21, and choose Shared or Not Shared.

14. Click Next.

15. Type in the HomeGroup password from Step 7 and then click Next.

16. Click Finish.

The two computers are now joined in a common HomeGroup, and you can share files and printers between them, as you'll learn in the upcoming sections of this lesson.

Set each resource type to the desired setting.

Figure 6-21

Browsing Other People's Shared Resources

What's out there to be discovered? You won't know until you start poking around in the shared folders on your network. Will it be buried treasure in the form of music and video clips, or just a boring old budget spreadsheet? In the following sections, you will learn how to browse the network for items that other people have shared, and how to map a network drive to make returning to a shared location easier. (If no folders on your network are currently shared, skip ahead to "Sharing Your Files and Printers" later in this lesson to learn how to change that.)

Browsing shared folders

When a network connection is established, you can access the network locations that have been made available to you by other users. These can include folders on a dedicated file server (in a large company, for example) and/or folders on individual PCs that the owners have chosen to share. The network locations available depend on the PC's network connectivity. Depending on your network type, you may see PCs, network storage devices, network-aware printers, media devices, and other resources.

One way to access a network location is to browse for it. You can do this by opening File Explorer and then clicking the Network link in the Navigation pane; a list of computers appears that are part of your workgroup or domain. From there, you can see what a computer is sharing by double-clicking the computer's icon.

In the following exercise, you will browse a network location.

1. **Open File Explorer, and click Network in the Navigation pane.**

   A list of computers, media devices, printers, and other network-shared items appears.

2. **Double-click the icon for one of the computers.**

   A list of the shared folders and printers for that computer appears. Figure 6-22 shows an example, but yours will have different folders and printers. Notice that the icons have a graphic of a cable underneath them, indicating that they're accessed from the network, rather than stored locally.

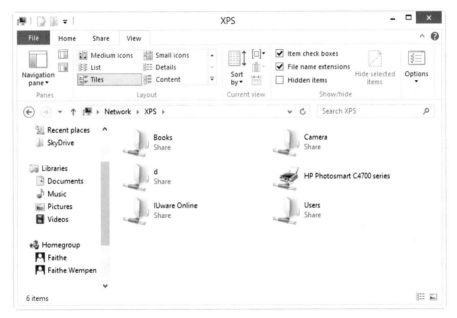

Figure 6-22

3. **Double-click the icon for one of the shared folders.**

   The content of the folder appears. You can work with this content just as you would local files.

Mapping a network drive

If you frequently access the same network location, you might want an easier way than browsing through the file system to access it. You can map that location to a drive with a specific letter assigned to it. The letter that represents the new drive appears in the Computer window, along with your other local drives, and then you can double-click that drive to quickly access the referenced location. In Figure 6-23, you can see that I've mapped a network location to the Z drive.

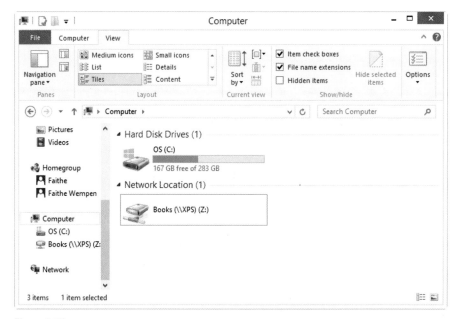

Figure 6-23

Any program can use the mapped drive, even programs that don't ordinarily support reading or writing from network locations. Network drive mapping is also a good tool to use when setting up systems for less experienced computer users because it's much easier for them to remember a simple letter than a complete path to a network location.

You can set up the mapping to reestablish itself automatically each time you log on, if desired. That way, you never have to think about the location being located on the network; as far as your system is concerned, the location is simply another hard drive on your own system.

In this exercise, you will map a network-shared folder as a drive on your PC.

1. **Open File Explorer, click Network, and navigate to the location that contains the folder you want to map.**

2. **Right-click the folder's icon and choose Map Network Drive from the menu that appears.**

   The Map Network Drive dialog box opens. See Figure 6-24. The default drive letter is Z, and that's fine for our purposes here — but you could change that if you wanted.

3. **Click Finish.**

4. **In File Explorer, click Computer.**

   Note that the mapped drive appears as an icon, along with local drives.

5. **Right-click the mapped drive and click Disconnect.**

   The drive mapping is disconnected.

Figure 6-24

Sharing Your Files and Printers

You can set up your PC to make certain folders, drives, and/or printers available to other computers on your network. For example, you can share your vacation photos with your whole family, or you can share a report you're writing with someone who has offered to help you proofread it.

Sharing libraries

As you saw in the previous section, you can choose certain libraries to share when you join a HomeGroup. You can also change your selections later at any time.

In this exercise, you will share and unshare libraries. There are two methods; you'll learn both of them.

1. **Open File Explorer, and in the navigation bar on the left, right-click HomeGroup and choose Change HomeGroup Settings from the menu that appears, as shown in Figure 6-25.**

   The HomeGroup dialog box opens.

2. **Click Change What You're Sharing with the HomeGroup.**

   The Change HomeGroup Sharing Settings dialog box opens.

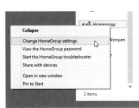

Figure 6-25

3. **Open the drop-down list in the Permissions column next to Videos, as shown in Figure 6-26, and click Not Shared.**

4. **If any other libraries are set to Not Shared, open the Permissions drop-down list and choose Shared for each one.**

5. **Click Next.**

6. **Click Finish.**

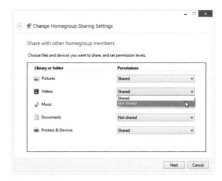

Figure 6-26

You can also share libraries individually, as shown in the following steps; this is useful for libraries you've created yourself, because these won't show up on the default list shown in Figure 6-26. Using this method, you can also choose whether to let others edit your shared files. With the method from Steps 1-6, other users get read-only access.

7. **In File Explorer, click Libraries.**

Icons for all your libraries appear.

8. **Right-click the Documents folder, point to Share With on the menu that appears, and then choose the HomeGroup (View and Edit) option. See Figure 6-27.**

The Documents folder is now shared with both Read and Write access.

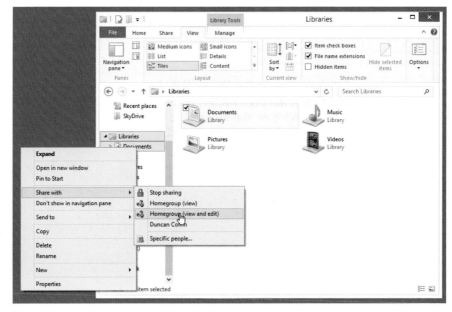

Figure 6-27

Sharing with other users

The sharing method you learned in the preceding section applies only to your fellow HomeGroup users. Some users on your network may not be part of the HomeGroup, perhaps because they use a version of Windows that doesn't support HomeGroups, or because they're in a different HomeGroup. (A computer can be a part of only one HomeGroup.)

You can share with everyone on your network at once by sharing with Everyone. Yes, that's right, there's a user named Everyone built into the networking in Windows. (Well, technically it's a group, not a user, but you get the idea.) The Everyone user represents all users who have access to the network.

To share with other individual users, you must either be part of a business network that's set up with domains (which you probably aren't), or you must create a local user account on your PC for each person with whom you want to share. You'll learn how to create user accounts in Lesson 7.

In this exercise, you will create a new folder on your hard drive and then share it with Everyone.

1. **In File Explorer, click the C drive in the Navigation pane.**

   The contents of the C drive appears.

2. **On the Quick Access Toolbar in the upper-left corner of the window, click New Folder.**

   A new folder appears, with the name New Folder highlighted so you can change it.

3. **Type Free and press Enter.**

   A new folder named Free is created.

4. **Right-click the Free folder, point to Share With on the menu that appears (as shown in Figure 6-28), and then choose the Specific People option.**

   The File Sharing dialog box opens. Your own username is already listed, with the permission level set to Owner.

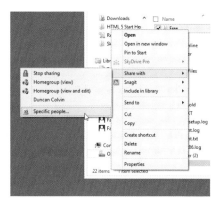

Figure 6-28

5. **Click the drop-down menu's down arrow and then choose the Everyone option, as shown in Figure 6-29.**

If other user accounts are set up on this PC, they also appear on this list, so you could share with a specific user instead of sharing with Everyone if you wanted to. (You can try that on your own if you like.)

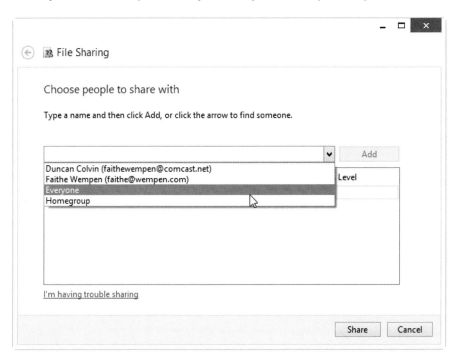

Figure 6-29

6. **Click Add.**

The Everyone group is added to the list of allowed users.

7. **As shown in Figure 6-30, under the Permission Level heading, click the down arrow next to Read on the Everyone line, and then choose Read/Write.**

The Read permission allows others to read but not change your files; the Read/Write permission allows both.

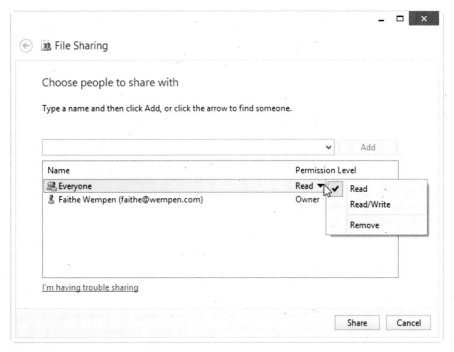

Figure 6-30

8. Click Share.

A confirmation box appears.

9. Click Done.

Configuring network sharing

On all networked computers, regardless of whether you use a HomeGroup, you can fine-tune the network sharing permissions. This includes things like whether file and printer sharing is turned on, whether other computers can see yours when browsing the network, and whether passwords are required for sharing.

There are three separate sets of properties for network settings: one used for Private networks, one used for Public or Guest networks, and one for All networks. The settings are different because you will probably want permissions for public networks to be very strict and limited, to prevent strangers from invading your privacy. Each set can be expanded (by clicking the down-pointing arrow) or collapsed (by clicking the up-pointing arrow). See Figure 6-31.

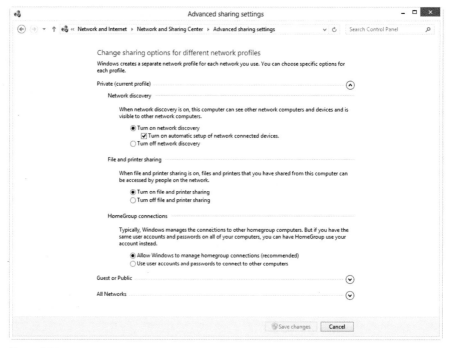

Figure 6-31

Here are the settings you can control:

🗸 **For Private and Guest or Public Networks:**

- *Network Discovery:* Determines whether others browsing the network can see you.

- *File and Printer Sharing:* Determines whether file and printer sharing (in general) is enabled on your PC.

- *HomeGroup Connections:* Determines how HomeGroup connections are authenticated. (You can adjust this only for Private networks.)

🗸 **For All Networks:**

- *Public Folder Sharing:* Determines whether the folder named Public is available to others.

- *Media Streaming:* Determines whether your music and video content is available for others to play on their computers by streaming it from yours.

- *File Sharing Connections:* Determines the level of encryption used to protect the connection when file sharing. A lower level of encryption is slightly less secure but allows more and different devices to have access.

- *Password-Protected Sharing:* Determines whether passwords are required when others try to access your files, folders, or printers.

In the following exercise, you will change some network settings on your computer.

1. **Right-click the Network icon in the notification area and choose Open Network and Sharing Center from the menu that appears.**

   The Network and Sharing Center appears onscreen.

2. **Click the Change Advanced Sharing Settings link.**

   The Advanced Sharing Settings screen appears. Refer to Figure 6-31.

3. **If the Private options aren't expanded, click the down arrow to the right of Private to expand them.**

4. **Make sure that Turn On File and Printer Sharing is selected.**

   See Figure 6-32.

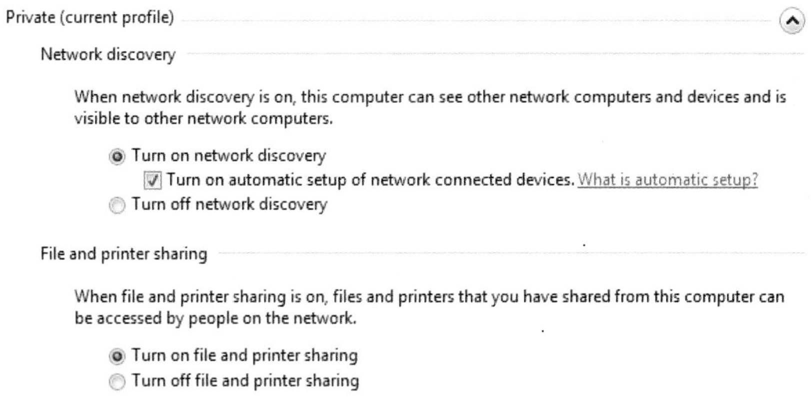

Private (current profile) ⌃

Network discovery

    When network discovery is on, this computer can see other network computers and devices and is visible to other network computers.

    ◉ Turn on network discovery
       ☑ Turn on automatic setup of network connected devices. What is automatic setup?
    ○ Turn off network discovery

File and printer sharing

    When file and printer sharing is on, files and printers that you have shared from this computer can be accessed by people on the network.

    ◉ Turn on file and printer sharing
    ○ Turn off file and printer sharing

Figure 6-32

5. **Click the down arrow next to Guest or Public to expand that category.**

   You may need to scroll down in the window to see that category.

6. **Make sure that Turn Off Network Discovery is selected, as shown in Figure 6-33.**

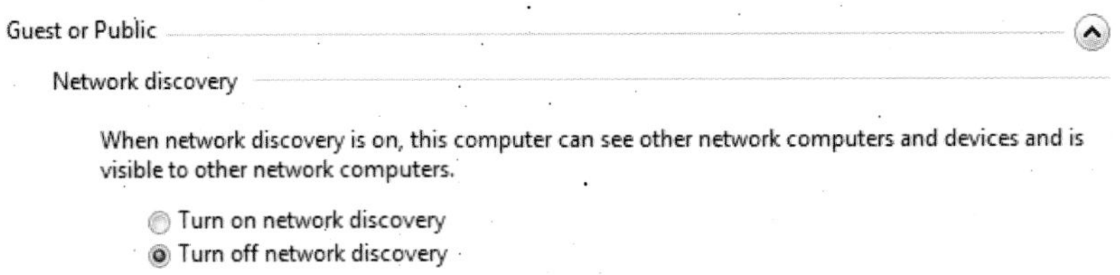

Guest or Public ── (^)

Network discovery ──

When network discovery is on, this computer can see other network computers and devices and is visible to other network computers.

○ Turn on network discovery
◉ Turn off network discovery

Figure 6-33

7. **Click the down arrow next to All Networks to expand that category.**

8. **Make sure that Turn Off Password Protected Sharing is selected.**

When password-protected sharing is turned on, users attempting to access resources on your PC must sign in with a valid ID and password; when this setting is turned off, that's not required.

9. **If you made any changes, click Save Changes.**

If you didn't make any changes, the Save changes button is unavailable.

10. **Close the Advanced Sharing Settings window.**

The window closes automatically if you saved changes in Step 9. Now your network security settings are configured such that on a private network, others may access your files without a password (for maximum convenience) but on a public/guest network, they can't even see that your computer exists (for maximum protection).

Sharing printers

If you have a local printer (that is, a printer that is directly attached to your computer), you can share it with other people on your network, so that they can send print jobs to the printer just as if the printer were locally connected.

Two types of printers can be available on a network: those that are truly network-aware, and those that are shared with an individual PC. A network-aware printer can be connected directly to the network's router, so that it doesn't rely on any particular PC being active in order to be available. A shared printer is dependent on the PC to which it's attached. When the PC

LINGO

A **network-aware** printer (also called a *network-ready printer*) has its own network interface card and its own network address. A **shared printer** is a locally installed printer on a PC that has been set up for sharing with others.

sharing is turned off or disconnected from the network, the printer becomes unavailable to network users.

Using a network printer

The Add Printers utility enables you to install either local or network printers. If you choose to install a network printer, it scans the network and presents you with a list of the available printers, both network-aware ones and shared ones. You can tell the difference because a network-aware printer has an IP address (a numeric address) listed for it; whereas a shared printer has a network path containing the name of the PC to which it's attached. For example, in Figure 6-34, the first printer on the list is network aware, and the last one is shared.

Figure 6-34

In this exercise, you will set up your PC to use a network printer.

1. **Open the Control Panel, and under the Hardware and Sound heading, click View Devices and Printers.**

   A list of the installed printers and devices appears. In Figure 6-35, you can see that one printer is already set up on my network — Brother MFC-9320CW Printer — as well as several other drivers that aren't technically printers, but are treated as printers for Windows' purposes: Fax, Microsoft XPS Document Writer, Send to OneNote 2013, and Snagit11.

Figure 6-35

2. **Click Add a Printer.**

   The Add Printer Wizard runs.

3. **Wait for the wizard to search for available printers, and then click the printer you want to use.**

   See Figure 6-34, but your available printers will be different. If the printer you want does not appear, make sure it's turned on and connected to the network or shared by another PC (as explained in the next section).

4. **Click Next.**

5. **Follow the prompts to complete the driver installation.**

For example, if you're prompted to install a driver, select the printer's make and model from the list, or click Have Disk and follow the prompts to select a driver.

6. **Click Next.**

7. **In the Printer Name box, type the name you want to use for this printer.**

You can accept the default name or change it.

Note: For a network-aware printer only, you may be prompted whether to share the printer with others. Sharing a printer with others isn't necessary because other PCs can access the printer directly, as you did.

8. **(Optional) Deselect the Set as the Default Printer check box if you don't want this printer to be the default.**

9. **Click Finish.**

Sharing a local printer on the network

You can make your own local printer available to other network users so that they can set it up on their PCs as described in the preceding section. A shared printer shows a sharing symbol on its icon, the same as with a shared folder.

If the other network users also run the same version of Windows, the needed driver is copied to their PCs automatically when they set up the printer. If other people on the network have other versions of Windows and would like to use the shared printer, however, you must make drivers available for those versions, or those users must supply their own drivers for the printer.

In this exercise, you will share one of your local printers with other people on your network.

1. **Open the Control Panel, and under the Hardware and Sound heading, click View Devices and Printers.**

2. **Right-click the desired printer and choose Printer Properties from the menu that appears.**

3. **Click the Sharing tab.**

4. **Select the Share this Printer check box, shown in Figure 6-36.**

Figure 6-36

5. **(Optional) Change the Share name, if desired, to more accurately describe the printer.**

   For example, you could name a printer according to what room of the house it is in.

6. **(Optional) To make other drivers available, follow these steps:**

   a. *Click the Additional Drivers button.*

   b. *Select the check boxes for the additional Windows versions to support.*

   c. *Click OK.*

   d. *If prompted, insert a disc containing the drivers for the other versions or navigate to the location that contains the needed files and click OK.*

   e. *Follow the prompts to finish installing the other drivers.*

7. **Click OK to close the dialog box.**

Sharing streaming media

LINGO

To **stream** is to view or play content from one computer on another computer without permanently transferring the content to the computer that's playing it.

If you have pictures, videos, or other media stored on your computer, you may want to share those files with other network users. You could copy the files onto a DVD and hand it to the person, or transfer the files via the network, but it may be more efficient to allow other users to access your media library from the network and stream what they want to view or hear. For example, you could put all of your music on one PC in your household, and every other computer in the house could access it.

Depending on your TV, DVR, or home theater equipment, you also may be able to stream media from your computer to your TV. Check the manual that came with your devices to find out how. You may also be able to discover additional devices to stream to by opening the Charms bar and clicking Devices. If any eligible devices are detected on your network, a command will appear enabling you to set them up.

The first step in sharing your media content with other computers and devices is to adjust your network settings to allow media streaming. You do this from the Network and Sharing Center, under Change Advanced Sharing Settings. (You learned this earlier in the lesson.) After enabling media server access, you can go to another computer on your network, display the Computer window, and double-click the Media Server icon to browse the media content available. You can also access the network media server from applications, just as if it were a drive. For example, in Windows Media Player, you can include network locations when creating playlists and playing music or videos.

In this exercise, you will enable media streaming on one PC, and then access shared music or video content on it from another PC.

1. **Right-click the Network icon in the notification area and choose Open Network and Sharing Center from the menu that appears.**

   The Network and Sharing Center appears onscreen.

2. **Click Change Advanced Sharing Settings.**

   The Advanced Sharing Settings appear.

3. **Click the down arrow to expand the All Networks section.**

4. **Under Media Streaming, click Choose Media Streaming Options.**

   The Media Streaming Options appear.

5. **Make sure that the Allowed check box shown in Figure 6-37 is selected.**

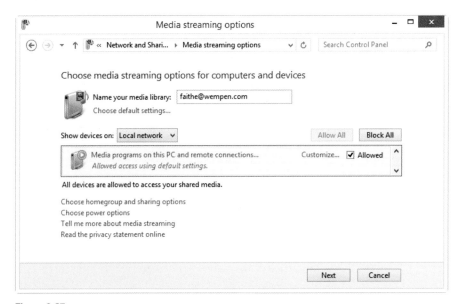

Figure 6-37

6. **Click Next.**

   The Share With Other HomeGroup Members dialog box opens.

7. **Make sure that the types of media you want to share are set to Shared.**

   For example, if you want to share music, make sure the Music library in set to Shared.

8. Click Next.

A reminder of the HomeGroup password appears.

9. Click Finish.

10. Close the Advanced Sharing Settings window.

11. On another PC on your network, open File Explorer, and click Computer in the Navigation pane.

A list of available drives appears. One of these is the media server you enabled in the earlier steps. You can access its content the same as you would your own hard drive.

If the media server doesn't appear in this step, on the Computer tab, click Media Access, and click Connect to Media Server. Then follow the prompts.

Summing Up

In this chapter, you learned how to set up and use a local area network on your Windows 8 computer. Here are some of the highlights:

- ✔ If you share an Internet connection among multiple computers in your household, you probably have both a broadband modem and a router, and you already have a basic network set up.

- ✔ You can check the network status by pointing at the Network icon in the notification area.

- ✔ The computer's network adapter (network interface card, or NIC) lets it participate in the network. Each network adapter has a unique IP address on the network.

- ✔ By default, the router doesn't have any security features enabled, but you can — and should — enable security by accessing the router's configuration page via your web browser.

- ✔ A HomeGroup enables all computers that are running Windows 7 or 8 on the network to easily share files and other resources with one another. Using a HomeGroup is optional.

- ✔ To browse other people's shared resources, open File Explorer and click Network.

- ✔ Mapping a network drive assigns a drive letter to a shared network folder for easy access to it.

✔ You can share libraries with other users, either by configuring sharing in the HomeGroup settings or by sharing individual libraries.

✔ To share with everyone, set up the resource to share with specific people and then share with the name Everyone.

✔ A network-aware printer has its own NIC and network address; a shared printer is a locally installed printer that is shared with others on the network.

✔ To set up a network printer, from the Devices and Printers screen, click Add Printer.

Know This Tech Talk

broadband modem: A device provided by your Internet provider (usually cable or DSL) that interfaces with your cable or phone line so you can use it for Internet connectivity.

Device Manager: A utility in Windows that provides a list of the installed hardware and enables you to access Properties boxes for configuring each of the devices and its driver.

Ethernet: The most common technology used for home and business networking.

HomeGroup: A collection of networked computers that trust one another, and therefore are allowed more simple and relaxed sharing permissions with one another than with the network at large.

local area network (LAN): A group of connected computers in the same room or building.

network: A group of connected computers.

network adapter: A communication interface that an individual computer uses to connect with a network. It may be a separate device, or it may be built into the device.

network-aware printer: Also called a *network-ready printer.* It's a printer that has its own NIC and its own network address.

network interface card (NIC): See *network adapter.*

router: An intelligent traffic-routing box through which all the computers in the network connect.

shared printer: A locally installed printer that's set up on the PC to be shared with others.

stream: To view or play content from one computer on another without permanently transferring the content to the computer that's playing it.

Wi-Fi: A shorthand way of referring to the type of wireless technology that computers commonly use for networking and Internet. Also called IEEE 802.11.

Lesson 7

Managing Accounts and User Settings

✔ Create new Windows user accounts.

✔ Change an account's password.

✔ Adjust mouse settings.

✔ Change the system date and time.

✔ Configure power management.

*W*ith Windows 8, each person can make the Windows environment his or her own. You can create multiple user accounts, each one with its own private areas for documents, music, videos, and so on, and each with its own customized user settings.

In this lesson, you'll find out how to set up new user accounts as well as how to protect a user account with a password. You'll also learn how to adjust Windows settings that affect basic usability, such as mouse sensitivity, region, date and time, and power management.

Managing Accounts

Windows 8 supports multiple user accounts, so each person who uses your computer can have his or her own login. Windows remembers the desktop preferences for each user account so that you don't have to adjust the color scheme, font sizes, or any of those other settings just because someone else has been using your PC. Each user account also has its own separate libraries for data files: Documents, Music, Videos, and Pictures.

When you install Windows, or when you buy a new computer with it preloaded and start it up for the first time, you're prompted to create a user account, so you already have one. Need more than one? You're in the right place; see the following sections.

Understanding account types

In Windows 8, the default Windows account type is a Microsoft account, which is a Windows account that has an e-mail address associated with it. The first time you sign into Windows with that account, that e-mail address is registered with Microsoft's servers via the Internet.

LINGO

A **Microsoft account** is a Windows account that's linked to an e-mail address. A **local account** is a Windows account that isn't linked to an email address.

When you sign into Windows 8 with a Microsoft account, you get all kinds of benefits, such as the ability to access your SkyDrive without having to perform a separate login. Your desktop preferences and settings also synchronize from one PC to another.

The alternative to that is to create a local account, which exists only on that specific PC. It isn't linked to anything. You don't need a Microsoft account for it.

Separate from the preceding choice, you also have a choice of making a particular account either standard or administrator in terms of its privileges. A standard account can use most software and change system settings that don't affect other users or the security of the PC. An administrator account has complete control over the computer — meaning that, with an administrator account, you can change any settings and access all of the files and programs stored on the PC.

LINGO

A **standard account** can use most programs on the PC, but can't make changes that affect other users, or the security of the PC. An **administrator account** can make all kinds of changes to the PC's configuration.

The first user account created on a PC is automatically set up as an administrator, because there needs to be at least one administrator account at all times. Subsequent accounts are set up as standard users by default, but you can change an account to administrator status after creating it. Microsoft recommends that everyone use standard accounts as they do their daily work, and that they log into an administrator account only to make specific changes as needed. That's because a user logged in with a standard account can't make system changes that will negatively impact other users.

Enabling the guest account

Every person who uses your computer doesn't necessarily have to have her own user account. If someone is a guest in your home, for example, and just wants to get online for a few minutes to look something up on a website, you wouldn't go to the trouble of setting her up with a separate account for the short time she's there.

LINGO

The **guest account** is a limited-access account that anyone may use to log into the computer. The guest account typically doesn't have access to apps that individual users have installed, but its users can use the desktop and Internet Explorer.

Windows 8 includes a guest account, which is an account with limited security privileges. The guest account isn't enabled by default, but you can easily enable it so that it shows up as one of the account choices when you log in.

In the following exercise, you will enable the guest account.

1. **Open the Control Panel and, under the User Accounts and Family Safety heading, click Change Account Type.**

   One way to open the Control Panel is to display the Charms bar (by pointing to the lower-right corner of the screen), clicking Settings, and then clicking Control Panel.

   The Manage Accounts screen appears, showing the current user accounts on this system. One of them is guest. (See Figure 7-1.)

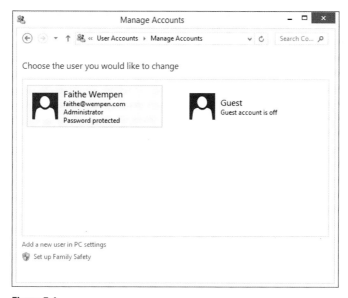

Figure 7-1

2. **If the guest account is off, as in Figure 7-1, click it.**

   A prompt appears, asking if you want to turn on the Guest account.

3. **Click Turn On.**

   The guest account is now enabled, and will appear next time someone logs into the computer.

Signing in as a different user

When you start up your PC, a sign-in prompt appears for the username that last signed into the PC. From here, you can click the left-pointing arrow button to the left of the current username to open a list of all the available user accounts. Click the one you want, and then type the password for it (if it has a password) to sign in.

To change users, sign out of whatever account is active, and then sign in with another one.

In the following exercise, you will sign in as the guest account that you enabled in the previous exercise.

1. **Sign out of Windows.**

   As you learned in Lesson 1, to sign out, click the username in the upper-right corner of the Start screen and choose Sign Out from the menu that appears. See Figure 7-2.

   The Date and Time screen appears, with a background graphic and the current date and time, as it does when you start up your PC.

Figure 7-2

2. **Press the space bar, or click anywhere.**

   Large icons for all of the available accounts appear. See Figure 7-3. They remain for 30 seconds, and if you don't do anything in that time, the Date and Time screen reappears, and you have to press the space bar again to get back to the icons again.

3. **Click the guest account.**

   The PC logs in to the guest account. The first time you log in with the guest account (or any new account), Windows may take a minute or two to prepare the

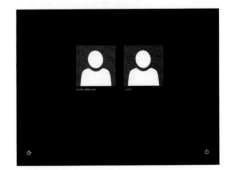

Figure 7-3

   account; this is normal. After Windows finishes loading, notice on the Start screen that there are very few tiles available. That's because the guest account doesn't have access to most of the applications. However, a guest can still use Internet Explorer and File Explorer. (See Figure 7-4.) Guests can also right-click and choose All Apps to get access to many of the built-in utilities in Windows 8.

Figure 7-4

4. **Click the word Guest in the upper-right corner of the Start screen.**

   A menu opens; the only command on the menu is Sign Out.

5. **Click Sign Out.**

   Windows signs out of the guest account and returns to the Date and Time screen.

6. **Press the spacebar, or click anywhere.**

   A list of user accounts appears, as it did after Step 2.

7. **Click your user account.**

   If your user account is password-protected, a password prompt appears. If not, Windows logs that account in immediately.

8. **If a password prompt appears, type your password and press Enter.**

   You are logged in under your regular account.

Adding a new user account

Create a new user account whenever someone else wants to use your computer on a regular basis. Creating a user account for someone also creates storage folders for their work, as well as libraries for their own use. It also enables them to save their own private list of favorites in Internet Explorer.

In the following exercise, you will create two user accounts: One with a Microsoft account associated with it, and one local account.

1. **Display the Charms bar, click Settings, and click Change PC Settings.**

   As you learned earlier, to display the Charms bar, point the mouse at the bottom-right corner of the screen — or on a touchscreen, swipe in from the right.

   The Start screen app-style PC Settings utility opens.

2. **Click the Users category on the left.**

   The Users options appear. (See Figure 7-5.)

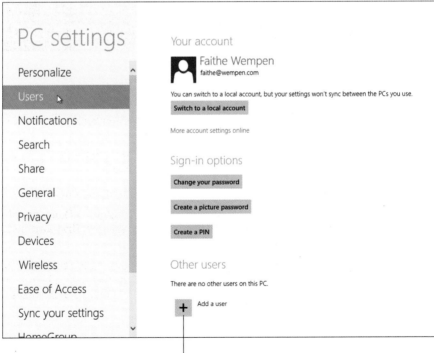

Click here to add a user.

Figure 7-5

3. Click Add a User.

The Add a User screen appears, as shown in Figure 7-6.

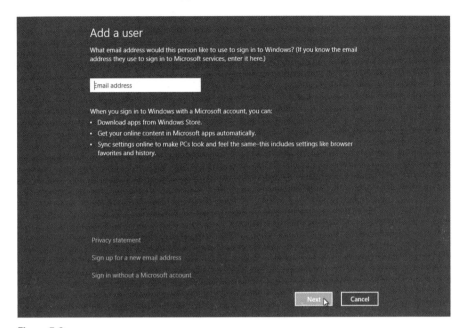

Figure 7-6

4. If you have another e-mail address besides the one you used when you set up your initial account in Windows, type it in the Email Address box, and click Next.

If you don't have another e-mail address, click Sign Up for a New Email Address, and follow the prompts to do so.

After you click Next, a confirmation screen appears.

5. In the text boxes provided (shown in Figure 7-7), enter information about this user account, including password, first and last name, country, and zip code. Then click Next.

See Figure 7-7. If the e-mail account you used in Step 4 has previously been used to create a Microsoft account (for example, on some other computer), you won't be prompted for this information, and you can skip directly to Step 7.

Figure 7-7

6. **In the prompts for security verification info, enter the information requested, and click Next.**

7. **At the Finish Up screen, enter the information requested, and click Next.**

This screen asks for your birth date and gender, and also permission to send you promotional offers from Microsoft. You can decline the promotional offers. See Figure 7-8.

After you click Next, the Finish Up screen may reappear with an extra prompt asking you to enter the characters you see onscreen; this is to ensure that you're a real person and not some software trying to mass-create a lot of new accounts. If prompted, enter the characters you see and then click next again.

8. **Click Finish.**

The new account is now created, and you are returned to the PC Settings utility.

Next you will create another user account, this one a Local account.

9. **Click Add a User.**

The Add a User screen appears, with a prompt for an e-mail address, as shown earlier in Figure 7-6.

Figure 7-8

10. **Click the Sign in without a Microsoft account hyperlink.**

    A description appears, explaining the two kinds of user accounts: Local accounts and Microsoft accounts.

11. **Click the Local Account button.**

12. **Type the requested information in the prompts shown in Figure 7-9 and then click Next.**

    Use a username of Chester. (You can use a different name if you like, but all the examples in this book will use Chester.) Leave the password text boxes empty so that no password is assigned.

13. **Click Finish.**

    The new account is now created.

14. **Drag the top of the PC Settings screen down to the bottom of the screen to close it.**

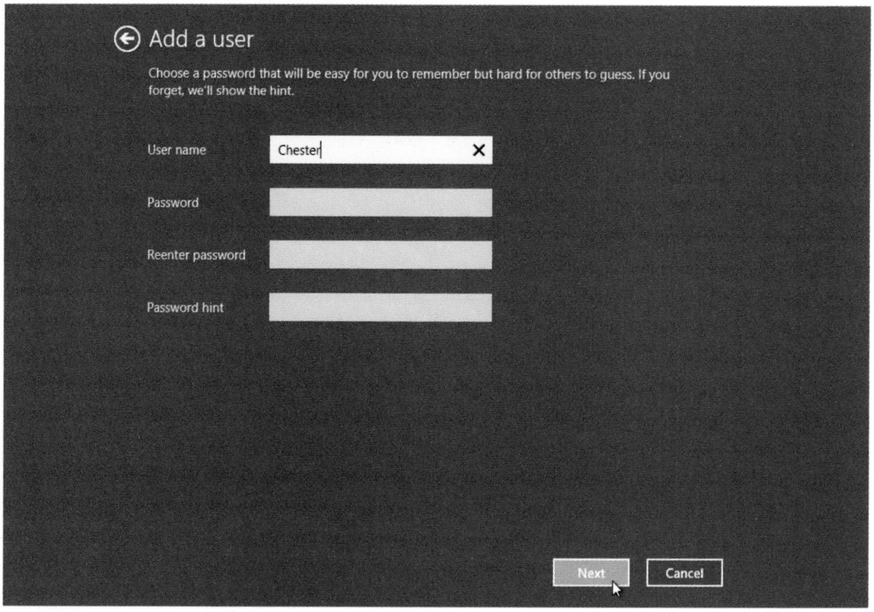

Add a user

Choose a password that will be easy for you to remember but hard for others to guess. If you forget, we'll show the hint.

User name   Chester   ✕

Password

Reenter password

Password hint

Next   Cancel

Figure 7-9

Changing account types

All accounts you create after the first one start out as standard accounts. You can upgrade one or more of them to administrator status to give them additional privileges to make system-level changes to Windows.

To see what the current account type is, look at the Manage Accounts screen, shown in Figure 7-10. (To get there, open the Control Panel and under the User Accounts and Family Safety heading, click Change Account Type.) If an account says Administrator under the name, it's an administrator account. If it doesn't, it's a standard account. (Exception: the guest account has its own special status, Guest, which is even more restrictive than standard.)

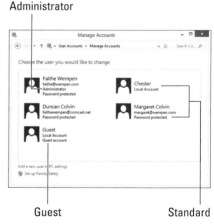

Administrator

Guest   Standard

Figure 7-10

In this exercise, you will change the local account that you created in the previous exercise to an administrator account.

1. **Open the Control Panel, and under the User Accounts and Family Safety heading, click Change Account Type.**

2. **Click the local account you created in the previous exercise (Chester).**

   A screen appears in which you can make changes to Chester's account. (See Figure 7-11.)

Figure 7-11

3. **Click Change the Account Type hyperlink.**

   The Change Account Type screen appears, with a list of available account types: Standard and Administrator. Standard is already chosen.

4. **Select the Administrator radio button, as shown in Figure 7-12.**

5. **Click the Change Account Type button.**

   The account type changes. Keep the Change Account Type window open for the next exercise.

Figure 7-12

This account currently has no password. You should not have an administrator account without a password because anyone can make system-level changes to your computer. In the next exercise, you'll learn how to assign a password to this account.

Working with account passwords

Each user account can have a password assigned to it or not. Microsoft strongly recommends that all administrator accounts have a password, to prevent unauthorized users from making changes that may inconvenience other users. Microsoft accounts are required to have passwords; it's only for local accounts that passwords are optional.

Make sure your passwords are strong — in other words, difficult to guess. Don't use words from the dictionary or proper names, and include a mixture of uppercase and lowercase letters, numbers, and symbols, at least eight characters total.

When you assign a password to an account, you're also prompted for a password hint. The hint can help you remember what you chose. For example, if your password is the address of the house you grew up in, your hint might be "old house."

In this exercise, you will assign a password to the user account you worked with in the preceding exercise, and then you will change that password.

1. **If you aren't already at the Change an Account screen for the desired account, do the following: Open the Control Panel, under the User Accounts and Family Safety heading click Change Account Type, and then click Chester (or whatever name you used for the account you created).**

2. **Click the Create a Password hyperlink.**

   The Create Password screen appears.

3. **In the New Password dialog box, type the password you want to use.**

4. **In the Confirm New Password dialog box, type the same password again.**

5. **In the Type a Password Hint dialog box, type the hint you want to use.**

   Figure 7-13 shows the completed dialog box. If you don't want to use a password hint, type **None** or some other word that will be no help to someone trying to guess the password. Windows doesn't allow you to omit the password hint entirely.

Figure 7-13

6. **Click the Create Password button.**

   You return to the Change an Account screen. The Create a Password hyperlink has been replaced by a Change the Password hyperlink.

7. **Click Change the Password.**

   The Change Password screen appears. The fields are the same as in Figure 7-13.

8. **Type and confirm the new password, and type a password hint. Then click Change Password.**

   The Change an Account screen appears again.

9. **Click Change the Password yet again.**

   The Change Password screen appears.

10. **Click Change Password without typing anything into the password text boxes.**

    The password is removed. The Change the Password hyperlink is replaced by a Create a Password hyperlink again. Keep the Change an Account screen open for the next exercise.

Deleting a user account

You can delete a user account whenever you find that you no longer have need of it. When you delete a user account, you can choose whether to keep or delete the user's data files. If you choose to keep them, they're moved to a new folder on the desktop with the same name as the deleted user account. The user's data files include his or her documents, music, pictures, and videos folders, plus any favorites that the user had set up in Internet Explorer.

In this exercise, you will delete the Chester account you created and changed in earlier exercises.

1. **If you aren't already at the Change an Account screen for Chester's account (shown in Figure 7-11), do the following: Open the Control Panel and under the User Accounts and Family Safety heading click Change Account Type, and then click Chester (or whatever name you used for the account you created).**

2. **Click the Delete the Account hyperlink.**

    A prompt appears, asking if you want to keep Chester's files. (See Figure 7-14.)

3. **Click Delete Files.**

    Figure 7-14

    Because you did not create any files under Chester's account, or any favorites, there would be nothing to save, so there is no reason to use Keep Files. A confirmation prompt appears.

4. **Click Delete Account.**

    The account is deleted, and no longer appears on the account list in the Manage Accounts window.

5. **Close the Manage Accounts window.**

Changing Mouse Settings

Your mouse — or other equivalent pointing device — is extremely important in
Windows. Yes, you can use Windows without one, but it's difficult. When the mouse
isn't right, it can throw a wrench into your
Windows productivity.

Different people have different opinions as
to what constitutes the perfect mouse settings. Some people like it when the pointer
zips across the screen at the least little
nudge, while other people like it to move just
a little at a time. And some people like the
mouse pointer to be all big and noticeable,
while others prefer it at a smaller and more
subtle size. In the next few sections, you'll
find out how to customize mouse setting to
make it your own.

Adjusting mouse performance settings

You can adjust several settings that control
how the mouse operates. Here are a few
examples:

- **Pointer speed:** How much the pointer moves onscreen in relation to the
  amount of movement you make with the mouse.

- **Double-click speed:** How quickly you have to click two times in a row
  for Windows to consider it a *double-click* and not two separate clicks.

- **Snap to:** Whether the pointer automatically jumps to the default button
  when a dialog box opens.

- **Pointer trails:** Whether trails appear behind the pointer as you move it.
  This option is especially useful for people who have limited vision and
  have a hard time seeing the pointer.

- **Button configuration:** You can switch the functions of the mouse's right
  and left buttons so that the right button is the primary one and the left
  one secondary. Some left-handed people find the mouse easier to use
  this way.

In the following exercise, you will adjust mouse performance settings and then experiment to see the results of them.

1. **Open the Control Panel and click the Hardware and Sound heading. Under the Devices and Printers heading, click Mouse.**

   The Mouse Properties dialog box opens.

2. **On the Buttons tab, drag the Double-Click Speed slider all the way over to Fast.**

   See Figure 7-15. Note that this tab is also where you can switch the primary and secondary buttons on the mouse, although you won't do that in this exercise.

3. **Click Apply.**

4. **Test the setting by double-clicking the folder icon to the right of the slider at various double-click speeds.**

   If the folder changes status (open or closed), you successfully double-clicked.

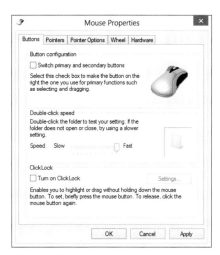

Figure 7-15

5. **Drag the Double-Click Speed slider to the halfway point between Slow and Fast, and click Apply.**

6. **Test the new setting.**

7. **Click the Pointer Options tab.**

   See Figure 7-16. Note that this tab is where you can set the Snap To and Visibility settings, in addition to the Motion setting (covered next).

8. **Drag the Motion slider all the way to Slow and then click Apply.**

9. **Test the new setting by moving the mouse pointer around onscreen.**

10. **Drag the Motion slider all the way to Fast and then click Apply.**

Figure 7-16

11. **Test the new setting.**

12. **Drag the Motion slider to the setting that works best for you.**

    It will probably be somewhere around the halfway point between Slow and Fast, but that's up to you.

13. **Click OK.**

Changing the mouse pointer appearance

In addition to changing how the mouse pointer operates, you can change how it looks. The pointer's appearance is controlled by a pointer scheme. Choosing a different pointer scheme may make the pointers easier for you to see, or you may just prefer a different look than the default.

In this exercise, you will change to a larger pointer scheme.

1. **If it's not already open, open the Control Panel and click the Hardware and Sound heading. Under the Devices and Printers heading, click Mouse.**

2. **Click Mouse.**

    The Mouse Properties dialog box opens.

3. **Click the Pointers tab.**

4. **Choose the Windows Black (Large) (System Scheme) option from the Scheme drop-down menu.**

    See Figure 7-17.

5. **Click Apply.**

    The new pointer scheme takes effect. The dialog box remains open.

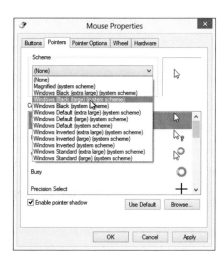

Figure 7-17

6. **Move the mouse onscreen to observe the new pointer.**

For more practice, try out some of the other pointer schemes. You can also try selecting a different individual pointer if you like. Select one of the pointers on the Customize list and then click Browse.

7. **Choose Windows Default (System Scheme) from the Scheme drop-down list and then click Apply.**

   The pointers return to the default.

8. **Click OK.**

   The dialog box closes.

Changing the Date and Time

If Windows is able to connect to the Internet, it can automatically keep the date and time accurate by consulting a date and time server online. You don't have to do anything special to make this happen. (You can, however, prevent Windows from doing this update if for some reason you *don't* want the current date and time to be accurate.)

You have to tell Windows which time zone you're in so that it can accurately display the time. If you travel frequently, you will get very accustomed to changing this setting.

In this exercise, you will change your computer's clock to a different time zone, and you'll make sure that your system's date and time are up to date.

1. **From the desktop, click the clock in the lower-right corner of the screen.**

   A monthly calendar and an analog clock appear. (See Figure 7-18.)

Figure 7-18

2. **Click the Change Date and Time Settings hyperlink.**

The Date and Time dialog box opens. See Figure 7-19.

3. **Click the Change Time Zone button.**

The Time Zone Settings dialog box opens. See Figure 7-20.

4. **Open the Time Zone drop-down list and choose a time zone that's different from the one you're currently in.**

5. **Click OK.**

The time zone changes, and the Time Zone Settings dialog box closes.

6. **In the Date and Time dialog box, click the Change Date and Time button.**

The Date and Time Settings dialog box opens.

7. **Click the calendar to change the date to tomorrow's date.**

8. **Click the up increment arrow in the Time box to advance the time by five hours.**

See Figure 7-21.

9. **Click OK.**

The Date and Time Settings dialog box closes.

10. **In the Date and Time dialog box, click the Internet Time tab.**

Figure 7-19

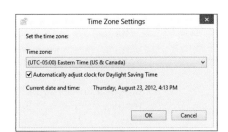

Figure 7-20

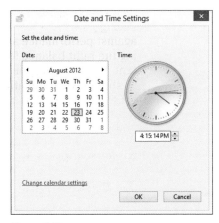

Figure 7-21

11. **Click the Change Settings button.**

The Internet Time Settings dialog box opens. (See Figure 7-22.)

12. **Click the Update Now button.**

The time returns to the correct time for the time zone you chose in Step 4.

13. **Click OK to close the Internet Time Settings dialog box.**

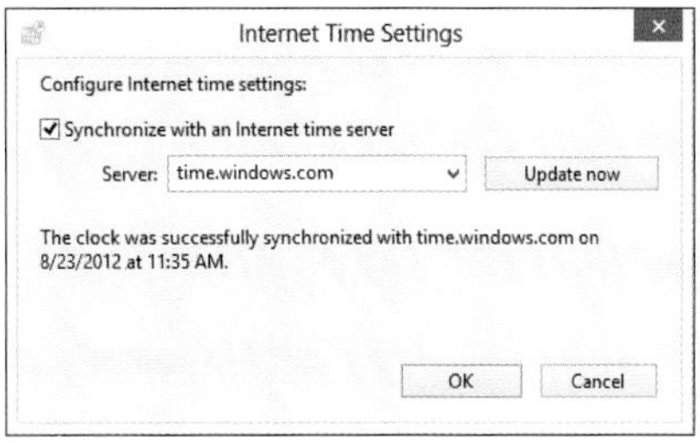

Figure 7-22

14. **In the Date and Time dialog box, click the Date and Time tab.**

15. **Repeat Steps 3–5 to reset the time zone to your actual zone.**

16. **Click OK to close the Date and Time dialog box.**

Configuring Power Options

Some people leave their computers on most of the time to avoid spending time rebooting every time they want to use it. However, leaving a computer on consumes a significant amount of electricity. Windows provides power-management settings that help you decrease the amount of electricity used — or battery power consumed, if you're using a portable device — without hampering performance or causing inconvenience.

You can choose a power plan in Windows to define how aggressive Windows should be about saving power. Power savings are a trade-off against performance and convenience, so finding the right balance for your situation is important. For example, you might not want your PC to shut down automatically if you leave it idle for five minutes at a time, but you also might not want it to remain at full power consumption for idle days at a time.

LINGO

A **power plan** is a collection of settings that define whether and how the computer will partially shut itself down to save power after a specified period of inactivity.

Windows comes with three default power plans:

- **Balanced:** A balance of power savings versus performance.

- **Power saver:** Aggressive power savings at the expense of some performance.

- **High performance:** Consistently high performance at the expense of most power savings.

Each of these power plans is fully customizable, so you can define what settings each plan uses. Then when your needs change on-the-fly, you can just apply one of the three power plans for instant application of your preferred settings for that situation.

Some of the settings in a power plan pertain to the low-power modes that the PC should be placed in after a certain period of inactivity. These modes include the following:

- ✔ **Sleep:** Keeps RAM and the CPU powered, but shuts down everything else so that the PC uses only a small amount of power. When the PC wakes up, it does so very quickly, within seconds.

- ✔ **Hibernate:** Copies the *system state* (that is, all the information required to reproduce the computer's current operational state) to the hard drive and then powers all components down. When the PC wakes up, it does so faster than it would from a cold startup.

- ✔ **Hybrid Sleep:** A combination of Sleep and Hibernate. It saves the system state to the hard drive, just the way hibernation does, but then instead of shutting down, it goes into Sleep mode. That way, you can wake the computer up quickly from Sleep provided the computer does not lose power or run out of battery life before you return. If it does, then it resumes from Hibernate.

Power plans contain many different settings. For example, you can control which components power down automatically, and after how much time. You can control whether the PC requires you to enter a password after waking up, and you can specify what function the PC's power button will activate. (For example, you can set it up so that pressing Power puts the computer into hibernation rather than shutting it down.)

In the following exercise, you will modify a power plan.

1. **Open the Control Panel, click the System and Security heading, and then click Power Options.**

   A list of power plans appears. (See Figure 7-23.) Windows provides three power plans, but some of them may be hidden; click the down arrow next to the Hide Additional Plans heading to see others. If you have a customized version of Windows that came with a new PC, the PC maker may have included other power plans, too.

2. **Click the High Performance radio button if it is not already selected.**

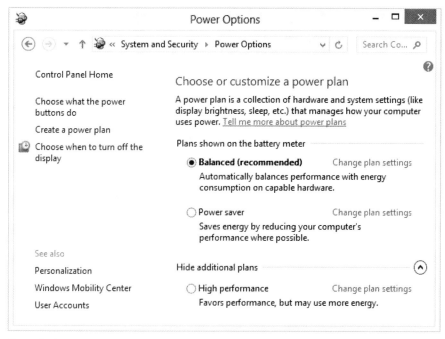

Figure 7-23

3. **Click the Change Plan Settings hyperlink next to High Performance.**

   The Edit Plan Settings screen appears, displaying a set of basic controls for that particular power plan. See Figure 7-24.

   Note: Depending on your computer type, you may not have all the same settings available to edit, as you see in Figure 7-24. For example, you may have only a single setting for each option, rather than separate settings for On Battery and Plugged In, and options for dimming the display and adjusting plan brightness might not be available.

4. **Choose 15 Minutes from the Turn Off the Display drop-down menu for both the On Battery and Plugged In settings.**

   You can choose a different setting if you prefer.

   Next, you will see how to fine-tune the settings even further for a particular power plan. Each power plan has many facets to it, and each is individually customizable.

5. **Click the Change Advanced Power Settings hyperlink.**

   The Power Options dialog box opens. Here you can fine-tune the settings for the power plan.

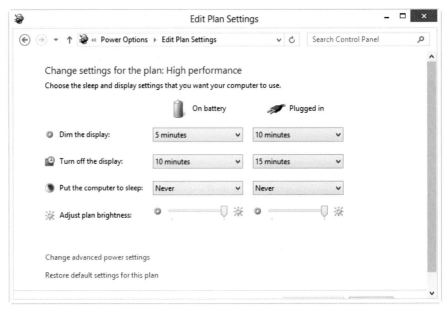

Figure 7-24

6. **If there is a plus sign next to Hard Disk, click it to expand that category.**

   A Turn Off Hard Disk After option appears below it. If you're working on a computer that has a battery, a plus sign appears next to it, because there are separate settings for battery and plugged in.

   Turning off the hard drive saves additional power. This is useful only for a mechanical hard drive; a solid state hard drive doesn't use much power, so it's only a negligible drain on your battery.

7. **If applicable, click the plus sign next to Turn Off Hard Disk After.**

   Separate options appear for On Battery and Plugged In.

8. **Change the Turn Off Hard Disk After setting (for Plugged In, if applicable) to 30 Minutes.**

   You can use some other setting if you prefer. See Figure 7-25.

Figure 7-25

9. **Click OK to close the Power Options dialog box.**

   You return to the Edit Plan Settings dialog box.

10. **Click Save Changes to save the changes to the power plan.**

    The Choose or Customize a Power Plan section of the Control Panel remains open. Next, you can undo what you just did by returning the power plan to its default settings.

Before going on to Step 12, you may want to experiment more on your own with the advanced settings for the power plan. For example, can you figure out how to change what happens when you press the PC's power button, or if you're on a notebook PC, what happens when you close the lid.

11. **Next to High Performance, click the Change Plan Settings hyperlink.**

    The Edit Plan Settings screen reappears. (Refer to Figure 7-24.)

12. **Click the Restore Default Settings for This Plan hyperlink.**

    A confirmation box appears.

13. **Click Yes.**

    Close all open windows.

EXTRA INFO

If you want to set an option to Never, you can either set the number of minutes to 0 or you can click in the text box where the number appears and type Never.

Summing Up

In this lesson, you learned how to manage user accounts as well as how to customize Windows in several important ways. Here are the highlights:

- A Microsoft account in Windows is linked to an email address, and has privileges like connecting to a SkyDrive account without a separate login. A local account is on the individual PC only.

- A standard account allows its user to make changes that don't affect other users or system security. An administrator account allows its users to make any and all changes.

- The guest account is disabled by default; enable it via the Control Panel, under User Accounts and Family Safety, Add or Remove User Accounts.

- To switch the logged-in user, click the username in the upper-right corner of the Start screen.

✔ To create a new user, go to Control Panel, under User Accounts and Family Safety, Add or Remove User Accounts, and then click Add a New User in PC Settings.

✔ To access mouse settings, open the Control Panel, set the View By to either Large Icons or Small Icons, and then click Mouse.

✔ To change the date and time, click the clock in the bottom-right corner of the screen.

✔ To work with power options, open the Control Panel, click System and Security, and click Power Options. Select the desired power plan, and then customize it if desired.

Know This Tech Talk

administrator account: An account that can make all kinds of changes to the PC's configuration.

Guest account: A limited-access account that anyone may use to log into the computer. The guest account typically doesn't have access to apps that individual users have installed, but it can use the desktop and Internet Explorer.

local account: A Windows login that isn't linked to a Windows Live account.

Microsoft account: A Windows login that's linked to an e-mail address.

pointer scheme: A collection of graphics that show how the pointer should look in a list of different situations, such as Normal Select, Working in Background, and Busy.

pointer: The arrow or other symbol that moves onscreen when you move or otherwise manipulate the mouse (or equivalent device).

power plan: A collection of settings that define whether and how the computer will partially shut itself down to save power after a specified period of inactivity.

standard account: An account that can use most programs on the PC, but can't make changes that affect other users, or the security of the PC.

Lesson 8

Keeping Your System Healthy and Secure

✔ Configure User Account Control (UAC) to prevent unwanted system changes.

✔ Configure Windows Defender to guard against malware.

✔ Optimize hard drive performance by defragmenting.

✔ Configure Windows Update to download and install important updates.

✔ Set up parental controls to prevent children from viewing inappropriate content.

*W*indows 8 is mostly self-maintaining. Updates download and install automatically, and several utilities monitor the system for various types of threats from the Internet and other networks. So even if you don't take any of the steps recommended in this chapter, you're probably still going to be okay.

However, you can make your system even safer, and work even better, by performing regular preventive maintenance tasks — or better yet, by scheduling those maintenance tasks to occur automatically on your behalf. You can also set up Family Safety in Windows 8 to limit the time and activities of specific users. In this chapter, you learn about Windows' security utilities and settings that keep you safe, and you find out how to use Windows' built-in family safety features to restrict the activities of some users.

Working with User Account Control

UAC is an extra layer of security that helps prevent system damage from viruses and rogue programs that might otherwise modify system settings without your permission. By restricting standard users' ability to make changes, it also prevents less experienced (or more reckless) people in your household from making changes to your PC's settings that you don't want.

LINGO

User Account Control (UAC) is a security feature that notifies you (and requests your permission) whenever a system or Windows settings change is about to occur.

Perhaps you've noticed that in the Control Panel, some of the items have a little shield next to them, as you see in Figure 8-1. The shield indicates that this is an item that triggers a UAC warning — or at least has the potential to do so. You may not always see a warning when you access one of those items, though. It depends on whether you're logged in as a standard- or administrator-level user, and it also depends on the User Account Control settings.

Shield icon means UAC will be triggered.

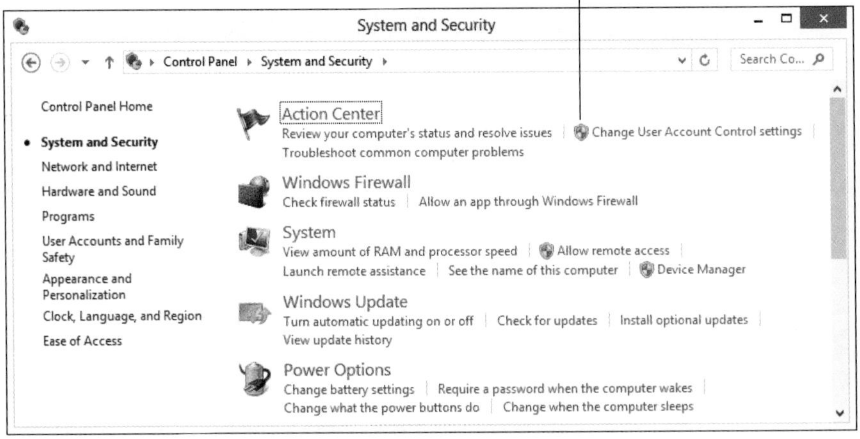

Figure 8-1

If you access an item that has UAC protection on it while you're logged in as a standard user, a prompt appears, asking you to provide an administrator password, as shown in Figure 8-2.

There are several variables for UAC — such as whether you'll be notified before an app makes changes to your PC, whether you'll be notified when Windows settings are changed that require administrator permissions, and whether those notifications will dim the rest of the screen — so you must approve or deny them before you can continue working.

Figure 8-2

The four settings you can choose from are summarized in Table 8-1.

Table 8-1	User Account Control Settings		
Setting	*Notified When Apps Make Changes to Your PC?*	*Notified When Windows Settings Changes Require Administrator Permissions?*	*Screen Dimmed When Notification Message Appears?*
Default — Always notify me when	Yes	Yes	Yes
Always notify me (and do not dim my desktop) when	Yes	Yes	No
Notify me only when apps try to make changes to my computer (don't dim my desktop)	Yes	No	No
Never notify me when	No	No	No

In the following exercise, you will set User Account Control to a moderate setting, and then you will test the setting by logging in as a standard user and attempting to make a Windows settings change.

1. **Log in with an administrator account.**

   Refer to Lesson 7 if you aren't sure what that means.

2. **Open the Control Panel, click the System and Security heading, and then click the Action Center heading.**

   The Action Center opens. The Action Center is a section of the Control Panel that contains links for identifying and solving system problems and resolving security issues.

EXTRA INFO

Yes, it can get annoying having to click a confirmation every time you want to make a change to a Windows setting, but keeping UAC at its highest setting keeps your system as safe as it can be from *malware* (harmful software). Most people find that it's worth the extra clicks.

3. **In the navigation bar at the left, click the Change User Account Control Settings hyperlink.**

4. **If a confirmation box appears, click Yes.**

   It may or may not appear depending on your current settings. The User Account Control Settings dialog box opens.

5. **Drag the slider to the highest position if it isn't already set there.**

   See Figure 8-3.

6. **Click OK to apply the new setting.**

   A User Account Control confirmation box appears.

7. **At the confirmation box, click Yes.**

   See Figure 8-4. The new setting is applied. The Action Settings window is still displayed.

8. **In the Action Center window, click the Change Windows SmartScreen Settings hyperlink.**

   The hyperlink has a shield next to it, indicating that UAC will be triggered when it's selected.

9. **At the confirmation box, click No.**

   The Windows SmartScreen settings window doesn't open.

10. **In the Action Center window, click Change User Account Control Settings, and then click Yes to confirm.**

    The User Account Control Settings dialog box reopens. (Refer to Figure 8-3.)

11. **Drag the slider to the next-to-highest position and click OK.**

12. **At the confirmation box (shown earlier in Figure 8-4), click Yes.**

    The Action Center window reappears.

Drag slider to change setting.

Figure 8-3

Figure 8-4

13. **Click Change Windows SmartScreen Settings.**

    This is the same option you clicked in Step 8, but notice the difference in what happens now. The Windows SmartScreen dialog box opens without any security prompt. See Figure 8-5.

14. **Click Cancel to close the dialog box without changing the setting.**

Figure 8-5

    Next, you will test the current UAC setting with a standard account. You should already have a standard account from your work in Lesson 7, but if you don't, you can either go back and create one now, or skip the rest of the steps in this exercise.

15. **Display the Start screen, and click the username in the upper-right corner.**

    A menu of usernames appears.

16. **Click the username for a standard user account, and sign in as that user.**

    You may be prompted to type a password to sign in.

17. **Open the Control Panel, click the System and Security heading, and under the Action Center heading, click Change User Account Control settings.**

    A dialog box appears, prompting you to enter the password for the administrator account you were previously using.

18. **Enter the password and click Yes.**

    The User Account Control Settings dialog box opens.

19. **Return the UAC slider to its original setting and click OK.**

    When prompted again for the password, enter it and click Yes again.

20. **Sign out, and sign back in with the user account you normally use.**

Preventing Attacks on Your Computer

Besides UAC, which you learned about in the previous section, Windows also provides several other tools and utilities that help keep you and your data safe and private. These include Windows Defender and Windows Firewall. In the following sections, you will learn about these features.

Checking for viruses and other malware

Earlier Windows versions have a malware checker called Windows Defender, but it included no virus protection . However, users could download a free antivirus program called Windows Security Essentials from Microsoft.

Windows 8 is different — its version of Windows Defender includes virus protection, too. That means that most people don't need a third-party antivirus application anymore. (Some people may still use one because of its extra options and features, and that's fine.)

Windows Defender works in these two ways:

- **Inspecting active files:** As the computer operates, its real-time protection component watches for threats in the files that are opened and executed as well as in the files that are transferred to and from the computer.

- **Scanning all files on the computer:** A scan component that scans all files — even those that aren't in use — for potential threats. You can perform a scan any time you suspect a problem, or just for general peace of mind.

Windows Update downloads and installs any updates for Windows Defender automatically. However, you can also do a manual update any time you like.

In this exercise, you will explore Windows Defender, check for updates, and perform a quick scan.

1. **At the Start screen, start typing** Defender. **When Windows Defender appears in the search results at the left, click it.**

   Windows Defender opens.

2. **Click the Update tab (shown in Figure 8-6) and then click that tab's Update button.**

   Windows Defender connects to the Internet and downloads any available updates.

3. **Click the Settings tab and then examine the settings there.**

   For example, on the Settings tab, click Advanced, and note that one of the settings is labeled Scan Removable Drives. (See Figure 8-7.) You can enable that feature if you suspect malware on your flash drive or some other external drive. Normally, you would leave this feature deselected.

4. **Click the Home tab (shown in Figure 8-8), make sure Quick is selected in the Scan Options section, and then click the Scan Now button.**

Figure 8-6

Figure 8-7

Windows Defender does a quick scan of your system. With a quick scan, it looks at only files that are most likely to contain malware or viruses.

Figure 8-8

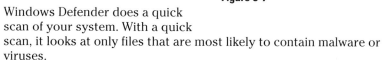

EXTRA INFO

It's unlikely that Windows Defender will find any problems, but if it does, follow the prompts that appear in order to respond to them. You can choose to either quarantine or delete the infected files. The Quarantine option keeps the files but segregates them from other files so they won't cause harm.

5. **When the quick scan has completed, click the Custom button and then click Scan Now.**

A Windows Defender dialog box opens, in which you can select the drives and folders you want to scan.

6. **Click the plus sign next to the C drive to expand its folders, and then select the Users folder's check box, as shown in Figure 8-9.**

The Users folder contains many of the data files that you and other users have created or downloaded, so it's a good location to check.

7. **Click OK.**

The Users folder is scanned.

8. **When the scan has completed, close the Windows Defender window.**

Figure 8-9

Using Windows Firewall

Have you ever wondered how it is that your PC's Internet connection can deliver various types of content without getting confused? It always sends your e-mail to your e-mail program, web pages to your browser, and so on. This works because each application — and in some cases each function within an application — uses a different port. For example, e-mail sent using an e-mail client like Microsoft Outlook or Windows Live Mail typically goes out on port 25 and comes in on port 110.

When a port is unused, any application can use it, and therein lies the security problem. Malicious programs can use unsecured ports to send commands to your system that compromise it. A firewall can prevent this from happening. Firewall software blocks port access requested by unknown programs, allowing only the programs you specify to get through. There are also hardware-based firewalls, especially in larger corporate networks, and some routers have firewall protection built in.

In this exercise, you will check the status of Windows Firewall, and turn it off and then back on again. Then you'll allow an individual program through the firewall. Why would you do that? Well, you might turn the firewall off temporarily if you were trying to do an online activity that the firewall was blocking, such as file sharing with a computer that uses a different operating system. Afterward, you would then make a point of turning the firewall back on.

1. **Open the Control Panel, click the System and Security heading, and under the Windows Firewall heading, click Check Firewall Status.**

   The Windows Firewall window appears, displaying the status of the firewall for private networks as well as for guest or public networks. (See Figure 8-10.) Note that you can have separate settings for the different network types. If the full details don't display, as in Figure 8-10, you can click the down-pointing arrow button on the right to expand the details for a network type.

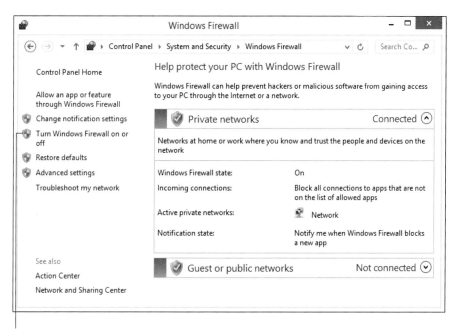

Click here to turn the firewall off.

Figure 8-10

2. **In the navigation bar on the left, click the Turn Windows Firewall On or Off hyperlink.**

   The Customize Settings window appears. (See Figure 8-11.)

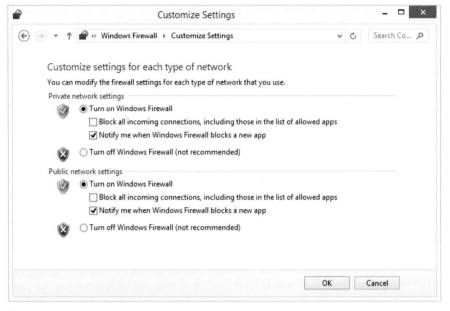

Figure 8-11

3. Under the Private Network Settings heading, click the Turn off Windows Firewall (Not Recommended) radio button.

It's okay to do this, even though it's marked as not recommended.

4. Click OK.

A warning appears in the notification area, alerting you that Windows Firewall is turned off and telling you how to turn it back on. (See Figure 8-12.)

Figure 8-12

5. Click the warning balloon in the notification area.

The firewall is enabled again.

Note: The balloon goes away in the notification area after a few seconds; if you missed clicking it in Step 4, you can instead click the Use Recommended Settings button in the Windows Firewall window to re-enable the firewall.

6. Back in the Windows Firewall window, click the Allow an App or Feature through Windows Firewall hyperlink in the navigation bar on the left.

A list of allowed apps and features appears. (See Figure 8-13.) You see check boxes for private as well as public networks.

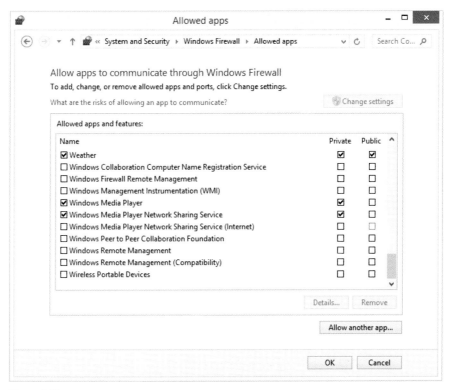

Figure 8-13

7. **Select the check box to the left of the Wireless Portable Devices item on the list.**

   Notice that doing so places a check mark in the Private column, but not in the Public column.

8. **Click OK to return to the Windows Firewall window.**

9. **(Optional) To restore the default settings for Windows Firewall, do the following:**

   a. Click the Restore Defaults hyperlink.

   b. Click the Restore Defaults button.

   c. Click Yes to confirm.

Tidying Up Your Hard Drives

Hard drives are the basis of most PCs' file-storage systems, and the more efficiently they run, the better the overall system performance.

Two things that slow down a hard drive's performance — maxed-out storage space and fragmented files. In the following sections, I show you how to fix these two problems.

Deleting unneeded files with Disk Cleanup

Over time, your hard disk may end up storing many files that you don't need, such as downloaded program files, temporary Internet files, Recycle Bin contents, and setup log files. If you have plenty of free space on your hard drive, that's not a problem. However, when you start running low on disk space (say, 10–15 percent free space left), you may want to consider getting rid of some or all of those unnecessary files. Doing so can not only give you more space to store files, but can improve system performance.

Windows' Disk Cleanup utility provides an easy way to identify and delete unneeded files. It points out files in a variety of categories, and you can choose the categories to include in the deletion.

In this exercise, you will delete some files using Disk Cleanup on your primary hard drive.

1. **In File Explorer, click Computer.**

   To open File Explorer, click the File Explorer icon on the taskbar. A list of the drives on your system appears.

2. **Right-click the C drive and choose Properties from the menu that appears.**

   The Properties dialog box opens for the C drive. (See Figure 8-14.)

EXTRA INFO

Perhaps you're wondering why lack of free hard disk space would affect system performance. It's because Windows relies on a technology called *virtual memory* as it operates. Virtual memory helps your computer not run out of memory when you're doing many different tasks at once. On an as-needed basis, Windows swaps data out of physical RAM and places it on the hard disk in a special holding area called a *swap file*. The swap file size fluctuates based on the amount of RAM you have and the amount of hard disk space that's free. If your system starts running low on hard disk space, Windows shrinks the size of the swap file, resulting in less swap file usage, which in turn can result in poorer Windows performance.

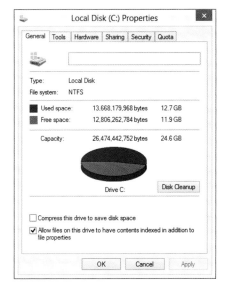

Figure 8-14

Figure 8-15

3. **Click the Disk Cleanup button.**

   After a quick analysis, the Disk Cleanup dialog box opens, presenting a list of categories of files that could potentially be deleted. (See Figure 8-15.)

   The files to be deleted don't currently include unneeded system files, such as files from previous Windows installations. Next, you'll re-create the list to include those files.

4. **Click the Clean Up System Files button.**

   If the User Account Control window opens, click Yes to continue. Disk Cleanup recreates the list of files to be deleted, this time including unneeded system files.

5. **Select the check boxes for the categories you want to delete.**

   In most cases, there is little reason to keep the files that have been recommended for deletion.

6. **Click OK.**

   A confirmation appears.

7. **Click Delete Files.**

8. **Wait for Disk Cleanup to delete the chosen files.**

9. **Close the C drive's Properties box.**

Optimizing a disk drive

When a file is stored on a disk, if there is room, the file is stored in multiple contiguous clusters on the drive surface. This makes the file easily accessible to the disk's read/write head, since all portions of the file are stored in one place. This *optimizes* (speeds up) disk access time. Over time, however, as the file is modified, the additional pieces are written to noncontiguous areas because there is no room adjacent to the original pieces, and the file becomes fragmented. The disk read/write heads must move around more to pick up the fragmented pieces, so the disk access time suffers. Defragmenting a disk can improve its performance by rewriting as many files as possible to contiguous clusters. Windows 8 calls the process of defragmentation *optimizing*.

Windows 8 automatically optimizes drives once per week, by default. You can set it to run daily or monthly if you prefer. The performance advantage of running it weekly instead of monthly is very small.

In the following exercise, you will manually run a disk optimization, and you will set the utility to run automatically on a monthly basis.

1. **In File Explorer, click Computer.**

   A list of the drives on your system appears.

2. **Right-click the C drive and choose Properties from the menu that appears.**

   The Properties dialog box opens for the C drive.

3. **Click the Tools tab, and then click the Optimize button.**

   The Optimize Drives window opens.

4. **Click the C drive (or other drive you want to optimize) and then click Analyze.**

   The utility analyzes the fragmentation of the drive and reports its status in the Current status column. (See Figure 8-16.)

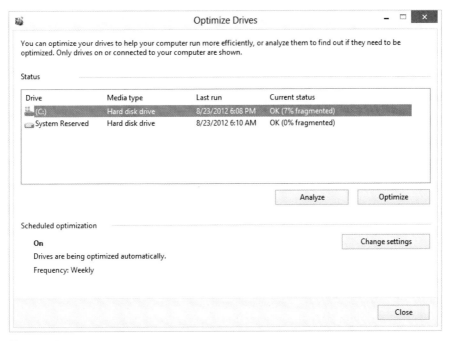

Figure 8-16

5. Click Optimize.

The defragmentation process begins.

The process may take up to several hours; you can minimize the window and do something else while you wait. You can also go on to the next step while it's still running.

6. Click the Change Settings button.

An Optimize Drives dialog box opens. See Figure 8-17. (This is a different dialog box from the previous one, even though they have the same name.)

7. Choose Monthly from the Frequency drop-down menu if it isn't already selected.

8. Click OK (if you changed the setting in Step 7), or click Cancel (if you didn't).

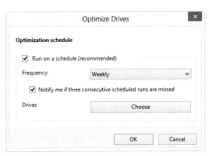

Figure 8-17

9. **In the Optimize Drives dialog box, click Close.**

   You don't have to wait for the optimization to complete; it will finish even if the dialog box is closed.

11. **Click Cancel to close the C drive's Properties box.**

Setting the Maintenance Window

In the previous exercise, you set up the Optimize Drives utility to run monthly. But when exactly will that be? The maintenance window setting determines that time. The date is determined by the last time the action was performed. For example, if you have Optimize Drives set to run monthly, and the last time it ran was on the 15th of the month, it will run on the 15th of next month.

You can change the maintenance window from the Action Settings section of the Control Panel. In the following exercise, you will change the time of the maintenance window to 1 a.m.

1. **Open the Control Panel, click the System and Security heading, and then click Action Center.**

2. **Click the down arrow to expand the Maintenance category.**

   Additional maintenance hyperlinks appear.

3. **Under Automatic Maintenance (see Figure 8-18), click the Change Maintenance Settings hyperlink.**

   The Automatic Maintenance screen appears.

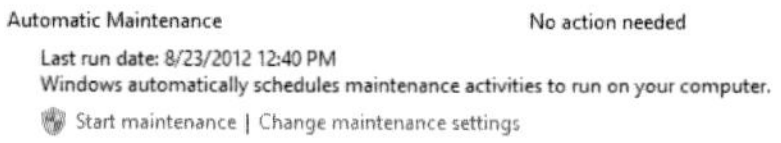

Automatic Maintenance   No action needed
Last run date: 8/23/2012 12:40 PM
Windows automatically schedules maintenance activities to run on your computer.
Start maintenance | Change maintenance settings

Figure 8-18

4. **Choose 1:00 AM from the Run Maintenance Tasks Daily At drop-down menu if it isn't already selected.**

   See Figure 8-19.

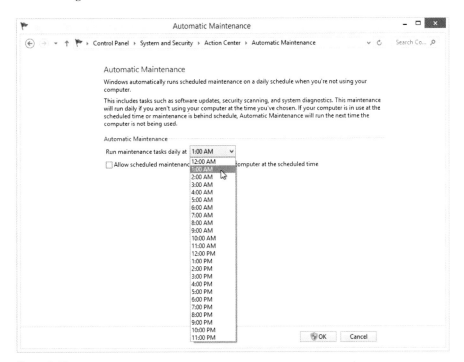

Figure 8-19

5. **Click OK.**

   When you return to the Action Center, the Maintenance category is collapsed again, so you have to re-expand it to do the next steps.

6. **Click the down arrow to expand the Maintenance category.**

7. **Click the Start Maintenance hyperlink. (Refer to Figure 8-16.)**

   The maintenance tasks start running.

8. **Close the Action Center.**

   The maintenance tasks continue running in the background.

Using Windows Update

LINGO

Windows Update is a free service from Microsoft that downloads the latest patches, fixes, and updates from Microsoft's servers for Windows 8 and other Microsoft products.

By default, Windows Update runs automatically behind the scenes, downloading updates as they become available. You don't have to do anything to get the updates, as long as you haven't modified the default settings that tell Windows to install available updates as they come in. You can also trigger an update manually.

Sometimes — rarely, but it does happen — an update will cause a problem with your system. When that happens, you do have some recourse. You can review updates that are already installed, and, in some cases, you can remove previously installed updates.

You can access Windows Update via the Control Panel. From the Windows Update screen, you can see when the system last checked for updates, when the last update was installed, and more. (See Figure 8-20.) Along the left side are links to common activities for working with Windows Update.

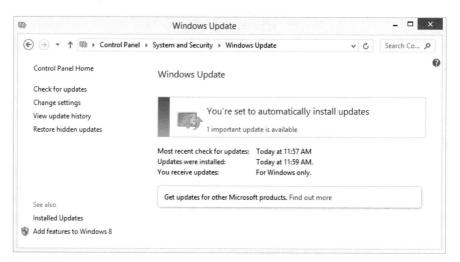

Figure 8-20

Some updates are more important than others to the system's functionality. For example, an update that patches a security hole is more important than one that slightly improves the functioning of a specialized utility that few people use. Windows Update categorizes the updates in one of three levels of priority:

✔ **Important:** Affects the system's stability and security. These updates are always included.

✔ **Recommended:** Fixes a problem with (or improves the performance of) a nonessential Windows 8 component or add-on. These updates are included automatically only if the check box is selected under Recommended Updates.

✔ **Optional:** Updates or enhances parts of Windows 8 that not everyone uses, such as support add-ons or foreign language packs. These updates aren't downloaded automatically; you must manually run Windows Update to acquire them.

As you will see in the next section, Windows handles each of these types of updates differently, and you can specify how each is handled.

Adjusting Windows Update settings

By default, Windows Update automatically checks for updates, downloads them, and installs them, all without any user intervention required. In most cases, that's great; but some people prefer to see what the updates are before installing them. In addition, in some business environments, the IT department would prefer that you not install Windows updates automatically, but instead wait until the department sends the updates out to all PCs on the network at the same time.

For important updates, you can choose one of the following options:

✔ **Install Updates Automatically (Recommended).** Updates are downloaded and installed at the specified time (unless the particular update requires user input or accepting a license agreement). If an update requires a restart, the restart occurs automatically. This is the default setting in Windows 8.

✔ **Download Updates but Let Me Choose Whether to Install Them.** Updates are downloaded, but then they wait for the user to trigger their installation. This is useful for people who might not always want every update that's offered.

✔ **Check for Updates but Let Me Choose Whether to Download and Install Them.** An update notice appears, but the download doesn't occur until the user triggers it. This is useful for people on dialup connections so that the download doesn't interfere with Internet performance at a critical time.

✔ **Never Check For Updates (Not Recommended).** Windows Update doesn't run automatically. This is useful in some managed corporate environments where updates are controlled by an administrator or provided by a company server rather than downloaded directly from Microsoft.

In the following exercise, you'll check your current Windows Update setting and change it so that updates aren't automatically installed. (Doing so will also prep your system to do upcoming exercises that have to do with manually choosing and installing updates.)

1. **Open the Control Panel, click the System and Security heading, and then click Windows Update.**

   The Windows Update screen appears. Your status may be somewhat different from the one shown.

2. **Click the Change Settings hyperlink in the navigation bar on the right.**

   The Change Settings window appears.

3. **In the Important Updates section, choose Download Updates but Let Me Choose whether To Install Them from the drop-down menu.**

   See Figure 8-21.

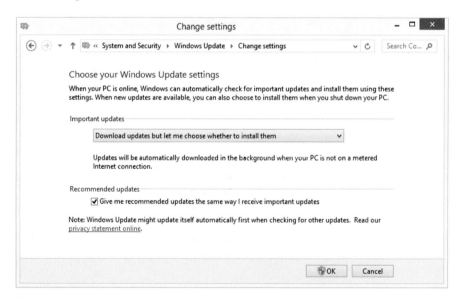

Figure 8-21

4. **In the Recommended Updates sections (if present), make sure the check boxes are selected.**

   If you select the check box in the Recommended Updates section, it ensures that your system receives all updates, not just those that are tagged as important.

If you select the check box in the Microsoft Update section, it ensures that you receive updates for other Microsoft products, such as Microsoft Office. You may not have this option available, depending on what other applications are installed.

5. **Click OK.**

Keep the Windows Update screen open for the next exercise.

Uninstalling an update

One possible source of system troubles in Windows is a bad update. An update might contain a bug in it, or there might be some unanticipated conflict between the update software and your specific combination of hardware that causes system performance to suffer. For whatever reason, you may at some point need to uninstall an update.

In the following exercise, you will view a list of installed updates and remove one of them. This exercise also preps your system for the next exercise, in which you'll install an update. (Removing an update now ensures that there will be one to install later.)

1. **If Windows Update isn't already displayed from the previous exercise, open the Control Panel, click the System and Security heading, and then click Windows Update.**

2. **In the bottom-left corner of the Windows Update window, click Installed Updates.**

   A list of installed updates appears.

3. **Under the Microsoft Windows heading, click the first update on the list.**

   You might need to scroll down to find the Microsoft Windows heading. Headings appear in blue. When you click an item, an Uninstall button appears above the list if the item is removable. (See Figure 8-22, in which there is only one update shown.)

EXTRA INFO

You might think that you'd want to choose View Update History in Step 2, but no. Choosing View Update History brings up a list of the installed updates but doesn't provide a way to uninstall them. You can remove updates only from the Installed Updates screen.

EXTRA INFO

Not all updates can be removed. Some of them make permanent changes to Windows system files that can't be undone. Updates that can't be undone lack an Uninstall button.

Go to the Microsoft Windows heading.

Figure 8-22

4. **Click Uninstall.**

A confirmation box appears.

5. **Click Yes.**

Don't worry about uninstalling an update here that might be important, because you're going to reinstall it in the next exercise.

Windows uninstalls the chosen update.

6. **If prompted to restart your computer, click Restart Now to do so.**

Applying an update

If your settings (from the previous exercise) don't specify that Windows will automatically check for updates, you must click the Check for Updates hyperlink in Windows Update screen to initiate a check. (The Check for Updates hyperlink appears in the navigation bar on the left side of the window.)

From the Windows Update screen, you can click Install Updates to download the important updates (if they aren't already downloaded) and install them. Even if Windows Update reports that no important updates are available, there may be some other useful updates you might want. For example, you might want a device driver update for a piece of hardware on your system.

1. **Open Windows Update in the Control Panel.**

Because you removed an update in the previous exercise, there will now be one available for you to install. And because you set Windows Update to download but not install new updates automatically earlier in the lesson, the update is waiting to be installed. See Figure 8-23.

Figure 8-23

2. **Click the Check for Updates hyperlink in the navigation pane at the left.**

Windows Update rechecks for any missing updates.

3. **Wait for Windows Update to complete its check, and then click the Install Updates button.**

If the button doesn't appear, click the hyperlink for the updates available, and then click Install.

The update(s) are installed. Wait for the installation to complete.

4. **If prompted to restart your PC, click Restart Now.**

Managing How Your Kids Use the PC

The Internet is designed primarily for adults, and a significant amount of what's out there is unsuitable for children: sexual content, violent images, profanity, and so on. And it's not just the Internet, either — video games can be violent and crude, too.

EXTRA INFO

If you want to see what the update is before you install it, click the hyperlink that reports how many updates are available. For example, in Figure 8-23, is the link looks like this: *1 important update is available.* Doing so takes you to a list of the individual updates available, and you can pick and choose which ones to install or not install.

The best way to keep children away from age-inappropriate content is to personally monitor their Internet usage 100 percent of the time. That's right; keep an eye on them every second they're online. The second-best solution is to employ the parental controls, like the ones built into Windows and Internet Explorer, to make inappropriate content as difficult for kids to get to as possible.

Windows' Family Safety controls enable you to do the following:

- **Restrict some online activities.** You set Windows to regulate activities such as website usage, search engine usage, and file downloads. Depending on how you choose to use the feature, it can prevent the user from accessing sites you have chosen to block, or it can prevent the user from accessing any sites that you haven't specifically allowed.

- **Restrict the user's access during certain times.** Allow the user to use the computer only during certain days and times of the week. This enables you to block computer use at times when you can't be there to supervise.

- **Choose which games the user can play.** Allow or block specific games, or games that have a certain rating (such as Adults Only).

- **Restrict the user's access to certain programs.** Allow or block specific programs installed on the computer.

Displaying the User Settings screen

The first step in setting restrictions is to display the User Settings screen for the account you want to restrict. After doing that, you can configure each of the types of family safety controls individually. You learn how to set up user accounts in Lesson 7.

In this exercise, you will access the User Settings screen for one of the users on your PC. Then in upcoming exercises, you will learn about each of the individual controls.

1. **Open the Control Panel and, under the User Accounts and Family Safety heading, click the Set Up Family Safety for Any User hyperlink.**

   The Family Safety screen appears, listing all the current users on the PC. (See Figure 8-24.) For this exercise, you can choose your own account to restrict, or one of the other users on your PC, such as one of the standard accounts you set up in Lesson 7.

Figure 8-24

2. **Click the user that you want to restrict.**

   The User Settings screen appears for that user.

3. **Under the Family Safety heading, click the On, Enforce Current Settings radio button.**

   The hyperlinks to the settings become available. (See Figure 8-25.)

Figure 8-25

From here, see the exercise that follows, which pertains to the type of control you want to set. Or if you want to know about all of them, work through all of the following sections.

Setting web filtering

The Windows web filter enables you to control web access by allowing certain sites, blocking other sites, and applying rules that help it decide what to do when a certain site is neither specifically blocked nor allowed. It can also be set to block all file downloads (since children can be rather gullible when it comes to "Click here for a special prize!" scams).

Many websites have content ratings associated with them, and when you visit the page, the page provides that rating to your web browser. (It's invisible to the user, so you probably never noticed it before.) Not all sites have ratings, of course, but many child-friendly sites do, to help parents control their children's usage.

Besides the Allow and Block lists, the Windows web filter lets you choose one of five options for other web content:

- ✔ **Allow List Only:** The user can view only websites that have been specifically allowed (on the Allow List, which you can set up by clicking the Click here to change the Allow List hyperlink).

- ✔ **Designed for children:** The user can view websites on the Allow list, and also any sites that are rated as child-friendly. All other sites are blocked.

- ✔ **General Interest:** The user can view websites on the Allow list, and also those with either child-friendly or general-interest ratings. All other sites are blocked.

- ✔ **Online Communication:** The user can view websites on the Allow list, and those in the following rating categories: designed for children, general interest, social networking, web chat, and web mail. All other sites are blocked.

- ✔ **Warn on Adult:** The user can view all websites, but a warning appears if the site contains suspected adult content.

Using any of the above settings also turns on Safe Search options for the major search engines, like Bing, Yahoo!, and Google. Safe Search prevents adult-oriented sites from appearing in search results.

You can also choose to allow only websites that are on the Allow list, regardless of their rating or content.

In this exercise, you will configure the Windows Web Filter settings.

1. **Open the User Settings screen for the user you want to restrict, and click On, enforce current settings.**

   See the previous exercise for the steps for navigating to the User Settings screen for a user.

2. **Click the Web Filtering hyperlink.**

   The Web Filtering screen opens for that user.

3. **Click the *Username* Can Only Use the Websites I Allow radio button.**

   See Figure 8-26.

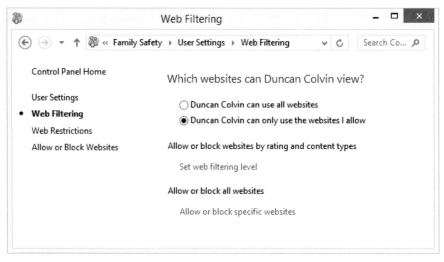

Figure 8-26

4. **Click the Set Web Filtering Level hyperlink.**

   A list of restriction categories appears. A description of each setting appears below it. See Figure 8-27.

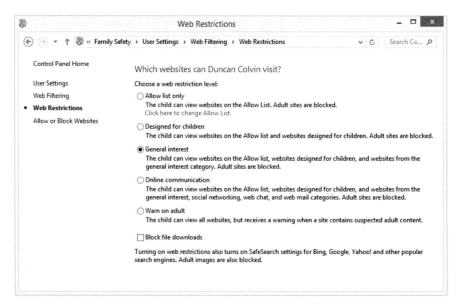

Figure 8-27

5. **Click the General Interest radio button in the Choose a Web Restriction Level section.**

6. **Select the Block File Downloads check box.**

7. **Click the Allow or Block Websites hyperlink in the navigation bar at the left.**

   The Allow or Block Websites screen appears.

8. **In the Enter a Website to Allow or Block text box, type** www.wiley.com **and then click Allow.**

   The site appears on the Allowed Websites list, as shown in Figure 8-28.

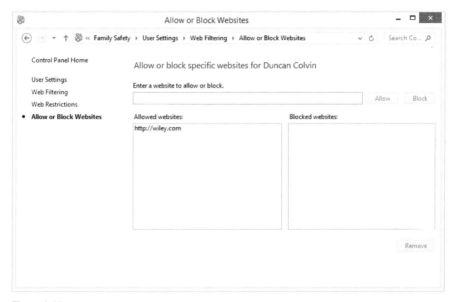

Figure 8-28

9. **Click the User Settings hyperlink.**

   The User Settings screen for the chosen user reappears. (Refer to Figure 8-25.)

10. **Keep the User Settings screen open for the next exercise.**

Setting time limits

Parents who aren't home all the time, or who aren't always awake when their kids are, will appreciate Windows 8's ability to specify time-based restrictions on user accounts. You can block a user account from using the computer at all during certain days of the week and certain times of day. You can also set an overall time allowance.

In the following exercise, you will block a user account from using the computer after 11 p.m. and set a time allowance of three hours per day.

1. **If it's not already open, open the User Settings screen for the user you want to restrict.**

2. **Click the Time Limits hyperlink, and then click the Set Time Allowance hyperlink.**

   The Time Allowance screen appears.

3. **Click the *User* Can Only Use the PC for the Amount of Time I allow radio button.**

   Controls appear for controlling the amount of time.

4. **Open the Hours drop-down list for Weekdays: Mon – Fri and choose 3 hours.**

   The number of minutes was already set to 30 by default, so now the total time for Weekdays is 3 hours and 30 minutes. See Figure 8-29.

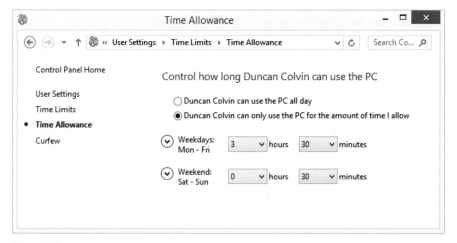

Figure 8-29

5. **Open the Hours drop-down list for Weekend: Sat – Sun and choose 8 hours. Open the Minutes drop-down list and choose 0.**

6. **Click the Curfew hyperlink in the navigation pane at the left.**

   A set of two radio buttons appears.

7. **Click *Username* Can Only Use the PC During the Time Ranges I Allow.**

   A grid appears. The white areas are the allowed time blocks. There aren't yet any restricted areas; if there were, they would appear in blue.

8. **Drag on the grid to select the rightmost column (11 to 12) and the six leftmost columns (12 to 6).**

See Figure 8-30.

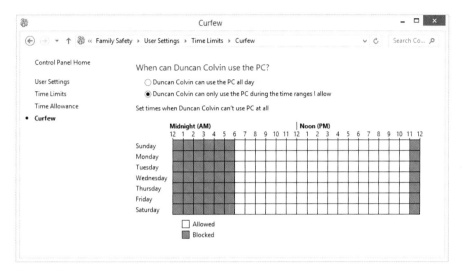

Figure 8-30

9. **Click the User Settings hyperlink in the navigation pane at the left.**

The User Settings screen for the chosen user reappears. (Refer to Figure 8-25.)

10. **Leave the User Settings screen open for the next exercise.**

Restricting games by rating

Games are rated by an independent organization called the Entertainment Software Rating Board (ESRB). Almost all games have a rating, which is built into the software and provided to Windows. The ratings are as follows:

LINGO

The **Entertainment Software Rating Board (ESRB)** is an organization that rates games to determine what age of children they're appropriate for.

- ✔ **Early Childhood (EC):** Suitable for ages three and older.

- ✔ **Everyone (E):** Suitable for persons ages six and older. There may be minimal violence, some comic mischief, and/or mild language.

- ✔ **Everyone 10+ (E10+):** Suitable for persons ages 10 and older. There may be cartoon, fantasy, or mild violence, mild language, and/or minimal suggestive themes.

✔ **Teen (T):** Suitable for persons ages 13 and older. May contain violent content and strong language.

✔ **Mature (M):** Suitable for persons ages 17 and older. May contain mature sexual themes, intense violence, and/or strong language.

✔ **Adults Only (AO):** Suitable only for adults, ages 18 and older. May include graphic depictions of sex or violence.

You can block games that have a certain rating or higher. You can also choose whether to block games that have no rating.

In this exercise, you will restrict gaming to Teen level and younger, or whatever level is appropriate for the user.

1. **If it's not already open, open the User Settings screen for the user you want to restrict.**

2. **Click the Windows Store and Game Restrictions hyperlink.**

   The Game and Windows Store Restrictions screen appears.

3. **Click the *Username* Can Only Use Games and Windows Store Apps I Allow radio button.**

   See Figure 8-31. The hyperlinks below the options buttons become available.

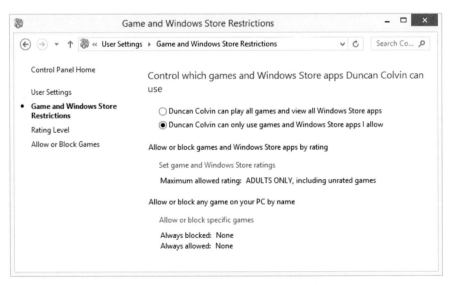

Figure 8-31

4. **Click the Set Game and Windows Store Ratings hyperlink.**

   The Rating Level screen appears.

5. Click the Teen radio button, or whatever button represents the appropriate level for this user.

See Figure 8-32. Notice that all the other ratings above it on the list are also selected, indicating that all of those are allowed.

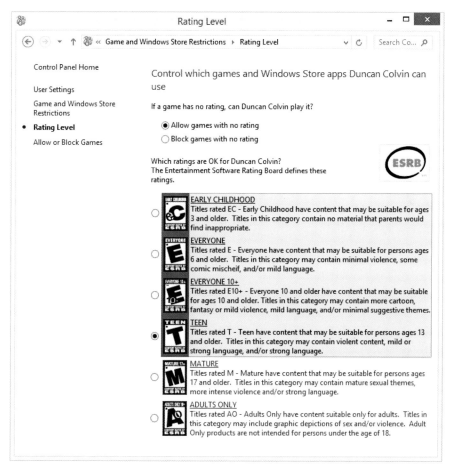

Figure 8-32

6. Click the User Settings hyperlink in the navigation pane at the left.

The User Settings screen for the chosen user reappears. (Refer to Figure 8-26.)

7. Keep the User Settings screen open for the next exercise.

Restricting applications

Another way to restrict programming is to limit the user to only applications that you specify. From a list of all the applications available, you can select check boxes for the ones you want to allow, and only those will be accessible.

In this exercise, you will restrict the user to only certain applications that you specify.

1. **If it's not already open, open the User Settings screen for the user you want to restrict.**

2. **Click App Restrictions hyperlink.**

   A set of two radio buttons appears. The default setting is that the user can use all apps.

3. **Click the *Username* Can Only Use the Apps I Allow radio button.**

   Windows builds a list of all the installed programs and displays the list in a table.

4. **Click the Check All button.**

   Check marks appear in all check boxes. (See Figure 8-33.) This is faster than selecting them one by one.

5. **Deselect the check box for wordpad.exe.**

   It's under the C:\Program Files\Windows NT\Accessories heading. If you prefer, you can instead deselect some other app that you'd like to restrict this user from accessing.

6. **Close all open windows.**

   If you have the user's login info, you can now take a look at how your settings are applied.

7. **Log in as the user whose account you just restricted.**

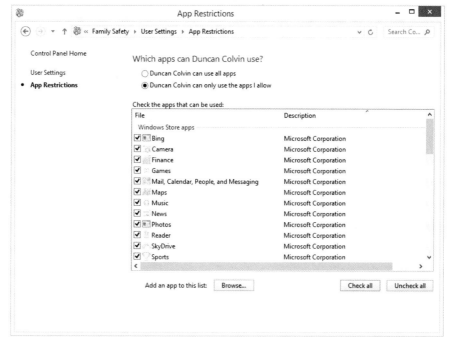

Figure 8-33

8. **From the Start screen, type** wordpad, **and then click WordPad on the Apps list.**

    A message appears that Family Safety has blocked this application. (See Figure 8-34.)

Figure 8-34

9. **Click Close.**

10. **Sign out of that user account, and sign back in with your original user account.**

11. **Reopen the Family Safety from the Control Panel.**

    From the Control Panel, click the Set Up Family Safety for Any User hyperlink under the User Accounts and Family Safety heading.

12. **Click the user that you set the parental controls for.**

13. **Under the Family Safety heading, click the Off radio button.**

    Parental controls are now off for this user.

14. **Click OK.**

15. **Close all open windows.**

Summing Up

In this lesson, you learned some ways to keep your computer operating safely and at maximum performance, as well as how to create a safer computing environment for young computer users. Here are the highlights:

- ✔ User Account Control (UAC) is what pops up those warning messages when you make system changes. You can make it more or less aggressive by adjusting its settings.

- ✔ Windows Defender guards against both viruses and other malware in Windows 8; virus protection within Defender is new to this version of Windows.

- ✔ Leave Windows Firewall turned on unless you have a third-party firewall that takes its place. You can allow individual programs through the firewall as needed.

- ✔ Disk Cleanup identifies and deletes files that you may not need on your hard disk, saving disk space.

- ✔ Optimizing a disk, also called *defragmenting*, relocates the parts of a file so that they're contiguous, making it quicker to read them from the disk.

- ✔ Windows Update automatically downloads and installs updates to Windows and to some Microsoft programs. You can configure it to hold off on either downloading or installing without your explicit permission each time.

- ✔ Windows Parental Controls offers several ways to keep your children away from inappropriate content. You can restrict web content, games, applications, and usage hours.

Know This Tech Talk

adware: Software that displays unwanted ads.

defragment: To reorganize the file storage so that as many files as possible are stored contiguously.

Entertainment Software Rating Board (ESRB): An organization that rates games to determine what age of children they are appropriate for.

firewall: Hardware or software that prevents unauthorized access to a port.

fragmented file: A file that's stored in multiple noncontiguous areas on a hard disk.

maintenance window: The time specified when Windows 8 should perform routine maintenance tasks on the system, provided the PC is powered up but not actively in use.

malware: A class of computer threats that includes both spyware and adware. Some people use the term *malware* even more generically, to include all software that harms a computer or compromises its security or privacy.

port: A numbered software channel that directs network input and output.

spyware: Software that spies on your usage and reports it to someone.

User Account Control (UAC): A security feature that notifies you and requests your permission whenever a system or Windows setting change is about to occur.

virus: Code that attaches itself to an executable file, such as a program file, and does something bad when that file executes, like slowing down performance or deleting certain files.

Windows Update: A free service from Microsoft that downloads the latest patches, fixes, and updates from Microsoft's servers for Windows 8 and other Microsoft products.

Troubleshooting Common Problems

✔ Shut down an unresponsive program.

✔ Find a lost file.

✔ Configure compatibility settings for older applications.

✔ Control which programs load at startup.

✔ Repair or reinstall Windows.

Computer problems can be frustrating, but here's the good news: it's never been easier to fix them than with Windows 8. Windows 8 has a variety of utilities and troubleshooters that can walk even the most clueless newbie through the troubleshooting and repair process. And if the problems are so severe that you can't go on, Windows 8 can repair itself, all the way back to a pristine new Windows installation.

In this lesson, you'll learn how to troubleshoot and fix several common problem types, and how to repair or reinstall Windows when everything less drastic fails to solve the problem.

Fixing Application Problems

Individual applications can run into a variety of problems, any of which can cause it to become unresponsive, or "crash." When a crash occurs, there may or may not be an error message associated with it, and the problem may or may not be confined to that individual application. In some cases, a crashed app can take the entire system down with it — so that even the mouse pointer stops working, and you have to restart the computer to clear up the problem. The problem may be a one-time fluke, or it might occur every time (or most times) you try to run that program.

So what do you do about an app crash? Here's a general troubleshooting process to go through:

1. If the app didn't shut itself down when it crashed, shut it down yourself. See "Shutting down an unresponsive program," later in this lesson.

2. Restart the computer and pretend it never happened. (See Lesson 1 if you need instructions for restarting the computer.) If the problem happens again, go on to the next step.

3. Go to the app developer's website and look in the Support section to see if any known bugs might be causing the problem, especially incompatibilities with certain hardware. (Display adapters and games frequently have incompatibility issues, for example.) Try whatever is recommended to fix it.

4. See if an updated driver is available for your display adapter. (Check with the company that made your PC if your display adapter came with the PC.) If so, install it using the setup program that you download from the manufacturer. It doesn't hurt anything to update to the latest version of a driver, and this has been known to fix problems with certain applications, especially games.

5. If it's a program designed for an earlier version of Windows, adjust its compatibility settings so that Windows provides it the environment it needs. See "Configuring compatibility settings" later in this lesson. If that doesn't fix the problem, go to the next step.

6. Repair the program, if there's an option to do so in the Control Panel. (See Lesson 2 for instructions.)

7. Uninstall and reinstall the program. (If the program files were corrupted in some way, that'll fix the problem.) Again, see "Installing, Repairing, and Removing Applications" in Lesson 2. If that doesn't fix the problem, go on to the next step.

8. Give up. No, I'm not being facetious here. Sometimes you just can't get a particular program to run on a particular PC, and it's more trouble than it's worth to keep chasing a solution. Sorry, but it's true.

Shutting down an unresponsive program

When a program crashes, it might terminate itself automatically, usually with an error message explaining what happened. However, in some cases, the program window stays open, and you must shut down the malfunctioning program manually.

In Windows 8, when a program stops responding to keyboard and mouse input, Windows displays that program's window with a white haze over it, and a message box appears, letting you know that the program has become unresponsive. From there, you can choose to restart the program or return to the program to wait for it to respond. (Some programs trigger false alarms because they take longer than normal to respond to certain commands.)

LINGO

Task Manager is an interface for viewing what programs are running and their statuses. It can also show detailed memory and CPU usage for each program when it's in More Details mode.

If Windows doesn't notice that the program has become unresponsive, you can display Task Manager, and shut down the program manually from there.

You shouldn't use the Task Manager method of closing a program under normal circumstances because it doesn't save your work in the program, and because there's a possibility for file corruption. Use this method only when you can't shut down the program by normal methods.

In the following exercise, you'll shut down a program using Task Manager.

1. **Start Notepad.**

   You can do this from the Start screen.

2. **Right-click the taskbar and click Task Manager from the pop-up menu.**

   The Task Manager window opens. Two views are possible: More Details and Fewer Details. If you see lots of numbers and multiple columns for each running program, click Fewer Details at the bottom of the window to switch to the simpler view shown in Figure 9-1.

3. **In the Task Manager list, click to select Notepad.**

4. **Click End Task.**

   Notepad closes.

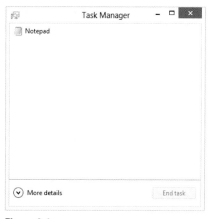

Figure 9-1

Configuring compatibility settings

Every version of Windows is a little different, and an application that works perfectly in an earlier Windows version may not work perfectly — or at all — in Windows 8. To combat this problem, Windows 8 offers Compatibility Mode.

You can set up compatibility for an application in the Properties box for the program file (that is, the executable file that runs the program), on the Compatibility tab. However, you may find it easier to use the Program Compatibility Troubleshooter utility, which is new in Windows 8. This utility helps you figure out the appropriate compatibility settings so you're not just guessing.

LINGO

Compatibility Mode simulates an earlier Windows version for the benefit of the program you're running, tricking it into thinking that it's running in that earlier version.

In this exercise, you will use the Program Compatibility Troubleshooter on an application, and then you will check out the compatibility settings it used in the program's Properties dialog box.

Since not everyone has the same older programs to work with for this exercise, you can use any older program that you happen to have installed, or you can download and install a program that's designed for an earlier Windows version. For the examples for this exercise, I'm using a free game called Pure Sudoku, which I downloaded from http://download.cnet.com. It's designed for Windows 2000/XP/Vista.

1. **Open File Explorer and navigate to the folder that contains the program file.**

   Most program files are stored in the C:\Program Files or C:\Program Files (x86) folder, in a subfolder named either for the application itself or for its maker. For example, in Figure 9-2, I navigated to C:\Program Files\Pure Sudoku.

   Note: On a system that runs a 64-bit version of Windows, there are two separate Program Files folders: one for 64-bit programs and one for 32-bit ones. The 32-bit programs are stored in the Program Files (x86) folder. On a 32-bit version of Windows, all program files are stored in C:\Program Files.

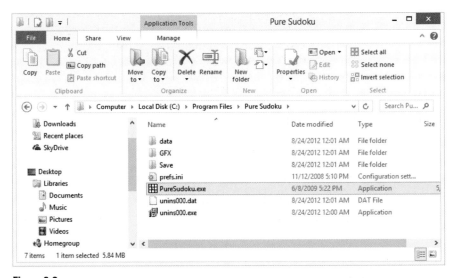

Figure 9-2

2. **Identify and select the executable file for the program.**

   If you have file extensions displayed, you can see the file's .exe or .com extension. (You can see Pure Sudoku's file extension in Figure 9-2.)

   If your file extensions are not visible, turn the display on so that you can identify the executable file. To turn on file extension display, click the Ribbon's View tab and select the File Name Extensions check box.

3. **Click the Ribbon's Manage tab.**

   Buttons appear on the Ribbon that pertain to managing the application. See Figure 9-3.

Figure 9-3

4. **Click the Troubleshoot Compatibility button.**

   The Program Compatibility Troubleshooter runs.

5. **Click Try Recommended Settings.**

   The utility may recommend a compatibility mode, as shown in Figure 9-4. It may recommend a different mode for your program than the one that's shown here, or you may see different options entirely, depending on the program. For example, you might be prompted to specify what problem you encountered or when the program last ran correctly. Follow the prompts presented if different from the ones shown here.

Figure 9-4

6. **Click the Test the Program button.**

   If a User Account Control box pops up, click Yes to allow the changes.

   Wait for the program to load. Check it out to see that it's working correctly, and then exit it.

7. **In the Program Compatibility Troubleshooter window, click Next to continue.**

EXTRA INFO

You can also use Compatibility Mode on setup utilities, for programs that won't install normally under Windows 8. To run a setup program in Compatibility Mode, navigate to that setup program's location; it may be a CD or DVD.

8. **If the program worked correctly, click Yes, Save These Settings for This Program.**

   Or, if your program didn't work correctly, click No, Try Again Using Different Settings, and then follow the prompts to try something else.

9. **Click Close the Troubleshooter.**

10. **In the File Explorer window, right-click the application's executable file and click Properties.**

    The Properties dialog box opens for that application.

11. **Click the Compatibility tab.**

    Notice that Windows has already chosen a Compatibility Mode, as you see in Figure 9-5. In the Compatibility Mode section, the Run This Program in Compatibility Mode For check box is selected, and a Windows version is selected from the drop-down list. The troubleshooter did that for you.

12. **Examine the other available options for compatibility.**

    For example, you can run in Reduced Color Mode, which allows programs written for lower-depth color modes than Windows 8 currently supports to run using their preferred color palette.

    You can also run the program in 640 x 480 screen resolution, a lower resolution than Windows 8 normally supports.

13. **Click OK to close the dialog box.**

Figure 9-5

Troubleshooting Problems with Files

Files . . . where would we be without them? There are all kinds of files, of course, from Windows system files to the drivers that help your devices operate. The files that you're probably most concerned about, though, are your own data files: word processing documents, spreadsheets, database files, and so on.

When a file is missing, or when you get an error message when you try to open it, the world seems pretty bleak. All the work that went into creating that data file seems wasted. But before you start with the tragic existentialism, check out this section, which may provide some recourse.

Searching for a file

First of all, maybe the file isn't really gone — maybe you just forgot where you put it. The application you were working with might have suggested a location, and you might have gone with the suggestion without really noticing where it was. Or perhaps someone else who uses your computer might have tried to be helpful and move some data files around to "organize" them in a way that hadn't occurred to you. Turn to in Lesson 4, and review the procedure for locating a file when you don't know where it's stored.

Accessing a file's history

More times than I care to count, I've made a change to a file, saved my work, and then thought, "Oh no! If only I could go back to the earlier version of the file." Windows 8 includes a File History feature that helps with this very problem. It saves backup copies of each previous version of a file, so you can go back to any version at any time.

The File History feature is turned off by default; you must enable it, and tell it where to save the backups. From that point on, you can just sit back and enjoy the benefits.

In the following exercise, you will enable File History on your system, create a new file, make a change to it, and then go back to the earlier version. To use this feature, you need some type of external storage connected to your PC (like a USB flash drive or an external hard drive), or an accessible network location you can use for the storage. A network location may have more disk space than a flash drive, making it a better choice for long-term use, but for this exercise, any of those locations will do. If you don't have any network or external storage locations available, you won't be able to do this exercise.

1. **Open the Control Panel, click the System and Security heading, and then click the File History heading.**

    If the Turn Off button appears, File History is already on; skip to Step 6.

2. **If the Turn On button is available, click it.**

   Turn On will be available if you have an external storage device connected to your PC, or if you have previously set up a network location for file history. If the location turns on successfully, skip to Step 6.

   Note: At some point in the setup process, you might see a message asking if you want to recommend this drive to other members of your HomeGroup. If you see that, click No.

3. **If the Select Drive screen doesn't automatically appear, click Select Drive in the navigation pane.**

   The Select Drive screen appears. Any available external drives appear on the list.

> **EXTRA INFO**
>
> File History saves copies of files that are in your libraries, contacts, favorites, and on your desktop. It doesn't save versions of files stored elsewhere unless you add that storage location to an existing library or create a new library for it. To add a location to a library, right-click the library's name in the navigation pane in File Explorer and choose Properties from the menu that appears. Then, in the library's Properties dialog box, click Add to add a new location to the library.

In the next steps, you'll choose a network location for your file history storage. If you don't have a network or don't want to use a network location, you can use a local external drive instead; select the drive from the Select a File History Drive and then skip ahead to Step 6.

4. **Click Add Network Location.**

   The Select Folder dialog box opens. See Figure 9-6.

5. **Navigate to the location where you want to save the file history and click Select Folder.**

   The selected folder appears on the Select Drive list now, and it's highlighted. See Figure 9-7.

   You can select any network location or any external drive, such as an external hard disk or USB flash drive. However, if you use a flash drive, be aware that File History won't be saved unless that drive is in place, so don't use a flash drive that you frequently disconnect to take other places.

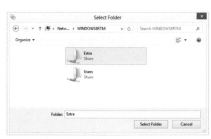

Figure 9-6

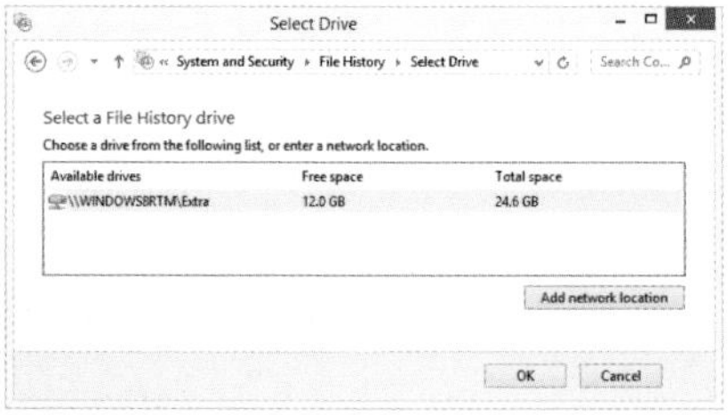

Figure 9-7

6. **Click OK to choose the network location you just set up, and then click Yes if asked whether you want to move your existing files too.**

7. **If you did not click the Turn On button earlier, click it now.**

   If a prompt appears asking if you want to recommend this drive to other members of your HomeGroup, click No.

   File history is now on. You can see proof of that fact, as well as the chosen location, on the File History screen.

8. **Click Advanced Settings in the navigation bar.**

   The Advanced Settings screen appears.

9. **Open the Save Copies of Files drop-down list and choose Every 10 Minutes.**

   This step increases the frequency at which the copies are synchronized so that you can complete the rest of the exercise more quickly. See Figure 9-8. Note that File History synchronizes the current copy with the backup only at the intervals you specify, or when you click Run Now in the File History window, and not when the files are actually modified.

Figure 9-8

10. **Click Save Changes.**

11. **Open File Explorer and navigate to the Documents library. Then right-click a blank area, point to New, and click Text Document.**

    A new text file appears.

12. **Type** Test **and press Enter.**

    The new file is named `Test.txt`.

13. **Double-click the Test file to open it in Notepad, and type** Version 1.

    See Figure 9-9.

Figure 9-9

14. **Close the Notepad window, and click Save when you're prompted to save your changes.**

15. **Return to the File History window and click the Run now hyperlink, or wait at least 10 minutes.**

    This ensures that a backup of the file's current state is saved to File History. As the backup is running, a Stop hyperlink appears. Wait until the Run Now hyperlink reappears, indicating the backup is complete.

16. **In File Explorer, double-click the Test file again, edit its contents to read** *Version 2,* **and then close it, saving your changes.**

17. **In the Control Panel, return to the File History screen and click Restore Personal Files.**

The Home – File History screen appears, listing the libraries and folders that it's protecting. See Figure 9-10.

Figure 9-10

18. **Double-click the Documents icon to display the Documents – File History window, and then double-click the Test file.**

The previous version of the file appears. You can tell it's the previous version because it still says Version 1. See Figure 9-11.

In Figure 9-11, notice the Next and Previous buttons at the bottom, with a Restore to Original Location button in the center. The Next and Previous buttons aren't available right now because you have only one older version of the file. If a file had multiple older versions saved, you could access them with the Previous button.

Figure 9-11

Next, you will discard the newer version of the file by overwriting it with the backup (version 1).

19. **Click the Restore to Original Location button (it's the big round green button at the bottom of the screen) to revert to version one.**

A Replace or Skip Files dialog box opens. See Figure 9-12.

20. **Click to select the Replace the File in the Destination Folder option.**

The My Documents folder opens, where Test.txt is stored.

Note: In Figure 9-12, notice that you had options other than the one we picked. You could have skipped this file (that is, cancelled its restoration), or you could have elected to choose which file to keep in the destination folder.

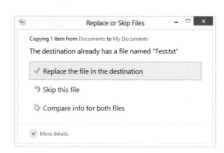

Figure 9-12

21. Double-click Test.txt.

The file opens in Notepad. The file's text reads *Version 1,* indicating that it's the prior version of the file.

22. Close all open windows.

Checking for disk errors

If you try to open a file and a message warns you that the file is corrupted or can't be opened, it's a sad day indeed. Here are some things you can try:

- ✔ **Restore an earlier version of the file.** You can do this by using File History, as you learned in the previous section.

- ✔ **Look for another copy of the file.** See if there's another copy of the file available somewhere. For example, if you use an online backup service, maybe there's a copy there.

- ✔ **Copy the file to another drive.** Sometimes copying a file fixes it. (Rare, but it does happen.)

- ✔ **Check the disk for file system errors.** If errors are found and repaired, there's a chance that the file may open normally.

Checking a disk uncovers and fixes both physical and logical errors on a disk. A *physical error* is a bad spot on the disk that the drive can't read. A *logical error* is an inconsistency in the disk's table of contents that prevents the drive from finding and assembling all the required pieces of the file.

In the following exercise, you will check your hard disk for errors using the Check Disk utility that comes with Windows 8.

1. Open File Explorer and click Computer in the navigation pane.

A list of drives appears.

2. Right-click the C drive and click Properties from its pop-up menu.

The Properties dialog box opens for the C drive.

EXTRA INFO

MS-DOS and some early versions of Windows called the disk checker *check disk,* which was a slightly expanded version of the utility file named *chkdsk.* Many seasoned computer professionals still call it that. So if someone tells you to "run check disk," she's referring to the utility covered in this section.

EXTRA INFO

A decade ago, disk errors were pretty common, and knowing how to check for them was an essential skill to have. However, hard disk technology and the Windows file system have both improved greatly, resulting in many fewer file storage errors. As a result, the error check you are about to perform will probably not find any errors, simply because there are none to be found.

3. **Click the Tools tab.**

   See Figure 9-13.

4. **Click the Check button.**

   A message may appear, saying you
   don't need to scan this drive. If you
   were doing this as part of troubleshooting a real problem, you could
   leave it at that and click Cancel. But
   let's pretend that there's a problem
   you're trying to solve, and continue.

5. **Click Scan Drive.**

   The check begins. If any errors are
   found, respond to the prompts to
   repair the error(s), if that's possible. When the check is complete,
   a message appears, reporting
   that your drive was successfully
   scanned.

Figure 9-13

6. **Click Close in the message dialog box.**

7. **Click Cancel to close the C drive's Properties box.**

Recovering from System Problems

System problems are the big ones — the problems that prevent Windows
from starting up correctly or from running at a decent performance level
once it's started, regardless of the application being used. Any of the following can cause system problems:

✔ Viruses or malware infections

✔ Disk errors, either physical or logical
(see the previous section)

✔ Corrupted Windows system files,
caused either by disk errors or by bad
or incomplete updates

✔ Bad changes made to the Registry
(usually by an overambitious would-
be techie or a poorly written driver or
setup application)

LINGO

The **Registry** is a database of
system settings that Windows
relies on to start Windows and
keep it running. It contains information about the computer's
hardware and software and the
users' preferences.

✔ Files that are supposed to load at startup but are missing or corrupted

✔ Bad updates to essential device drivers, like the display adapter's driver. The driver update might have been corrupted, or the wrong driver for the device might have been installed.

✔ Programs that are no longer installed still trying to load automatically at startup

✔ Incompatibility between the PC's hardware and a driver

✔ Incompatibility between the PC's hardware and a recent Windows update

✔ Incompatibility between the PC's hardware and a recently installed application

As you can see, there's quite an array of reasons why Windows might be acting up. In the following sections, I'll show you some of the most common things you can do to solve such thorny problems.

Booting to Safe Mode

If Windows won't boot normally, you might try booting in Safe Mode, which works where regular booting won't in cases where the problem is a program or nonessential driver that's trying to load at startup.

Booting to Safe Mode doesn't fix anything by itself. It's simply a means to an end. After you've booted in Safe Mode, you can use one of the utilities in the following sections to perform actions that may fix the problem.

In this exercise, you will boot into Safe Mode.

LINGO

Safe Mode is a no-frills startup mode that loads only the essential device drivers and doesn't load any of the programs that are scheduled to load at startup.

This exercise assumes that you can access the Windows desktop, which may not always be the case when you want to go into Safe Mode. However, if the PC fails to restart normally and you can't access the Windows desktop, the Advanced Boot Options menu will automatically appear when you try to start the PC, so in the event of an actual emergency, you would start at Step 8.

1. **From the desktop, display the Charms bar, and click Settings.**

   Remember, to display the Charms bar, either point the mouse pointer to the bottom-right corner of the screen or swipe in from the right if you're using a touchscreen.

   The Settings bar appears, as show in Figure 9-14.

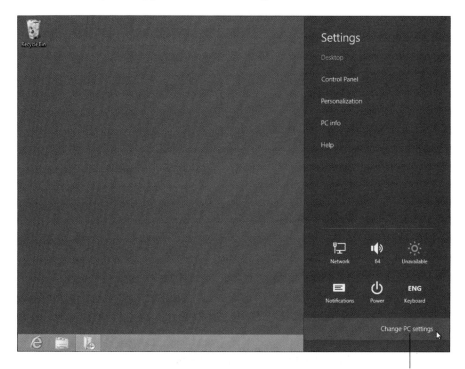

Click here to open the PC settings screen.

Figure 9-14

2. **Click Change PC Settings near the bottom-right corner of the Settings bar.**

   The PC Settings app opens.

3. **Click the General category at the left) and then, in the right pane, scroll down to the Advanced Startup section and click Restart Now. See Figure 9-15.**

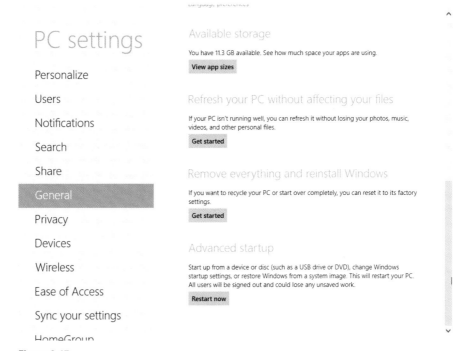

Figure 9-15

The computer restarts, and the Choose an Option screen appears, as shown in Figure 9-16.

4. Click Troubleshoot.

The Troubleshoot screen appears. See Figure 9-17.

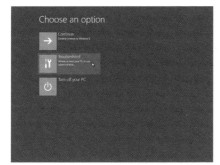

Figure 9-16

Figure 9-17

5. **Click Advanced Options.**

   The Advanced Options screen appears. See Figure 9-18.

6. **Click Startup Settings.**

   The Windows Startup Settings screen appears.

7. **Click Restart.**

   Windows restarts, and the Advanced Boot Options screen appears. See Figure 9-19.

Figure 9-18

8. **Type 4 to choose Enable Safe Mode.**

9. **Log in to Windows, typing your password if prompted.**

   Windows is now in Safe Mode, as shown in Figure 9-20. You can tell you're in Safe Mode because the display resolution is lower than usual, no wallpaper is displayed, and *Safe Mode* appears in the corners of the screen and a Windows Help and Support window appears. The sound and network features aren't functional. You may also

Figure 9-19

notice that commands take longer to execute in this mode.

At this point, if you were doing actual troubleshooting, you might use System Restore, as described in the following section, "Restoring the system to an earlier state," or you might prevent certain programs from loading at startup, as described in the "Controlling which programs load at startup" section after that. Because this was just a test, though, we'll now reboot normally.

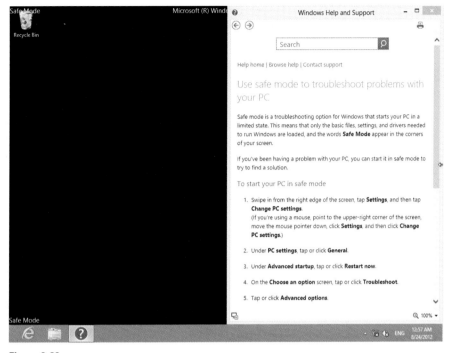

Figure 9-20

10. **Display the Charms bar, click Settings, click the Power icon, and click Restart. See Figure 9-21.**

    Remember, to display the Charms bar, either point the mouse pointer to the bottom-right corner of the screen or swipe in from the right if you're using a touchscreen.

    Windows restarts normally.

Figure 9-21

Restoring the system to an earlier state

Windows system files contain lots of information about every aspect of your system's current state, including what hardware you have, what applications are installed, which users are authorized, and what those users' preferences are. These system files are a complex, frequently changing group of files, stored in multiple hidden locations on your hard drive. In short, they're a mess to mess with on your own.

Whenever you install a new application, driver, or anything else, it affects your system files. That means you're only one poorly written driver away from big problems at any point.

If Windows starts malfunctioning or just "acting funny" after you do something that affects system files, the easiest fix is often to use System Restore. This utility enables you to roll back the system files to earlier saved versions, presumably wiping away whatever error was recently introduced. System Restore is among the first of the tricks I pull out of my troubleshooting bag whenever a system is acting up.

Windows 8 creates a restore point every day. A *restore point* is a copy of all the important system files that you would need for a System Restore operation (which takes your computer back to a happier time when all your programs played together nicely). You can also manually create additional restore points whenever you like.

A good time to create a restore point, for example, is right before you install some unknown program or driver that you aren't sure is 100 percent Windows 8 compatible.

In the following exercise, you will manually create a system restore point. Then you will roll back to the restore point you created. It won't make any changes to do so, because the restore point is the same as your current system state, so this is harmless to experiment with. Completing this exercise is good practice for a later time when you may need this skill to get your computer up and running again.

1. **Open the Control Panel, click the System and Security heading, and click the System heading.**

2. **In the navigation bar at the left, click System Protection.**

Figure 9-22

The System Properties dialog box opens with the System Protection tab displayed, as shown in Figure 9-22.

3. **Click the Create button near the bottom of the dialog box.**

   The System Protection dialog box opens, prompting you to create a restore point.

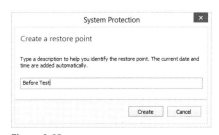

4. **Name your restore point by typing** Before Test **in the dialog box, then click Create.**

Figure 9-23

   See Figure 9-23. If you were doing this for real, you might want to name it something more descriptive, such as "Before Installing Photoshop."

5. **At the message that the restore point was created successfully, click Close.**

   If you want to, at this point you can make some system changes, which will be reversed when System Restore completes. That's entirely optional, though, and ultimately a waste of time since anything you do (or have done since you created the restore point in Step 4) will be undone in the next steps.

6. **In the System Properties dialog box, on the System Protection tab, click the System Restore button.**

   The System Restore screen opens.

7. **Click Next.**

8. **Click the Before Test restore point, as shown in Figure 9-24, and click Next.**

9. **Click Finish.**

   A warning appears, telling you that once you start the process, System Restore can't be interrupted.

10. **Click Yes.**

    The System Restore process begins. Wait for it to finish and for Windows to reboot.

Figure 9-24

11. **When Windows reboots and a System Restore message appears letting, you know it was successful, click Close.**

Controlling which programs load at startup

Some programs start automatically when Windows starts. For example, a utility that controls a multifunction printer might load automatically, as might an antivirus program that needs to stay running all the time.

Having programs load at startup has both advantages and drawbacks. It's handy to preload programs that you frequently use — but choose wisely because programs that take up space in memory but don't actively contribute to your productivity can be a waste of resources. Having a lot of programs running at once can slow down system performance, and having a lot of programs loading automatically at startup can make Windows take longer to start.

The default for some programs is to start automatically when you start your computer. In a perfect world, only programs that legitimately need to be running all the time will do this, but reality is somewhat different. A lot of programs seem to think they're special and worthy of being always-on, but they often don't contribute to your computer's success on a daily basis. For example, a device that you have Windows 8 installed on might have global positioning system (GPS) capabilities. If you have a map update service for your GPS, it might be always on by default so that it can constantly monitor the GPS service's server for available updates. It's up to you to decide whether you want to let that kind of background activity go on, on a case-by-case basis.

To disable an automatic startup, open Task Manager and choose the app to disable from the Startup tab. See Figure 9-25. If Task Manager doesn't appear with tabs as shown in Figure 9-25, click the More Details button to make the tabs appear.

Figure 9-25

Then there's the opposite case: Perhaps you can think of a program that you would like to start up automatically at Windows startup, but it doesn't. For example, if the first thing you do every day, without fail, is to open your e-mail program, why not have it start up automatically and save you that daily click or two?

It's possible to modify the Registry to set a program up for automatic loading, but there's a much easier and safer way that works just as well. Just place a shortcut to that program in a hidden Startup folder, located at here:

```
C:\Users\username\AppData\Roaming\
        Microsoft\Windows\Start
        Menu\Programs\Startup
```

Note: On your computer, you'll see your user account name in place of *username*.

In the following exercise, you'll make a program load at startup that does not normally do so, and then you'll find out how to disable a program from starting up automatically.

1. **Open C:\Windows\System32 in File Explorer.**

   This is the folder that contains the executable files for many of the Windows accessory programs.

2. **Hold down Alt and drag notepad.exe to the desktop.**

   A shortcut is created there for Notepad. See Figure 9-26.

Hold down Alt and drag notepad.exe to the desktop.

Figure 9-26

3. **Navigate to the system's Startup folder using the following path, where *username* is the user account name.**

   ```
   C:\Users\username\AppData\
        Roaming\Microsoft\
        Windows\Start Menu\
        Programs\Startup
   ```

4. **Drag the Notepad shortcut from the desktop into the Startup folder as displayed in the main File Explorer window.**

   The shortcut is added to the system's Startup folder. See Figure 9-27.

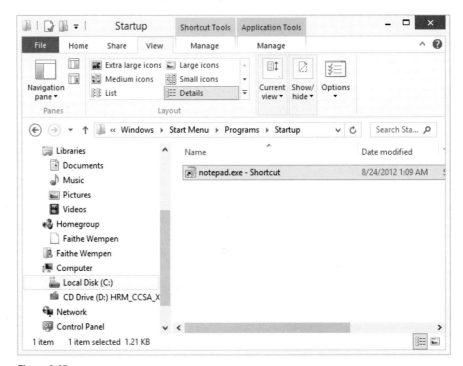

Figure 9-27

5. **Restart the PC.**

   Notepad starts automatically.

6. **Right-click the taskbar, as shown in Figure 9-28, and choose Task Manager.**

   Task Manager opens.

Figure 9-28

7. **If no tabs are visible in Task Manager, click More Details.**

8. **Click the Startup tab, as shown in Figure 9-29.**

   Notepad appears on the list of startup applications.

9. **Click Notepad, and click the Disable button.**

   This is how you would disable any unwanted startup program.

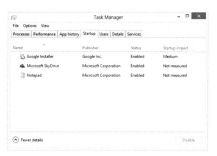

Figure 9-29

10. **Close the Task Manager window.**

11. **Open File Explorer and navigate this path:**

    ```
    C:\Users\username\AppData\
         Roaming\Microsoft\
         Windows\Start Menu\
         Programs\Startup
    ```

12. **Select the Notepad shortcut and press Delete.**

    Windows will no longer open Notepad at startup.

13. **Close all open windows.**

EXTRA INFO

When an app is disabled from startup from Task Manager, it won't load at startup, but information about its startup still appears in the Registry. The larger the Registry, the longer it takes Windows to start up, so there's a minor benefit to removing the shortcut from the Startup folder.

Refreshing or reinstalling Windows 8

Sometimes no matter what you try, Windows won't behave. Maybe it's molasses-slow to start up, or there's an annoying delay between clicking a command and something happening. Perhaps applications crash, or Windows spontaneously reboots itself or displays cryptic and ominous error messages.

In earlier versions of Windows, when that sort of problem occurred, you didn't have many options, and the ones that you did required inviting a tech-savvy friend over for dinner. Windows 8, though, offers two options that make the repair process just about as idiot-proof and painless as possible:

LINGO

To **refresh** Windows is to repair it without losing any of the current settings or files. To **reinstall** Windows is to completely start over, eliminating all nondefault files and settings.

- ✔ **Refresh:** Spruces up your Windows installation by replacing any missing or changed system files, while enabling you to keep your photos, music, videos, and other personal files.

- ✔ **Reinstall:** Wipes the slate clean on your PC, completely reinstalling Windows in a factory-fresh condition. You lose everything that was on your hard disk.

When problems occur, try Refresh first, because it's less invasive and you have less work to do afterward to restore all your files and applications. Then if that doesn't work, resort to Reinstall. Both commands are found in the General section of PC Settings.

In the following exercise, you'll refresh your Windows 8 installation. You may want to skip this exercise unless there's really something wrong with Windows, because it takes a long time and there's a chance that the process might change something that you didn't want changed.

Before doing this exercise, you may want to locate your Windows 8 installation media. You might be asked for it as part of the exercise process.

1. **Display the Charms bar, and click the Settings charm.**

   Remember, to display the Charms bar, either point the mouse pointer to the bottom-right corner of the screen or swipe in from the right if you're using a touchscreen.

2. **At the bottom of the Settings panel, shown in Figure 9-30, click Change PC Settings.**

   The PC Settings app opens.

3. **On the left side of the window, click General.**

   A variety of general settings appear.

Figure 9-30

4. On the right side of the window, scroll down to the bottom.

Options for refreshing and reinstalling Windows appear there. See Figure 9-31.

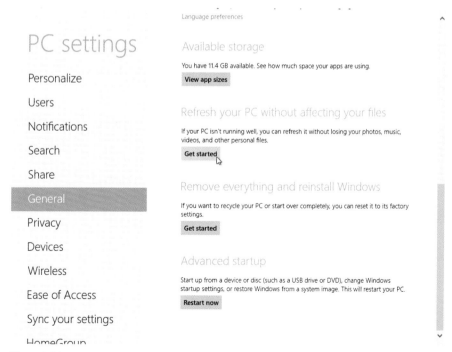

Figure 9-31

5. **Under the Refresh Your PC without Affecting Your Files heading, click Get Started.**

An explanation appears, describing what will happen.

6. **Click Next.**

7. **If prompted, insert your Windows installation or recovery media.**

In simple terms, that means to insert the Windows DVD or plug in the other device that you installed Windows from.

8. **Click Refresh.**

9. **Wait for Windows to refresh and restart.**

 Summing Up

In this lesson, you learned what to do when you have a problem with Windows, from losing an important file to fixing system performance problems. Here are the highlights:

✔ You can resolve most application crashes by shutting down the offending app via Task Manager and then rebooting. Reinstall or repair the application if needed, or look for an online patch or fix.

✔ Programs designed for earlier Windows versions may require that you use Compatibility Mode in order to get them to work.

✔ To locate a missing file, use the Search feature in Windows, as you learned in Lesson 4.

✔ You can retrieve an earlier version of a file with the File History feature, provided it was enabled on your system prior to the file being lost.

✔ You can check for disk errors, which, if present, may prevent a file from opening or saving correctly, or an application from running properly. Open the Properties dialog box for the drive, click the Tools tab, and click Check.

✔ Booting into Safe Mode may be useful if Windows won't start normally. While in Safe Mode, you can disable faulty startup programs or make other corrections.

✔ System Restore returns system files to an earlier state to correct system problems that are caused by a bad recent change made to a system file.

✔ You can control which programs load at startup from the Startup tab of Task Manager.

✔ If Windows won't work right and you can't find another way to fix it, use the Refresh or Reinstall feature. Refreshing repairs Windows without losing any of your file settings; Reinstall resets it to the original factory state.

Know This Tech Talk

Compatibility Mode: An execution mode that simulates an earlier Windows version for the benefit of the program you're running, tricking it into thinking that it's running in that earlier version.

crash: A condition that occurs when a program stops responding to user commands. *Crash* is only a metaphor; physical items aren't crashing into each other.

refresh: To repair Windows without losing any of the current settings or files.

reinstall: To completely start over in Windows, eliminating all nondefault files and settings.

Registry: A database of system settings that Windows relies on to start Windows and keep it running. It contains information about the computer's hardware and software and the users' preferences.

restore point: A copy of the system files from a certain point in time. See also *System Restore.*

Safe Mode: A no-frills startup mode that loads only the essential device drivers and doesn't load any of the programs that are scheduled to load at startup.

System Restore: A utility that enables you to roll back the system files to earlier saved versions.

Task Manager: An interface for viewing a list of running programs and their statuses. It can also show detailed memory and CPU usage for each program when it's in More Details mode.

Lesson 10

Using Windows 8 Apps

- ✔ Understand Windows 8 apps.

- ✔ Check the weather.

- ✔ Browse and manage photos.

- ✔ Track appointments.

- ✔ Organize contacts.

- ✔ Check your e-mail.

- ✔ Get driving directions.

A s you learned in Lesson 4, Windows 8 apps are the new style
of application unique to Windows 8. They're optimized for use
on touchscreen computers, although you can use them on any
Windows 8 device. In this lesson, you will learn about some of the most
popular Windows 8 apps.

Windows 8 Apps: A Quick Review

As you learned in Lesson 2, Windows 8 apps are
applications that are designed specifically for
the Windows 8 interface. Windows 8 apps have
an entirely different look and feel, compared to
traditional desktop apps, and the rules for navigating them are different, too.

In a Windows 8 app, the most important thing to
remember is *right-click*. Right-clicking brings up
a bar across the bottom of the screen that contains commands you can select. For example,
Figure 10-1 shows the commands that appear
when you right-click in the Calendar app. The
exact commands depend on the app, and
also on what you right-clicked. (You used the
Calendar app in Lesson 2, so this lesson doesn't
cover it again in detail.) If you're using a touchscreen, swipe down on the tile instead; that's
the equivalent of right-clicking for touch users.

EXTRA INFO

If you want to find and install
more Windows 8 apps, turn back
to Lesson 2, where you learn how
to shop for Windows 8 apps in the
Windows Store.

EXTRA INFO

Windows 8 apps run full-screen.
However, as I mentioned in Lesson
2, if you have a high-resolution display, you have the option of snapping open Windows 8 applications
to take up either one-third or two-
thirds of the screen, so you can
run two apps side by side.

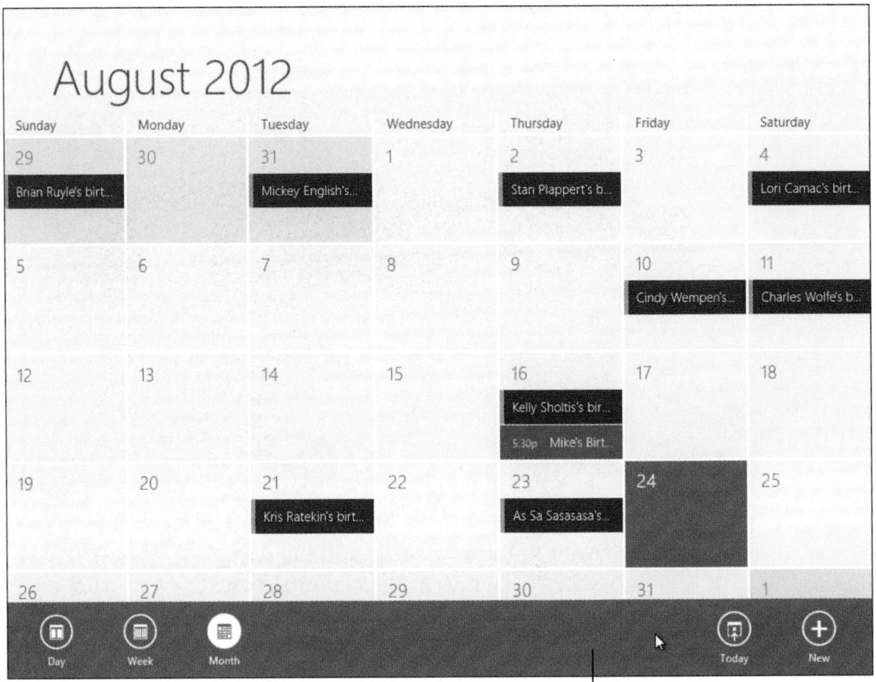

Right-click to display a command bar.

Figure 10-1

Windows 8 apps don't show up in the taskbar on the desktop, even when they're still running. If you're in another application and need to switch back to an open Windows 8 app, point the mouse pointer to the upper-left corner of the screen, and a thumbnail of the running Windows 8 app appears. You can click it to switch to it. Or if you're running more than one Windows 8 app, move the mouse pointer downward to display a bar along the left side of the screen with thumbnails for each of the running Windows 8 apps, and then click the one you want. (See Figure 10-2.) For a touchscreen, it's even easier than that: just swipe in from the left to switch among applications.

To exit a Windows 8 app, drag downward from the top of the screen to the bottom. You can do this with the mouse, or by dragging down with your finger on a touchscreen.

These apps are running – click one to switch to it.

Figure 10-2

As you drag downward from the top of a Windows 8 app, you might notice that right before the app closes entirely, it becomes a thumbnail image. At this point, if your screen resolution is high enough, instead of completing the drag to the bottom, you can drag to the right or left side to snap the app into either one-third or two-thirds of the available screen space. You can then switch to another Windows 8 app to fill the remaining screen space, and have two apps going side-by-side, as in Figure 10-3. If your screen resolution is not at least 1366 pixels wide, the option to show more than one app side by side isn't available.

To return one of the apps to full-screen and hide the other, drag the divider line between the two windows all the way to the left or right.

EXTRA INFO

Four of the Windows 8 apps — Mail, People, Messaging, and Calendar — are part of a single package. This lesson covers three of them; the fourth one, Calendar, is covered in Lesson 2.

If you ever need to uninstall one of them — to correct a problem, for example — all four are uninstalled. To get them back, go to the Store, go to Top Free, and install the Mail, Calendar, People, and Messaging app.

Two apps running side by side

Drag the divider to adjust the relative sizes.

Figure 10-3

Lesson 2 contains several exercises that familiarize you with Windows 8 app usage. Return to these exercises now if you need to review:

✔ Starting an application, page 39

✔ Switching among applications, page 42

✔ Closing an application, page 46

✔ Working in a Windows 8 app, page 50

✔ Arranging Windows 8 apps, page 55

The remainder of this lesson looks at individual apps that come with Windows 8. As you work through these exercises, you'll get lots of practice with the Windows 8 interface.

Getting a Weather Report with the Weather App

The Weather app is one of the simplest Windows 8 apps, but one that you will probably use and appreciate every day. It tells you the current weather conditions at your location (or some other location of your choice) and lets you know the forecast.

The first time you run the Weather app, you may be asked, "Do you want to turn on location services and allow Weather to use your location?" Click Allow to permit the Weather app to determine your location by looking at your Internet provider's address and automatically enter that location for weather-reporting purposes.

The Weather screen scrolls to the right to show different data. You can move the mouse pointer to the bottom of the screen to activate a scroll bar, or you can drag your finger from right to left with a touchscreen to scroll the display to the right.

The default weather information appears for your current location, but you can also request weather information for other locations. To do so, right-click and then click Places in the command bar that appears at the top of the screen.

In the following exercise, you will check the weather in your current location, and then add a new location and check the weather there, too. These steps use a mouse, but you can use a touchscreen instead if you have one.

1. **From the Start screen, locate the Weather tile.**

   If you've already set up your home location, the current temperature and weather for your location appears on the tile, as shown in Figure 10-4. That's useful because you don't have to start the Weather app just to find out the current conditions.

Figure 10-4

2. **Click the Weather tile.**

   If this is the first time you've used the Weather app, click Allow to allow Windows to derive your current location from your Internet provider's address.

   The current weather conditions and a five-day forecast appears. In the upper-left corner of Figure 10-5, you can see that the Weather app has determined that my location is Fishers, IN. Don't worry if the app didn't get it quite right. In the steps that follow, I tell you how to select additional locations.

Scroll bar

Figure 10-5

3. **Move the mouse pointer to the bottom of the screen to display a scroll bar, and then scroll to the right.**

   An hourly forecast appears, along with links to various maps. (See Figure 10-6.)

4. **Right-click or swipe downward anywhere on the screen.**

   Icons appear across the top: Home, Places, and World Weather.

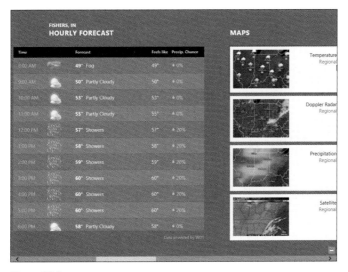

Figure 10-6

5. **Click Places.**

   A list of favorites appears, as shown in Figure 10-7. So far, there may only be one: The one for your current location.

   The blank tile with the plus sign on it is for adding new locations.

6. **Click the plus sign.**

   An Enter Location prompt appears.

7. **Type** Moweaqua**; when Moweaqua, Illinois, United States, appears on the list beneath the text box, as shown in Figure 10-8, click it to select it, and click Add.**

   After you click to select the new location, a thumbnail for it appears on the Favorites list.

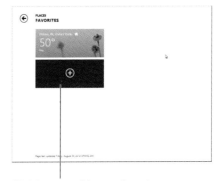

Click here to add a new location.

Figure 10-7

Figure 10-8

8. **Click the Moweaqua tile in the Favorites list.**

   Weather information for this new location appears.

9. **Click the left-pointing arrow (back arrow) in the top-left corner of the screen.**

   The Favorites list reappears.

10. **Right-click the Moweaqua tile.**

    A command bar appears. See Figure 10-9.

Figure 10-9

11. **Click the command bar's Set as Default option.**

    Now Moweaqua, Illinois, is your new home location. Notice that it now has a house symbol next to the location name.

    Depending on the graphic for the weather conditions, you may or may not be able to see the house icon. When it's sunny and clear, there's a white sunburst on the graphic exactly where the house icon is.

12. **If you're ready to exit the Weather app, use the mouse or your finger (on a touchscreen) to drag the top of the screen down to the bottom to exit it.**

If you'd like to remove a location tile, right-click to select it and click Remove on the command bar. You can't remove the default location, so if you want to remove the Moweaqua tile, you must first set your other location as the default.

Viewing and Importing Photos with the Photos App

The Photos app enables you to view photos that you've stored in a variety of locations within a single interface. These locations can include network storage that you have permission to access, your own local Pictures library, your SkyDrive, Facebook, and Flickr.

While the Photos app doesn't have a lot of complicated features like some desktop-based photo apps have, it's more than adequate for quickly showing off your photos to a friend or quickly importing some new photos into your library.

Viewing photos

When you open the Photos app, you see tiles for several locations arranged along the bottom of the screen, as shown in Figure 10-10, including your Pictures library, any shared picture libraries from other PCs on your network or HomeGroup, your SkyDrive, your Facebook account, and your Flickr account. Each tile shows one of the following:

- ✔ **One of your pictures in that account:** The tile is a preview of one of the pictures at that location. (A little later in this section, I tell you how to choose which picture displays there.)

- ✔ **A plain solid color:** The tile is simply a solid color if you don't have pictures stored at that location or you haven't configured the app to connect to that location.

EXTRA INFO

If you don't store pictures on SkyDrive, Facebook, or Flickr, you can click the Hide hyperlink in the tile's upper-right corner to remove its tile from the Photos app.

Figure 10-10

To place pictures on your SkyDrive, open a web browser and go to www. skydrive.com. You can't import pictures to your SkyDrive directly from within the Photos app. The same goes for Facebook; you'll need to go to www.facebook.com to manage your stored photos there. For Flickr, it's www.flickr.com. The Photos app only *displays* pictures from these locations; it doesn't allow you to do any file management.

If you have a Facebook account associated with the same e-mail address that you use to sign into Windows itself, click the Facebook tile on the Photos app and follow the prompts to link your Facebook account to the Photos app. You may also want to copy some files to your SkyDrive, as you learned in "Working with Your SkyDrive" in Lesson 4, just to see them show up here in Photos.

As you're viewing a particular picture within the Photos app, you can right-click it and then click the command bar's Set As option to open a menu of places where you can set this picture as the default. (See Figure 10-11.) Here are your choices:

  ✔ **Lock screen:** This is the picture you see prior to signing in to Windows, or when the PC is locked.

  ✔ **App tile:** In the Photos app, this is the picture on the tile that represents the account it links to, such as Facebook or Flickr.

  ✔ **App background:** This is the picture behind the tiles on the opening screen of the Photos app.

Figure 10-11

For the following exercise, you will need at least two pictures in your Pictures library on your PC. If you don't have any, get some (the Internet is rife with them), and place them there. Then follow these steps to check out how the Photos app displays photos.

1. **From the Start screen, click Photos.**

   The Photos app opens. (Refer to Figure 10-10.) Tiles appear at the bottom of the screen for the locations from which you might want to browse photos.

2. **Click the Pictures Library tile.**

   Large previews of the pictures in that location appear. You can scroll to the right to see more, if not all of them fit onscreen at once.

If you have folders in your Pictures library, each folder appears as a tile. Pictures that aren't in any particular folder within the Pictures library appear on their own here.

3. **Move the mouse pointer to the bottom of the screen.**

   In the lower-right corner, notice the tiny – (minus) and + (plus) signs, shown in Figure 10-12. These allow you to zoom in and zoom out. If you don't see them, move the mouse to the bottom of the screen to make them appear, along with a scroll bar if there are more pictures than can be displayed at once.

Figure 10-12

4. **Click the – (minus) sign.**

   The images appear much smaller, so you can see more of them at once. Figure 10-13a and 10-13b show before-and-after examples.

Figure 10-13

5. **Click the + (plus) sign.**

   The images return to their earlier sizes.

6. **Click the first (leftmost) picture.**

   The picture appears in full-screen size. If the picture isn't the same shape as the monitor screen, black panels appear in the empty areas.

7. **Move the mouse pointer.**

   A right-pointing arrow button appears at the right edge of the screen.

8. **Click the right-pointing arrow button.**

   The next picture appears.

9. **Move the mouse pointer again to display the arrow buttons, and then click the left-pointing arrow button.**

   The original picture reappears. In the steps that follow, I tell you how to set this picture as the Photos app background.

10. **Right-click the picture.**

    Icons appear in the command bar at the bottom of the screen, including Set As, Delete, and Slide Show. (See Figure 10-14.)

> **EXTRA INFO**
>
> Make sure you click the first picture, not the first folder (if you have any folders). If all your pictures are in folders, click a folder, and then click the first picture within it. You can distinguish a picture from a folder because a folder has a name under the picture, along with a number (representing the number of pictures in that folder).

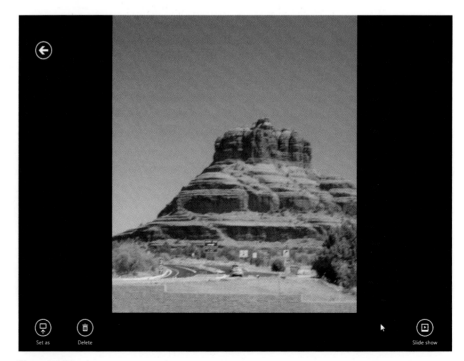

Figure 10-14

11. **Click Set As.**

   A menu appears. (Refer to Figure 10-11.)

12. **Click App Background.**

   This photo is now the app background image for Photos.

13. **Press the Escape key to return to the Pictures library.**

   The Pictures Library screen reappears.

14. **Right-click and then choose the command bar's Browse by Date option.**

   The files are grouped according to the dates associated with them.

15. **Right-click and then choose the command bar's Browse by Album option.**

   The files are grouped according to folder, or if you have no folders in your Pictures library, each photo appears separately.

Importing photos

The Photos app enables you to import pictures from external drives, such as flash drives or cameras; it places them in albums in your Pictures library.

In the following exercise, you will see how to import a photo from an external drive, such as a USB flash drive.

1. **Connect an external drive that contains a picture file.**

2. **In the Photos app, right-click and then click Import on the command bar.**

   The Choose a Device to Import From dialog box opens. (See Figure 10-15.)

3. **Click the external drive's letter.**

   Thumbnails of all the pictures on that drive appear. You may need to scroll to the right to see them all. The display shows all pictures in all folders and subfolders on the drive, not just the ones at the root (top) level.

Figure 10-15

4. **Click Clear Selection if you want to import only one photo.**

   This is necessary because by default every picture on the drive is selected.

   At the bottom of the screen is a text box that shows today's date. That's the default name for the folder into which the pictures will be imported.

5. **(Optional) If you want to change the name of the folder into which the pictures will be imported, change the text in the text box at the bottom of the screen from today's date to some other name.**

6. **Click a picture you want to import and click Import.**

   The picture is imported into a folder (also known as an album) that the app created within your Pictures library based on the name you specified in Step 5. If you already have a folder with that name, the picture is placed into it.

   A message appears letting you know the picture was imported, and an Open Album button appears.

7. **Click the Open Album button.**

   The contents of the folder appears.

8. **Click the Back button (left-pointing arrow) in the upper-right corner of the screen.**

   The starting screen of the Photos app reappears. The image you chose in the previous exercise appears as the background image.

9. **Drag the top of the Photos app down to the bottom of the screen to close the app.**

> **EXTRA INFO**
>
> The date on a Photos file is the date the file was created on the disk on which it currently resides. This may or may not be the date on which the picture was actually taken. For example, if you copied the picture from your camera to your hard disk many months after you actually took the picture, the picture file's date will be the date the copy was made, not the date the picture was taken.

Organizing Contacts with the People App

You probably have contact information for different people stored in all kinds of different online and offline locations. For example, maybe all your high school friends are accessible via Facebook, your coworkers via Microsoft Exchange, and your current BFFs through Twitter.

The People app enables you to look up people's contact information from one convenient location. You have two choices for how you load that contact info into the People app.

> ✓ **Include multiple contact entries from your existing accounts.** The People app automatically pulls in contact data from different accounts or services — including Twitter, Microsoft Exchange, LinkedIn, and Facebook — and present them to you all at once. If you're registered with any of those services with the same e-mail address as the one you use to sign into Windows, the People app will automatically pick up the contacts there.

> ✓ **Type a contact entry for each person who isn't already in your other contact lists.** You can manually enter new contact information in the People app for folks who aren't already a part of any of your existing contact databases.

In the following exercise, you will link the contacts from an existing service to your People app.

1. **From the Start screen, click the People tile.**

   The People app opens.

2. **In the upper right corner, click the Connected To hyperlink.**

   The Accounts panel appears, showing any accounts that are already set up.

3. **Click Add an Account.**

   The Add an Account panel appears, showing icons for available services. See Figure 10-16.

4. **Click the service you want to connect to, and enter the information requested.**

   Login information appears for that service. The exact prompts depend on the service you chose. Figure 10-17 shows the prompts for Hotmail, for example.

5. **Click Connect.**

   That service is connected to the People app. It may take a few minutes after you set up a new account before the data is linked/synchronized.

Leave the People app open for the next exercise.

Figure 10-16

Figure 10-17

In the following exercise, you'll enter a new contact manually into the People app, and update some information about yourself.

1. **If the People app isn't already open from the previous exercise, open it. To do so, from the Start screen, click the People tile.**

   The People app opens.

2. **Right-click and then click New in the command bar that appears.**

   The New Contact screen opens.

3. **Fill out the new contact info with someone's contact information that you want to add, as shown in Figure 10-18.**

   If there's nobody you want to add, use the contact info shown in Figure 10-18

   Note: In the Account field, you can specify which of your accounts this contact is associated with if you've linked to more than one account that supports this feature. If in doubt, leave it set to the default.

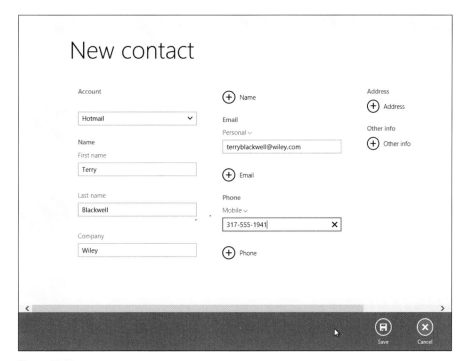

Figure 10-18

4. **Click Save.**

   The information you entered appears as a new contact.

5. **Click the Back button (left-pointing arrow) to return to the list of people.**

   Names are sorted alphabetically; Figure 10-19 shows how the list looks with many contacts. Notice that the names are sorted by first name, not last name.

   If you chose to link another account to the People app, you may have many more contacts than just the ones you entered manually.

Figure 10-19

For more practice, enter several more people's contact information.

6. **Click the Me graphic at the left side of the screen.**

   Your own name appears, along with a View Profile button.

7. **Click View Profile.**

   A Contact Info screen appears, showing all the info that you've entered about yourself so far.

If you haven't entered any information about yourself yet, the only thing that appears is the name you signed into Windows with.

8. **Right-click and then choose the command bar's Edit option.**

   The Windows 8 version of Internet Explorer opens, and your profile page appears. (See Figure 10-20.)

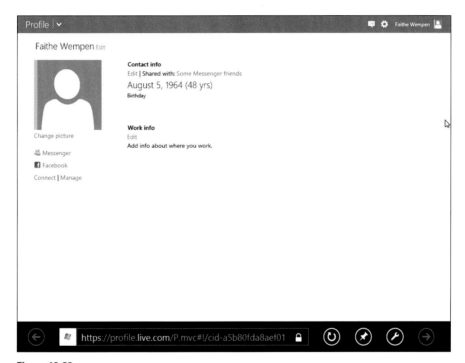

Figure 10-20

9. **Next to Contact info, click Edit.**

   Fields appear for entering and editing contact information.

10. **In the Birth Date fields, enter the month, day, and year of your birth.**

    See Figure 10-21.

11. **Click Save.**

12. **Drag from the top of the screen to the bottom to close the web browser.**

    The Start screen reappears.

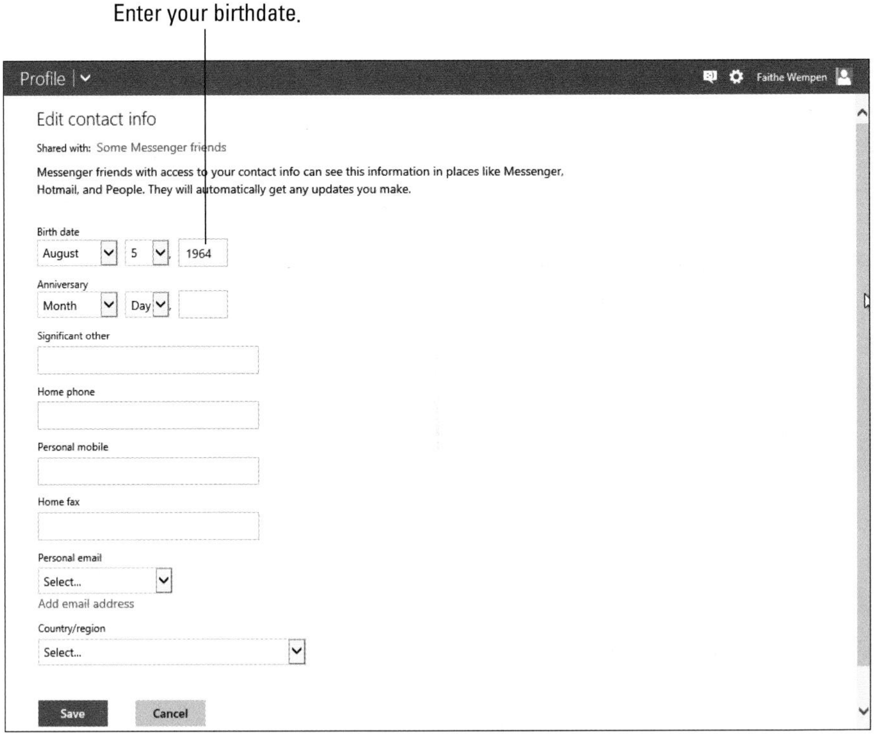

Enter your birthdate.

Figure 10-21

Sending and Receiving E-mail

The Mail app provides a basic e-mail send-and-receive interface for Exchange, Hotmail, and Gmail accounts. The Mail app is not as full-featured an application as some dedicated mail programs like Outlook or Eudora, but it is very convenient to use, especially on a touchscreen tablet where desktop applications may be more unwieldy.

LINGO

Microsoft Exchange is a type of mail server commonly used by large companies to implement their employee e-mail system. Many companies that provide Exchange-based e-mail use Microsoft Outlook as the e-mail client program.

Setting up an e-mail account

The first time you run the Mail app, you may see a prompt to set up your e-mail account (the one for the address that you signed into Windows with, associated with your Microsoft account) if it's one of the mail systems that the Mail app recognizes. It asks for your server type: Exchange, IMAP, or POP. POP is the most likely guess if you aren't sure. See Figure 10-22. However, if you choose POP, you'll get a message explaining that Mail doesn't support POP accounts, and you'll need to click Cancel to continue.

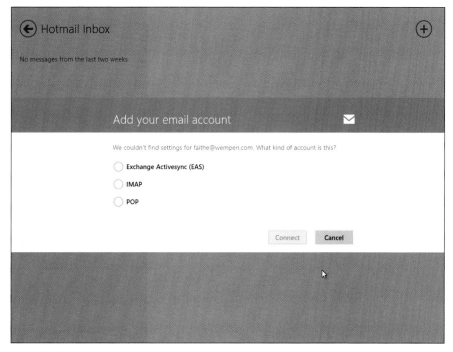

Figure 10-22

By the time you read this, Mail may support other mail services, but at this writing, these services are supported:

- ✔ **Hotmail:** This includes e-mail addresses that end in hotmail.com, live. com, and MSN.com.

- ✔ **Outlook:** This includes e-mail addresses configured in Microsoft Exchange, Office 365, and Outlook.com.

✔ **Google:** Accounts that end in gmail.com.

✔ **Yahoo!:** Accounts that end in yahoo.com.

✔ **Other Account:** Any e-mail account that uses an IMAP server. (If you don't know what that is, ask your e-mail provider or tech support person.)

For the exercises in this lesson, we'll use a Gmail account (Google). If you don't have one, go to www.gmail.com and get one for free. Alternatively, you can use any other e-mail account you already have from any of the services on the preceding list.

In the following exercise, you will add an existing Gmail account to the Mail app, allowing you to send and receive messages via the Mail app with that account. (You can do this exercise with a Hotmail account instead if you have one.)

1. **Make sure you know your e-mail address and password.**

2. **From the Start screen, click Mail.**

   If any messages appear about setting up Exchange or other e-mail, click Cancel.

3. **Open the Charms bar and click Settings.**

   The Settings panel appears.

4. **Click Accounts.**

   A list of your current mail accounts, if any, appears, along with an Add an Account hyperlink. See Figure 10-23.

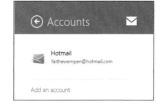

Figure 10-23

5. **Click Add an Account.**

   A list of the types of accounts you can connect to appears: Hotmail, Outlook, Google, Other Account, and Yahoo.

6. **Click Google (or Hotmail, as appropriate).**

   An Add Your Google Account prompt appears, with text boxes for your e-mail address and password. (See Figure 10-24.)

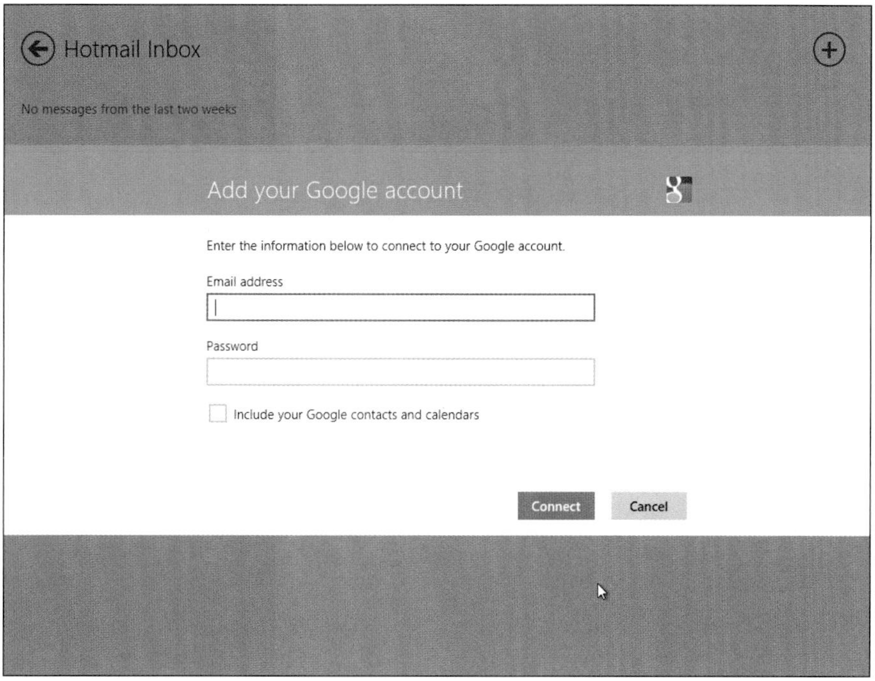

Figure 10-24

7. **Enter your e-mail address and password and then click Connect.**

   The account is added, and its inbox appears.

8. **Click the back arrow in the upper-left corner of the screen.**

   You're returned to the folder list for your mail accounts. The folders and other shortcuts for them appear in the navigation pane at the left, including Inbox, Draft, Sent Items, and so on. See Figure 10-25.

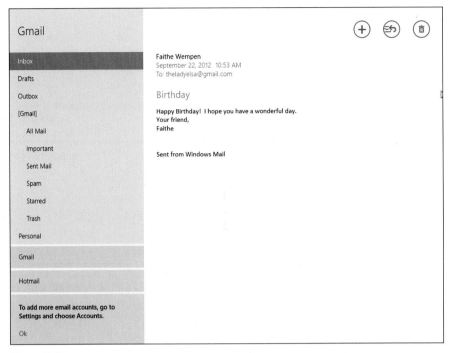

Figure 10-25

After you set up an e-mail account in the Mail app, that account appears as a set of folders in the left pane. If you've configured more than one mail account , the mail account names appear at the bottom of the folder list, as shown in Figure 10-25. (Gmail and Hotmail are shown in that figure.) You can jump to the inbox for an account by clicking the account's name there, and return to that account's folder list from the inbox by clicking the back arrow.

Sending an e-mail message

You can send an e-mail message from any account that you've set up in the Mail app. You can specify recipients by typing their e-mail addresses manually, or you can select them from your contacts in the People app.

Here are the fields you can complete when composing an e-mail message in the Mail app:

- ✔ **Subject:** The message's title.

- ✔ **Message body:** The main part of the message.

- ✔ **To:** The primary recipient(s).

- ✔ **Cc:** (optional) Additional recipient(s).

- ✔ **Bcc:** (optional) Additional recipient(s) that the other recipients won't know about.

- ✔ **Priority:** (optional) A flag that identifies the message as High, Normal, or Low priority; this makes a difference only if the recipient sorts incoming mail by priority or importance.

- ✔ **Attachments:** (optional) Files that you want to send along with the message.

LINGO

Cc stands for courtesy copy, a copy sent to someone other than the main recipient(s). **Bcc** stands for blind courtesy copy, a courtesy copy sent privately to a recipient so that the other recipients aren't aware of it.

In the following exercise, you will compose an e-mail message to a recipient that you select from the People app, and Cc yourself on it. You'll also attach a file to it and set its priority to High.

1. **In the Mail app, if you have more than one e-mail account set up there, select the account you want to use for this exercise.**

   To select an account, click its name in the navigation pane at the left. For this example, I'll use a Hotmail account.

2. **Click the New button (plus sign) in the upper-right corner of the screen.**

   A new message opens. (See Figure 10-26.)

3. **Click the plus sign next to the To box.**

   The People app opens.

EXTRA INFO

Notice in Figure 10-26 that the Mail app automatically inserted the text *Sent from Windows Mail* at the bottom of the message body. It does that for all messages sent via the Mail app. You can't turn that off, unfortunately, but you can delete that text individually in each e-mail message before sending.

Click here and type the subject.

Faithe Wem... ˅
faithewempen@hotmail...

Add a subject

To

⊕

Cc

⊕

Show more

Sent from Windows Mail

Click here to access the people app.

Click here and type the message.

Figure 10-26

4. **Click a person whose e-mail address you've entered in this app, and who won't mind receiving a test message.**

   The person's name is highlighted, and an Add button becomes available. (See Figure 10-27.)

5. **Click the Add button.**

   You return to the Mail app with that person's name filled into the To box.

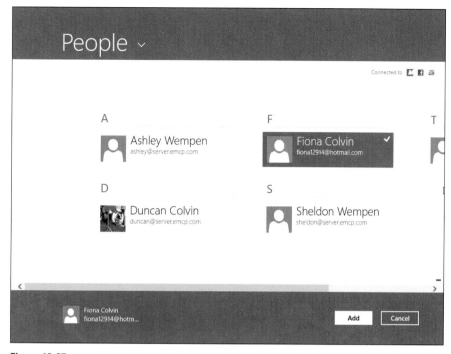

Figure 10-27

6. **Type your own e-mail address in the Cc box.**

7. **If you'd like to add an attachment, right-click and click the Attachments icon in the command bar.**

   A Files list appears, showing the last location you worked with in a Windows 8 app. If you've been doing the exercises in this lesson in order, that's probably a folder containing some pictures. (See Figure 10-28.)

8. **Click a file to attach.**

   You can attach any file you like; a picture would be ideal. Don't send this person a file containing private information you don't want him to have, though.

9. **Click the Attach button.**

   The file is attached, and a preview of it appears in the message body area.

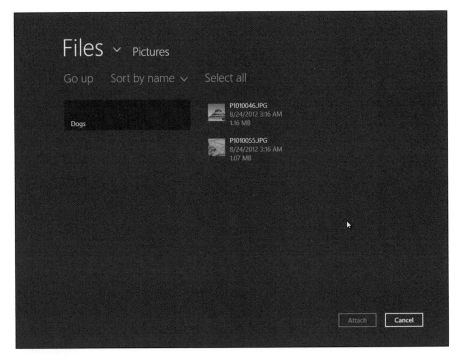

Files ⌄ Pictures

Go up   Sort by name ⌄   Select all

Dogs

P1010046.JPG
8/24/2012 3:16 AM
1.16 MB

P1010055.JPG
8/24/2012 3:16 AM
1.07 MB

Attach   Cancel

Figure 10-28

10. **Click below the attached file in the message body, and type** This is just a test.

11. **Click in the Add a Subject line and type** This is a test.

12. **Click the Show More link in the navigation pane at the left.**

The Bcc and Priority fields appear.

13. **Open the Priority drop-down list and click High Priority.**

The completed e-mail will resemble Figure 10-29, except you'll have a different file attached and different e-mail addresses in the To and Cc boxes.

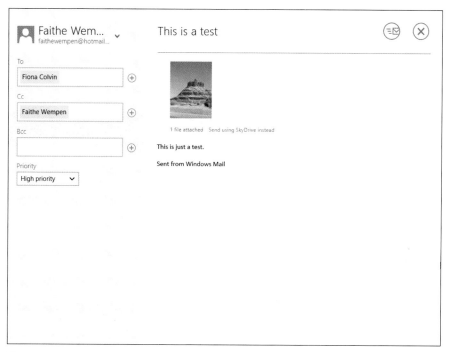

Figure 10-29

14. Click the Send button in the upper-right corner of the screen.

Your message is sent to your Outbox, and then sent to the recipient the next time the Mail app syncs to your mail server for that account. (You can right-click and choose the command bar's Sync option to make it do so immediately.)

Go on to the next exercise to receive the copy you sent to yourself.

LINGO

To **sync**, in the Mail app, is to perform a send/receive operation. The app checks the mail server for any new mail, and sends any mail in your Outbox.

Receiving and reading messages

The Mail app receives messages as well as sending them. It automatically checks for new messages at an interval you specify, and you can also manually issue the Sync command to send and receive at any time.

New messages appear in the Inbox folder, and their text appears bold to distinguish them from already-read messages.

Notice in Figure 10-30 that the new message has an exclamation point on it; that means it's High Priority. The paperclip symbol on it indicates that it has an attachment.

In the following exercise, you will receive the copy of the message you sent in the previous exercise, save its attachment to your hard disk, and reply to it.

EXTRA INFO

To set the send/receive interval for a mail account, display the Charms bar and click Settings, and then click Accounts. Click the desired account to manage, and then open the Download New Email drop-down list and choose a different interval. If you don't see a Download New Email drop-down list, that setting isn't editable for the mail account you're working with.

1. **In the Mail app, right-click and then choose the command bar's Sync option.**

Any e-mail still in your Outbox is sent, and any new mail is received.

High Priority

Attachment

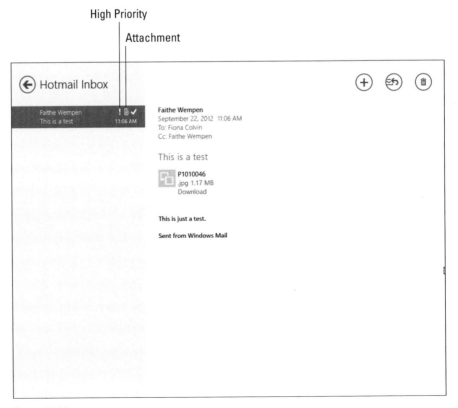

Figure 10-30

2. **If the test message you sent in the previous exercise doesn't appear as a new message, wait a few minutes and then repeat Step 1.**

Repeat Step 1 every few minutes until the test message arrives.

3. **Click the test message to select it.**

The message body appears in the right pane. Depending on the type of file you sent as an attachment, a preview of it may appear, or a gray box may appear with the filename and a paperclip icon, as shown earlier in Figure 10-30.

4. **Click the Download hyperlink under the attachment.**

If a preview of it didn't appear before, it appears now.

5. **Right-click the attachment and then choose Save from the pop-up menu.**

See Figure 10-31. The Files screen appears. The location displayed is the same one you used when you selected the attachment in the previous exercise.

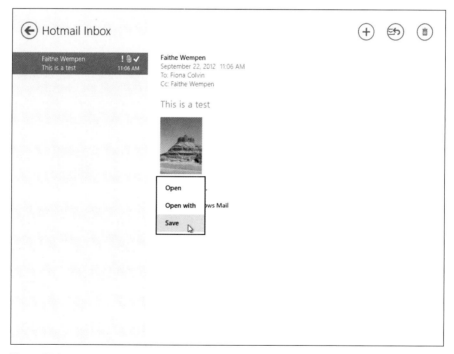

Figure 10-31

6. **In the filename text box at the bottom of the screen, type** test.

Leave the file type as-is. (The file type is the drop-down list immediately to the right of the filename, as shown in Figure 10-32.)

File type

Figure 10-32

7. **Click the Save button.**

A copy of the attachment is saved back to the original location, with the name of *test*.

8. **Click the Respond button in the upper-right corner of the message.**

A menu appears. (See Figure 10-33.)

Respond button

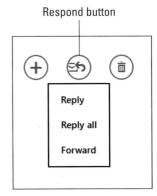

Figure 10-33

9. Click Reply.

A reply screen appears. The recipient is already filled into the To box, and the subject line is the same as the original with the addition of RE: (short for *regarding*) at the beginning. The insertion point is at the top of the message body area.

10. Type Received, thank you.

See Figure 10-34.

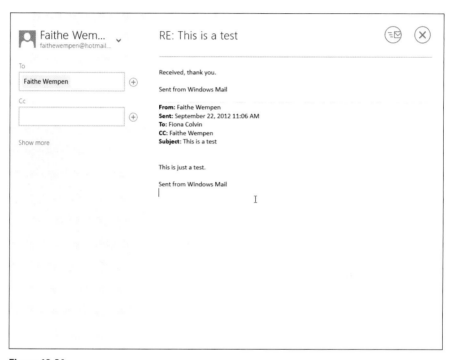

Figure 10-34

11. Click the Send button.

The reply is sent (back to yourself, in this case).

12. If you'd like to delete the original message, select it and click the Delete button.

It's the button that looks like a trash can in the upper-right corner of the message. The message is deleted.

13. Close the Mail app.

Remember, to close a Windows 8 app, drag from the top of the screen down to the bottom, either with the mouse or with a finger on a touch-screen.

Chatting with Friends via Messaging

Messaging is a chat program, also called instant messaging, or IM. It enables you to chat with friends who use a Microsoft service called Messenger. Also, if you've connected your Windows account to other supported services, such as Facebook, you can chat with people via those services here too.

The nice thing about the Messaging app is that it's seamlessly connected to the People app, so you can start conversations with anyone who appears in your People list. If you've set up People to include your contacts from multiple services, perhaps Facebook and LinkedIn, then you can access all those contacts in one place.

In the following exercise, you'll start an IM conversation with someone from your People list who is online now.

1. **From the Start screen, click Messaging.**

   The Messaging window opens.

2. **Click New Message in the upper-left corner of the screen.**

   The People app opens.

3. **Click the Online Only heading.**

   The list is filtered to show only people who are available for chat right now. (See Figure 10-35.)

Click Online Only.

Figure 10-35

4. **Click the person you want to chat with and then click the Choose button in the command bar.**

You return to the Messaging app, to a new conversation window.

5. **Type your message in the text box at the bottom of the window, and press Enter.**

The message appears in a shaded block. When the person replies to you, the reply appears in a different-colored block. (See Figure 10-36.)

6. **Say goodbye to your friend.**

Figure 10-36

7. **If you want to destroy all evidence of the conversation, right-click and then click the command bar's Delete option.**

   A confirmation box appears. (See Figure 10-37.) Deleting will remove all record of this conversation from your computer.

8. **Click the Delete button.**

9. **Close the Messaging app.**

Figure 10-37

Summing Up

In this lesson, you learned how to navigate several of the most popular Windows 8 apps. Here are the highlights:

- ✔ To open a Windows 8 app, click its tile on the Start screen. To close a Windows 8 app, drag from the top of the screen down to the bottom, either with the mouse or your finger (on a touchscreen).

- ✔ When using a Windows 8 app, remember that right-clicking almost always brings up a bar containing commands you can choose.

- ✔ In the Weather app, scroll to the right to see additional types of reports for your area. For different locations, right-click and then click the Places tile.

- ✔ The Photos app enables you to show off the photos from your Pictures library. You can also browse pictures from your SkyDrive, from Facebook, and from Flickr. You can't upload pictures to any of those services from the Photos app, however.

- ✔ The People app enables you to store and retrieve contact information. You can store individual contacts there, and you can pull contact info from other services you already participate in, including Microsoft Exchange, Twitter, LinkedIn, and Facebook.

- ✔ The Mail app enables you to send and receive e-mail from Microsoft Exchange, as well as from Hotmail and Gmail.

- ✔ To compose an e-mail message, click the New button, fill out the form, and click Send. To receive messages, right-click and choose the command bar's Sync option.

- ✔ The Messaging app enables you to have real-time conversations (instant messaging) with friends who are connected to the same services as you. The supported services include Windows Messenger and Facebook.

Know This Tech Talk

album: A folder, in the language of the Photos app.

Bcc: Blind courtesy copy, a courtesy copy that the other recipients aren't aware of.

Cc: Courtesy copy, a copy of an e-mail sent to someone other than the main recipient(s).

instant messaging (IM): A real-time chat in which you type a message, and the recipient sees it pop up on her screen immediately. She can then type one back to you. It's like texting, but on a computer instead of a phone.

Microsoft Exchange: A type of mail server commonly used by large companies to implement their employee e-mail system.

sync: In the Mail app, to perform a send/receive operation.

About the CD

This Appendix contains information to help you get started using *For Dummies* eLearning. This course requires no installation.

System Requirements

For Dummies eLearning will provide all required functionality on the following Microsoft operating systems: Windows 8, Windows 7, Windows Vista, Windows XP, Windows 2000, and Windows 2003 Server.

The following browsers will be supported under Windows: Microsoft Internet Explorer 6.0 or higher, and Mozilla Firefox 2.x or higher.

To run the CD-ROM, the system should have the following additional hardware/software minimums:

- Adobe Flash Player 8
- A Pentium III, 500 MHz processor
- 256MB of RAM
- A CD-ROM or DVD-ROM drive

A negligible amount of disk space must be available for tracking data. Less than 1MB will typically be used. Your purchase of this *For Dummies* eLearning Kit includes access to the course online at the *For Dummies* eLearning Center. If you have purchased an electronic version of this book, please visit www.dummies.com/go/getelearningcode to gain your access code to the online course.

Launch Instructions

Keep in mind that course functionality relies heavily on mini-windows known as *pop-ups* for delivering its content. Many web browsers have *pop-up blockers*, on the (mistaken) assumption that all pop-ups must be advertising that no one really wants to see. These browsers also let you enable pop-ups if you so desire. Please make sure to enable pop-ups before starting to use the CD or the course online. If you don't enable pop-ups, some pop-up blockers may restrict the course from running.

Setup instructions for Windows machines:

1. **Put the CD in the CD drive and, if prompted, click on the** Run shellexe. exe **option in the AutoPlay window that displays.**

2. **If the course does not autoplay:**

   a. Double-click the My Computer icon to view the contents of the My Computer window.

   b. Double-click the CD-ROM drive icon to view the contents of the *For Dummies* eLearning CD.

   c. Double-click the start.htm file to start the *For Dummies* eLearning CD.

   Your computer may warn you about active content. Click Yes to continue starting the CD. The CD may create new tabs in your browser. Click the tab to see the content.

The browser offers the option of using the lessons from the CD or from the website, as spelled out in the next sections.

Accessing the course on the website

When you launch your *For Dummies* eLearning CD, you have two options for accessing your eLearning course: Access Course(s) Online and Access Course(s) on CD. To access the course online, do the following:

1. **In the Activate Your FREE Online Course Now! section, click the Access Course(s) Online button.**

   Note: You will need the online course access key found behind the CD-ROM in this book to complete your online registration.

2. **In the *For Dummies* eLearning home page that appears, click the Already Have an Access Code? button on the right-hand side of the page**

   In the new browser page that appears, notice the Access Key field for entering your personal access key.

3. **Enter your personal access key (found behind the CD-ROM in this book) into the Access Key field and then click the Send button.**

   You're brought to a Terms and Conditions of Use browser page.

You only have to use the access key once. In fact, if you try to enter an access key after it has already been accepted, you'll end up getting an error code.

4. **Read through the terms and conditions of use for the online course, then click the Accept button.**

5. **On the Registration page, fill in the required personal information (including username and password); then click the Submit button.**

   You are brought to the My Courses page of the *For Dummies* eLearning website.

6. **In the My Courses page, click the link for the course you want to work on.**

   The course launches.

After you launch the course, it plays an introductory animation. To watch more animations on the topic, click the Next button (the arrow pointing right) at the bottom of the screen to play the next one.

If you want to switch to another lesson or another topic, click the Topic List button on the controls at the bottom of the screen and choose a topic from the expanded list.

Some topics have an active tab for resources on the right side of the window. By default, Windows opens this content in a new window. If you have another compressed file manager installed, such as WinZip, your system may behave differently.

This course has a preassessment to allow you to test your level of knowledge of Windows 8 before taking the course. The preassessment is optional. You can answer all or some of the questions, or skip the preassessment altogether. To start the course at any time, click the Topic Map button and choose your starting place. (Lesson 1 is a good place to start!)

Here are some things to keep in mind when working with your online course:

🖋 You can come back and resume your course as many times as you like over the six-month subscription period.

🖋 Your online course "home base" can be found at www.dummieselearn-ing.com. Whenever you want to return to your online course, just point your browser to that address. (You may want to use your browser's Bookmark feature to store this address for quick access later on.)

🖋 After landing at the dummieselearning.com site, just enter your user-name and password in the appropriate fields in the upper right and then click the Login button to return to your My Courses page. (If you click the Remember Me check box, the dummieselearning.com site will store your username and password for you, so when you return, all you need to do is click the Login button to get to your My Courses page.)

🖋 Once back at your My Courses page, you can click one of your courses and either start over from the beginning or pick up where you left off.

🖋 For a quick overview of other online courses available from the dummieselearning.com site, click the Catalog tab on the site's home page to access the online catalog. From there, you can choose to purchase new courses.

Accessing the course on the CD

When you launch your For Dummies eLearning CD, you see a browser page that offers you two options for accessing your eLearning course (online or on CD). If you choose to use the CD version of the course, just click the Access Course(s) on CD button in the Activate Your FREE Online Course Now! section. Doing so brings you to the home page of your *For Dummies* eLearning course. From here, you can choose a lesson (or topic within a lesson) to work with.

Whenever you want to return to the CD version of your eLearning course, just launch the CD and click the Access Course(s) on CD button

After you launch the course, it plays an introductory animation. To watch more animations on the topic, click the Next button (the arrow pointing right) at the bottom of the screen to play the next one.

As is the case with the online version of the course, if you want to switch to another lesson or another topic, click the Topic List button on the controls at the bottom of the screen and choose a topic from the expanded list.

Troubleshooting

What do I do if the page does not load?

It is possible that you have a security setting enabled that is not allowing the needed Flash file to run. Be sure that pop-up blockers are off, ActiveX content is enabled, and the correct version of Shockwave and Flash are on the system you are using.

Please contact your system administrator or technical support group for assistance.

What do I do if I launch the course from the CD and my bookmark isn't remembered?

Remember that, when viewing the CD version of the course, your bookmark is stored locally on your machine. If you use the CD on another computer, your previous bookmark can't be accessed.

What do I do if I click a Launch button but nothing happens?

This may occur on machines that have AOL installed. If you are using the course from a CD-ROM and you are an AOL subscriber, follow the following steps:

1. **Exit the course.**

2. **Log on to AOL.**

3. **Restart the course.**

What do I do if the Shockwave installer on the CD says that I have a more recent version of the plugin, but the software still says that I need to install version 8.5 or higher?

Download the latest version of the Shockwave plugin directly from Adobe's website:

```
www.adobe.com/downloads
```

If prompted to install Flash Player to view the CD's content, you can download the latest version from the same URL.

Index

• *B* •

J

K

L

Q

End-User License Agreement

restrictions for these individual programs that are detailed in the "About the CD" appendix and/or on the Software Media. None of the material on this Software Media or listed in this Book may ever be redistributed, in original or modified form, for commercial purposes.

5. **Limited Warranty.**

   (a) WILEY warrants that the Software Media is free from defects in materials and workmanship under normal use for a period of sixty (60) days from the date of purchase of this Book. If WILEY receives notification within the warranty period of defects in materials or workmanship, WILEY will replace the defective Software Media.

   (b) WILEY AND THE AUTHOR(S) OF THE BOOK DISCLAIM ALL OTHER WARRANTIES, EXPRESS OR IMPLIED, INCLUDING WITHOUT LIMITATION IMPLIED WARRANTIES OF MERCHANTABILITY AND FITNESS FOR A PARTICULAR PURPOSE, WITH RESPECT TO THE SOFTWARE, THE PROGRAMS, THE SOURCE CODE CONTAINED THEREIN, AND/OR THE TECHNIQUES DESCRIBED IN THIS BOOK. WILEY DOES NOT WARRANT THAT THE FUNCTIONS CONTAINED IN THE SOFTWARE WILL MEET YOUR REQUIREMENTS OR THAT THE OPERATION OF THE SOFTWARE WILL BE ERROR FREE.

   (c) This limited warranty gives you specific legal rights, and you may have other rights that vary from jurisdiction to jurisdiction.

6. **Remedies.**

   (a) WILEY's entire liability and your exclusive remedy for defects in materials and workmanship shall be limited to replacement of the Software Media, which may be returned to WILEY with a copy of your receipt at the following address: Software Media Fulfillment Department, Attn.: *Windows 8 eLearning Kit For Dummies,* John Wiley & Sons, Inc., 10475 Crosspoint Blvd., Indianapolis, IN 46256, or call 1-800-762-2974. Please allow four to six weeks for delivery. This Limited Warranty is void if failure of the Software Media has resulted from accident, abuse, or misapplication. Any replacement Software Media will be warranted for the remainder of the original warranty period or thirty (30) days, whichever is longer.

   (b) In no event shall WILEY or the author be liable for any damages whatsoever (including without limitation damages for loss of business profits, business interruption, loss of business information, or any other pecuniary loss) arising from the use of or inability to use the Book or the Software, even if WILEY has been advised of the possibility of such damages.

   (c) Because some jurisdictions do not allow the exclusion or limitation of liability for consequential or incidental damages, the above limitation or exclusion may not apply to you.

7. **U.S. Government Restricted Rights.** Use, duplication, or disclosure of the Software for or on behalf of the United States of America, its agencies and/or instrumentalities "U.S. Government" is subject to restrictions as stated in paragraph (c)(1)(ii) of the Rights in Technical Data and Computer Software clause of DFARS 252.227-7013, or subparagraphs (c) (1) and (2) of the Commercial Computer Software - Restricted Rights clause at FAR 52.227-19, and in similar clauses in the NASA FAR supplement, as applicable.

8. **General.** This Agreement constitutes the entire understanding of the parties and revokes and supersedes all prior agreements, oral or written, between them and may not be modified or amended except in a writing signed by both parties hereto that specifically refers to this Agreement. This Agreement shall take precedence over any other documents that may be in conflict herewith. If any one or more provisions contained in this Agreement are held by any court or tribunal to be invalid, illegal, or otherwise unenforceable, each and every other provision shall remain in full force and effect.

Apple & Mac

iPad 2 For Dummies,
3rd Edition
978-1-118-17679-5

iPhone 4S For Dummies,
5th Edition
978-1-118-03671-6

iPod touch For Dummies,
3rd Edition
978-1-118-12960-9

Mac OS X Lion
For Dummies
978-1-118-02205-4

Blogging & Social Media

CityVille For Dummies
978-1-118-08337-6

Facebook For Dummies,
4th Edition
978-1-118-09562-1

Mom Blogging
For Dummies
978-1-118-03843-7

Twitter For Dummies,
2nd Edition
978-0-470-76879-2

WordPress For Dummies,
4th Edition
978-1-118-07342-1

Business

Cash Flow For Dummies
978-1-118-01850-7

Investing For Dummies,
6th Edition
978-0-470-90545-6

Job Searching with Social
Media For Dummies
978-0-470-93072-4

QuickBooks 2012
For Dummies
978-1-118-09120-3

Resumes For Dummies,
6th Edition
978-0-470-87361-8

Starting an Etsy Business
For Dummies
978-0-470-93067-0

Cooking & Entertaining

Cooking Basics
For Dummies, 4th Edition
978-0-470-91388-8

Wine For Dummies,
4th Edition
978-0-470-04579-4

Diet & Nutrition

Kettlebells For Dummies
978-0-470-59929-7

Nutrition For Dummies,
5th Edition
978-0-470-93231-5

Restaurant Calorie Counter
For Dummies,
2nd Edition
978-0-470-64405-8

Digital Photography

Digital SLR Cameras &
Photography For Dummies,
4th Edition
978-1-118-14489-3

Digital SLR Settings
& Shortcuts
For Dummies
978-0-470-91763-3

Photoshop Elements 10
For Dummies
978-1-118-10742-3

Gardening

Gardening Basics
For Dummies
978-0-470-03749-2

Vegetable Gardening
For Dummies,
2nd Edition
978-0-470-49870-5

Green/Sustainable

Raising Chickens
For Dummies
978-0-470-46544-8

Green Cleaning
For Dummies
978-0-470-39106-8

Health

Diabetes For Dummies,
3rd Edition
978-0-470-27086-8

Food Allergies
For Dummies
978-0-470-09584-3

Living Gluten-Free
For Dummies,
2nd Edition
978-0-470-58589-4

Hobbies

Beekeeping
For Dummies,
2nd Edition
978-0-470-43065-1

Chess For Dummies,
3rd Edition
978-1-118-01695-4

Drawing For Dummies,
2nd Edition
978-0-470-61842-4

eBay For Dummies,
7th Edition
978-1-118-09806-6

Knitting For Dummies,
2nd Edition
978-0-470-28747-7

Language &
Foreign Language

English Grammar
For Dummies,
2nd Edition
978-0-470-54664-2

French For Dummies,
2nd Edition
978-1-118-00464-7

German For Dummies,
2nd Edition
978-0-470-90101-4

Spanish Essentials
For Dummies
978-0-470-63751-7

Spanish For Dummies,
2nd Edition
978-0-470-87855-2

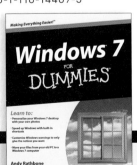

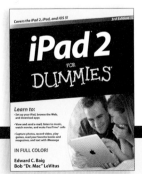

Math & Science

Algebra I For Dummies,
2nd Edition
978-0-470-55964-2

Biology For Dummies,
2nd Edition
978-0-470-59875-7

Chemistry For Dummies,
2nd Edition
978-1-1180-0730-3

Geometry For Dummies,
2nd Edition
978-0-470-08946-0

Pre-Algebra Essentials
For Dummies
978-0-470-61838-7

Microsoft Office

Excel 2010 For Dummies
978-0-470-48953-6

Office 2010 All-in-One
For Dummies
978-0-470-49748-7

Office 2011 for Mac
For Dummies
978-0-470-87869-9

Word 2010
For Dummies
978-0-470-48772-3

Music

Guitar For Dummies,
2nd Edition
978-0-7645-9904-0

Clarinet For Dummies
978-0-470-58477-4

iPod & iTunes
For Dummies,
9th Edition
978-1-118-13060-5

Pets

Cats For Dummies,
2nd Edition
978-0-7645-5275-5

Dogs All-in One
For Dummies
978-0470-52978-2

Saltwater Aquariums
For Dummies
978-0-470-06805-2

Religion & Inspiration

The Bible For Dummies
978-0-7645-5296-0

Catholicism For Dummies,
2nd Edition
978-1-118-07778-8

Spirituality For Dummies,
2nd Edition
978-0-470-19142-2

Self-Help & Relationships

Happiness For Dummies
978-0-470-28171-0

Overcoming Anxiety
For Dummies,
2nd Edition
978-0-470-57441-6

Seniors

Crosswords For Seniors
For Dummies
978-0-470-49157-7

iPad 2 For Seniors
For Dummies, 3rd Edition
978-1-118-17678-8

Laptops & Tablets
For Seniors For Dummies,
2nd Edition
978-1-118-09596-6

Smartphones & Tablets

BlackBerry For Dummies,
5th Edition
978-1-118-10035-6

Droid X2 For Dummies
978-1-118-14864-8

HTC ThunderBolt
For Dummies
978-1-118-07601-9

MOTOROLA XOOM
For Dummies
978-1-118-08835-7

Sports

Basketball For Dummies,
3rd Edition
978-1-118-07374-2

Football For Dummies,
2nd Edition
978-1-118-01261-1

Golf For Dummies,
4th Edition
978-0-470-88279-5

Test Prep

ACT For Dummies,
5th Edition
978-1-118-01259-8

ASVAB For Dummies,
3rd Edition
978-0-470-63760-9

The GRE Test For
Dummies, 7th Edition
978-0-470-00919-2

Police Officer Exam
For Dummies
978-0-470-88724-0

Series 7 Exam
For Dummies
978-0-470-09932-2

Web Development

HTML, CSS, & XHTML
For Dummies, 7th Edition
978-0-470-91659-9

Drupal For Dummies,
2nd Edition
978-1-118-08348-2

Windows 7

Windows 7
For Dummies
978-0-470-49743-2

Windows 7
For Dummies,
Book + DVD Bundle
978-0-470-52398-8

Windows 7 All-in-One
For Dummies
978-0-470-48763-1

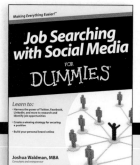

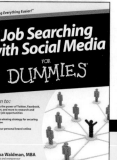